KU-158-839

LYN JAUNTON.

The Guardian
Guide to Running
a Small Business

THE GUARDIAN
GUIDE TO RUNNING
A SMALL BUSINESS

Edited by Clive Woodcock

Kogan
Page

First published 1980. Second edition published 1981 by
Kogan Page Ltd, 120 Pentonville Road, London N1 9JN

Copyright ©1980, 1981 The *Guardian*
All rights reserved
British Library Cataloguing in Publication Data
    The Guardian guide to running a small business
    — 2nd ed
    I. Woodcock, Clive
    658'.022'0941   HD69.S6
ISBN 0-85038-476-1 (Hb)
ISBN 0-85038-477-X (Pb)

Printed in Great Britain by the Anchor Press Ltd
and bound by William Brendon & Son, both of Tiptree, Essex

Contents

5. Marketing *132*

6. Planning the Office *156*

7. Benefiting from the Tax System *170*

8. Franchising *214*

9. Further Information *231*

DIRECTORS RUN OWN PENSION SCHEME

What made you decide to do it?

As we run our own Company, we wanted a scheme we could run ourselves rather than tie up all our money in an insurance company scheme.

I thought you already had a pension scheme?

Right – but there were significant financial advantages to setting up a self administered scheme for the directors of the company.

What are these advantages?

Apart from all the tax advantages we have complete control and flexibility. There are numerous other advantages – ask P.A.L.

How can the fund be invested?

The choice is almost unlimited — the company can even borrow from the fund or use it to buy office premises, with substantial tax savings.

Wasn't it difficult to establish?

No, it was easy. Pensions Associates Limited (P.A.L.) did everything necessary to set up our scheme. They are specialists in self-administered plans.

**FOR FURTHER INFORMATION
CALL BOB RIVERA ON 01-836 1018**

OR WRITE TO:

**Pensions Associates Limited
Suite 24, 91 St. Martins Lane
London WC2H 0DG**

1
Introduction

CLIVE WOODCOCK

Running a small business can often seem like a game of snakes and ladders in which the snakes are everywhere and the ladders are reserved for the larger firms. The pitfalls in the way of small firms in their constant fight for survival are such that the wondei is not that Britain has a relatively low proportion of small businesses contributing to the economy, but that so many believe it worthwhile continuing.

There is, in fact, a low birth rate and a high mortality rate for small firms in Britain. The relative size of the small business sector in the United Kingdom is much less than that in many other developed, industrialised countries: one-quarter of that in the US, one-fifth of that in West Germany, and one-sixth of that in France. A connection is sometimes made between this situation and the increasing depression of the British economy compared with the Western world in general.

Those firms which do survive (one in three fails in the first 12 months of life while only one in five makes it to five years) have to cope with the veritable landslide of government legislation with which they are supposed to be familiar and the myriad statistical returns they are asked to make, while at the same time trying to get on with the essential business of actually running companies profitably.

The rhetoric produced by the sudden awakening of interest in the small business sector in recent years has not so far produced much of practical value to help the small businessman make his business sufficiently profitable. Nor has action been taken to engender the growth needed to enable firms to take on more people (a role they are increasingly being looked upon to play) and thus ease unemployment problems.

Finance for growth is a case in point. Frequently it is said that there is a shortage of finance for small firms, but it could be rather that there is an information gap, that small firms are unaware of the range of institutions which want to and are able to provide them with funds, or of the scope of the services available.

9

The banks and other institutions actually go to considerable lengths to give information on their financial and advisory services. Yet the common complaint from businessmen is that their desire to expand production or develop new ideas is thwarted by the caution and conservatism of bankers, who seem to want a 200 per cent guarantee that they are not going to lose money. This division would continue to exist to some extent even if the financial system was working perfectly, and the evidence suggests that there is a serious problem in this area. But it is possible partly to close this information gap in a number of ways.

When, in 1977, the *Guardian* started its section devoted to the interests of small firms, under the title of *Small Business Guardian*, one of the aims was to try to bridge the information gap by providing a national forum for discussion of the problems of small businesses and to disseminate the facts which would point the bewildered businessman in the right direction. It is, for example, possible to describe the best ways of preparing the kind of business plan which will enable the businessman to extract money from bankers to whom risk-taking is anathema, and signpost the path to improved methods of marketing, an area in which small firms have often shown weakness.

This has led to a series of clear, succinct and essentially practical articles on a wide variety of topics appearing in *Small Business Guardian* over a period of four years. They have dealt with subjects such as starting a new business, budgeting and cash flow, sources of finance, marketing, office planning and ways of getting the best out of the tax system. They do not pretend to be comprehensive in scope or to provide the answer to every problem encountered in managing a small business, but together they provide the hard-pressed businessman with an easily assimilable outline of how problems can be approached, an indication of possible solutions, and a guide to where more detailed and expert advice can be obtained.

Where there are gaps in coverage, it is hoped to fill these in the pages of *Small Business Guardian* every Friday and to incorporate them in future editions of this book. In the meantime it is hoped that the articles from *Small Business Guardian* collected here will help the small businessman to avoid some of the many pitfalls in managing his business.

2
The First Steps

2.1 Drawing up a plan
Clive Woodcock

While luck naturally plays its part, the main reason for the success of a business is that it has developed a sound strategy and persisted in implementing it, a course which can substantially reduce the high risks of failure. An important element in this strategy is the basic plan for the business and, if this is well thought out, it will not only clarify the path which has to be taken through the first year of the firm's existence, but it will also help considerably if a need to raise money for the venture should exist.

For many just beginning the idea of drawing up a plan seems rather daunting, but it is a simple process. One of the best guides to drawing up a plan has been prepared by Enterprise North, the voluntary service based at Durham University Business School, which provides advice to help companies to get off the ground.

The proposal should begin with personal details, such as schooling, any apprenticeship served, qualifications, experience, jobs done and positions held in industry or commerce. If other people are involved their function in the proposed business should be explained.

The next step is to explain the idea, invention, manufacturing method or service on which the business will be based. The crux of the idea should be given in the first few lines and not buried in a mass of words.

The potential market for the product should then be explained with as much support as possible from documents, statistics, or other written evidence from prospective buyers. If it has been possible to make a sample, some indication of market reaction to it should be given.

An area of weakness with many small businesses is selling, so the plan should go into some detail on how the product will be sold. If there are partners involved in the project, it is a good idea if one has some knowledge of, or skill at, selling.

A sales forecast then has to be made and should be supported with as much evidence as possible. Cautious realism should be the tone of the forecast, leaving a little in hand in case of emergencies. The forecast should not be for more than one year ahead, but there is no reason why the possible growth of the business beyond that should not be discussed in less precise terms.

The question of price is also an important one. If the product proposed is better and more expensive than similar ones already available, an explanation should be given as to why the market will prefer it or why a particular method of marketing will produce the forecast sales. A margin should be allowed in the price for agents, wholesalers or retailers, depending on how the product or service is sold. These margins are likely to be quite substantial as the selling costs of most products represent a substantial proportion of the price. New firms quite often start out by charging too little for their products and then have to go through the embarrassing process of explaining to customers why prices have to go up, or go out of business.

The costs of the whole operation must then be thoroughly detailed. If the business is manufacturing these will include raw materials, components bought in, direct labour, supervision and inspection costs, wastage, fuel and any other overheads. Drawings of, for example, engineering products will need to be submitted along with any other appropriate manufacturing information so that independent checks can be made of the costings. An effective system of financial control is essential to the survival and success of any business and this should be discussed with an accountant and put into operation from the inception of the business.

The next step is to draw up a budget for overheads which do not arise from the manufacturing process itself, such as costs of selling, accounts, development, packing, plant depreciation, interest charges. Once this has been done it will be possible to make some assessment of the likely profit of the business.

A small business should aim at making a return of at least 15 per cent on its turnover, which, as a rough guide, would leave 10 per cent after tax. If the returns are any less than this the owner/manager might just as well start giving away the bricks and mortar.

It should also be remembered that in addition to the proprietor paying himself a fairly meagre salary in the initial stages, it will probably be necessary for profits to be ploughed back into the business for a number of years in order to avoid borrowing too much money. Using your own funds is the cheapest way of expanding.

Pensionplus
–for people who mind their own business.

When we designed Pensionplus we built in a great deal of flexibility — because that's what is needed in a personal pension plan.

Flexibility of contributions, of pension benefits and of retirement age — you'll find them all in Pensionplus ... **plus** flexible Family Security Benefits.

Pensionplus
– designed for people who mind their own business.

There are pensions experts at every Gresham Life Area Sales Office and at our Head Office. Call us, or write FREEPOST, no stamp required, to:

Gresham Life Assurance Society Limited
FREEPOST
Bournemouth BH4 9BR

Telephone: 0202 767655.

A member of the Life Offices' Association.

13

You're never too small for Telex.

Our service is your cost-effective link with the world of business.

Only £45.00 p.a. plus cost of messages.

7 days/week, 24 hour, reliable, discreet.

Over 20 teleprinters at your service.

Plus: *Telephone answering (private or shared line)*
Private Mail Boxes
Word processing service
Registered office facilities

Call us now **British Monomarks Limited** (established 1925)
27A Old Gloucester Street, London WC1N 3XX
Telephone: 01-405 4442
01-404 5011

All the information now gathered together will give the budding entrepreneur the means to draw up a cash flow forecast. This will show how much money is coming in and going out of the business and, most important, when this is likely to arise, and enable the businessman to make appropriate plans for this contingency. It is a particularly useful tool of control when a business is starting out as the flow of cash will be all in one direction – outwards. Several forecasts will probably be needed to arrrive at the best arrangement to get the business moving and make sure that it is done with the minimum amount of cash. The forecast will also indicate whether the proposal is too ambitious and may enable the project to be scaled down to one of more manageable proportions which has a greater chance of success.

Any other information in support of the proposal should then be written down, but only that which has been thoroughly thought out and tested. The plan is then ready to be typed out and presented to the prospective financier of the new small business.

2.2 Choose your experts

Margaret Dibben

At the first sign of wanting to launch your own business, you will rush for professional help to your accountant, your bank manager and solicitor. Just what sort of advice will you get from this expensive panel?

All will prescribe monochrome leaflets on the theme of starting our own business, but these will tell you very little except how indispensable your accountant, bank manager and solicitor will be. Then you will find an overlap in the advice each gives. For example, all three are willing to help you through the foggy maze of taxation. Remember, though, that your bank manager does not charge for the advice he gives, only for operating the account, whereas accountants and solicitors make an hourly charge for talking to you. Each will point out immediately if he does not think your plan is viable.

Before all else you need to decide what kind of business you want to start. You have the choice of forming a partnership or a limited company, becoming a sole trader or buying an existing business. The decision depends largely on questions of taxation and the extent of liability you take on. If your personal tax position is complicated you will need an accountant to advise you, otherwise your solicitor can handle it.

As a limited company you can take money out either by paying yourself a salary from the profit or you can reward yourself with dividends which are treated as investment income. The business itself attracts Corporation Tax on the profits. The legal requirements and expenses are greater with a limited company. You can buy a 'shelf' company for about £100, but by law you must file audited annual accounts at Companies House. Even the most straightforward accounts now cost a three-figure sum to audit and there is a £20 charge to file the annual returns. If the financial risks of your business are high, however, the advantage is that your personal liability if anything goes wrong is limited to the amount you have put into the company, and your house and own possessions are safe.

One advantage of forming a partnership is privacy, as there are no legal requirements to file accounts. But if the business goes bust there is no limit to how far the liquidator can confiscate your personal property. The partners have joint and several liability so it is crucial that your solicitor draws up a watertight partnership agreement. Then, if a creditor sues one partner there is no dispute as to how the responsibility is divided. A simple one-page partnership agreement might cost £100 from your local solicitor but, if it is highly complex with various personal taxation consequences, the cost could reach four figures.

How do you find the best solicitor or accountant to suit your needs? Be prepared to shop around; if you openly admit that you are seeing two or three solicitors before deciding, they will almost certainly meet you for a quarter of an hour without charge. In fact they will probably be glad of the opportunity to size you up as well. The large city practices will, undoubtedly, be more expensive than smaller local firms where the overheads are lower. Ask around, see who your friends and competitiors use, quiz your bank manager. But if you find you are not happy with your accountant or solicitor, perhaps because his dull, plodding attitude jars on your bright, thrusting personality, move to another quickly before you both waste too much time.

As there are certain grey areas covered by both solicitors and accountants, it is a good idea to bring the two together at a very early stage. They can then chew over your problems with the minimum waste of time and avoid any duplication of work.

The accountant, as well as worrying about figures and the spectre of taxation, can also help decide what form your company should take. Particularly if you are buying a going concern, he will be able to say if you are paying a fair price.

If no one in your business has the necessary skills, a chartered accountant can handle the company secretarial work for you and he will look after the pay-roll and bookkeeping. He will also advise on what books and registers you need to maintain.

Unless you can keep all the records and handle all cash totally by yourself, there will need to be simple controls to guard against error and fraud. An accountant will suggest that each employee's responsibilities are carefully defined and that accounting entries are checked.

The fees charged by accountants vary enormously, depending on the area, size of firm and the kind of advice it is giving. Get a broad idea of what it will cost before your accountant embarks on your accounts as the price may range from £15 to £50 a day.

How does the bank manager help? His role is to lend the money to get the business off the ground and to keep it running but he needs to be sure that your proposition is sound and sensible. Strolling into his office with a vague idea that you might like to open a greengrocer's shop in the High Street will not convince him that you are a fit person to make a success of it.

However, if you have been working for several years in the fresh

National Westminster knows a lot about small businesses

The great majority of our business customers are small businesses – 50% of them employ fewer than 10 people.

We can help you if you are setting up in business

Our venture capital scheme for small businesses – the Capital Loan Scheme – is unique.

We are participating jointly with the Department of Industry in the Government Loan Guarantee Scheme.

We can help you if you wish to expand your business

Our Business Development Loans are specially tailored for the growing small business and are appropriate for both working capital needs and for investment in new fixed assets.

We can provide a whole range of other services...

including unrivalled advice and information.

All you have to do is to contact your local NatWest manager. He's there to help you.

♻ National Westminster Bank

fruit and vegetable department of a supermarket and take your accountant with you to present a budget, he will know that you have thought out the plan and have a track record in the field. Even so, before he agrees to make a loan, the bank manager will expect you to know how much you will need to spend on a lease, on stock, and on vehicles and he will be much more impressed if you have a lump sum of your own already saved.

He will then, after making a personal assessment of your ability, decide what type and size of loan is most appropriate. His interest does not end there as he will continue to keep a paternal eye on your (that is, the bank's) money, which will probably mean showing him a quarterly cash flow statement.

Each of the banks has its own pet schemes to help small businesses and the manager's advice will be coloured by this. But all banks are now keen to help the independent company, provided of course they feel their money will be safe. Some plans are tailored to a particular region and all the banks have close links with COSIRA at a local level. You may find that your bank runs regional conferences for local small businessmen.

The banks can also be helpful if you want to export, guiding you through the tangle of red tape and forms. The Midland Bank launched a Smaller Exports Scheme at the beginning of the year designed for customers with very few or intermittent exports, whereby the bank takes out umbrella ECGD cover.

As for the cost of a bank account, on top of the interest you pay, the bank will charge a business account commission for debit and credit payments and for services such as using the night safe.

Then, when your business is off the ground, take your professional advisers completely into your confidence and tell them frankly when you run into problems. If you have chosen well, these experts are fully trained to help.

2.3 Finance from tax
Joe Horner

Mrs Thatcher and Sir Geoffrey Howe have taken a huge gamble in hoping that the country will respond to direct tax cuts with increased productivity and increased employment opportunities.

Whether they were right to take this gamble is a matter of

political opinion but, having taken it, I imagine that nobody will be particularly pleased if they fail in their purpose. The small business sector, together with high taxpayers, can play an important part in trying to make the gamble work.

At a recent meeting, when the subject of raising finance for new enterprises was discussed, the old fallacy that other countries give tax incentives to new businesses but this country does not was heard. This is quite untrue. There are incentives to start new businesses in this country. It is just that they are not as obvious as everybody would like and therefore are not properly understood.

We have an unfortunate habit of making financial and fiscal matters so complicated that the good ideas are often lost sight of or are viewed with suspicion.

There is no shortage of new ideas. Some may be brilliant; others may be mediocre; others may end in failure. With a few exceptions, it is impossible to predict accurately which ideas are in which category. Banks are often criticised for only supporting the certain winners and not taking a risk on ventures which are unable to prove a market need in advance.

While the critic may himself be at fault for researching and presenting his case badly, there might nevertheless be some truth in the criticism. However, with demand for capital exceeding supply, it is a little unreasonable to expect the lenders not to favour the ventures which appear to carry the least risk.

Those who can, however, afford to take a risk on a new venture are people who paid tax at very high rates in the past three years. If such people were to form partnerships (or even begin on their own) to start new businesses they would be taking very little risk.

Provided that the enterprise was not a silly one but stood a genuine chance of being successful in a reasonable time, they would be substantially protected against loss. If the business did make a loss in its early years, they could set that loss against their income of three years earlier and reclaim the tax.

The Inland Revenue would therefore carry the lion's share of the risk. With the new scales of higher rate tax, one of the old deterrents (the fact that any profit also went almost wholly to the government) has been greatly modified.

The people in the highest tax brackets are presumably in the main anxious to see the present government succeed. By starting a new enterprise they will, at the least, be providing a few jobs and therefore helping both the individuals they employ and the government.

The opportunity to do that, with the prospect for making a profit for themselves and the Inland Revenue putting a safety net under them if the venture is unsuccessful, should be almost irresistible.

There are, of course, difficulties. The person in the highest tax bracket does not necessarily have large immediate cash resources. He may have little time to devote to a new enterprise.

There are commercial risks in branching into a field where one has no personal experience. These, and many others, are all genuine problems but in many cases they can be solved satisfactorily. Perhaps the biggest problem of all is 'how does the person with the new idea get in touch with the person who can afford to promote it?'

What seems to be lacking is an introductions bureau where the two can meet. Perhaps some of the business schools could develop an organisation to help these people get together.

The right to set business losses against gross income from other sources has existed for a long time. The right to choose to carrry them back against income of three years earlier was introduced by Mr Healey and was designed specifically to encourage people to try new ventures with the minimum of risk.

It will be a pity if this particular government incentive fails to achieve its objective because it is under-appreciated or because there is no coordinating body or place where the parties with the different contributions to make can get in touch with each other. There are some commercial organisations already trying to provide the organisation but it is desirable that a body with conference facilities should be involved, and this is where business schools could be so useful.

There are also other types of government incentive to risk-taking and to investing in areas of the economy which, by agreement of all political parties, deserve encouragement. They could also be explored and developed by an organisation with the right prestige and facilities.

2.4 The right premises
Robert Waterhouse

Suitable premises are obviously a key factor in the decision to set up in business. Not that many start in ideal premises, or that even the most modern and well-serviced buildings are exactly right for any one operation. Like most of life, they are a compromise which can be made to work when there is sufficient will and effort. The important thing is to have somewhere; otherwise the experience is similar to starting a marriage without a home.

Many ventures begin in somebody's back room, study or garage. For a few months, maybe even a year or two, the business is nurtured over its crucial early stages by the fact that there is no rent or rates to pay. But quite soon, if business begins to grow (and four out of five new ventures still fail to get off the ground) there will be pressure to move out of the home and into commercial premises.

What and where depend on what is needed, what is on offer, and the price. The best advice at this stage, if not before, is to contact the Department of Industry's Small Firms Service. Get on their books, see if you are eligible for a set-up grant, and have at least one interview (it's free) with their counselling service, picking the brains of an experienced and sympathetic voluntary counsellor. He or she may tell you that, in their opinion, the best thing to do is forget about the venture altogether; but you don't have to follow their advice.

The service will put you in touch with estate agents or commercial clients who do have space to offer. Alternatively, you may just qualify for an advance factory nursery unit built either by the Department, the Development Commission, the Scottish or Welsh Development Agency, a new town development corporation, or by a local authority.

There is a bewildering array of governmental help for the small business (at least before the quangos are put to death) compounded by the partnership and other schemes set up to revive inner cities. But the idea of the Small Firms Service is to create shop-front access to potential customers, and the Department of Industry through its regional centres is ready and willing to provide specific guidance. And it seems, by a marvel of coordination and goodwill, red tape has been overcome and that the links between the various authorities are valid and working.

Since the election of the present government the whole approach to assistance has been revised. This means the downrating of large parts of the north from its present intermediate area status, and a concentration of selective assistance (often on a higher level) for areas of persistently high unemployment. But this new policy does not come into effect for most places until August 1982, so small businesses starting in the next year or so can claim the kind of assistance which has been normal for several years.

Details of present and future regional development grants are too intricate to list here, but can be obtained from any of the authorities mentioned above. One point to remember is that the authorities building advance factories do have the ability to reduce or waive rent and rates for the first year or two to help a promising firm survive the transition to commercial premises. This discretionary system makes advance units highly desirable, and they are usually over-subscribed by a factor of 10, but it is still worth trying to get hold of one.

Rent and rates vary, even in advance factories, with the usual laws of supply and demand. The going rent on Merseyside is about £1.40 per square foot, in Manchester perhaps £1.60, and so on. Commercial rents may be much lower, or higher. For instance, space on the top floor of an old, unserviced mill in the Burnley area might be offered at as little as 20p per sq ft, but the question remains how suitable this would be to most businesses. In the more affluent parts of the country, costs could be well over £3 per sq ft for less than brilliant premises, and would-be industrialists may find local authorities far less accommodating than in development areas.

Planning permission is, of course, needed for any change of use involving industrial or commercial premises. This means, for instance, that an empty house may look very desirable for office space, but the idea could be blocked by a local policy of protecting and encouraging housing in that area.

It is now generally recognised that the comprehensive approach to slum clearance and urban redevelopment practised throughout the 1960s and early 1970s swept away thousands of small businesses along with their premises. Some relocated themselves in the new towns or on industrial estates, many simply vanished without trace. There has since been a sincere desire on the part of the authorities to try to undo the damage. Small businesses (or light industry) are by and large allowed to co-exist with housing and shops in a way unthinkable only 10 years ago.

There could be no better time for the small capitalist, with the approval and often assistance of the state, to set himself up. How long the fashion will last is quite another question, so quick decisions are the order of the day.

2.5 Tenants' rights

Clare Dyer

1979 was the twenty-fifth anniversary of the Act of Parliament which gave a measure of security to the tenant of business premises – the Landlord and Tenant Act 1954. The last 25 years have seen growing protection for the residential tenant, but the businessman's right to carry on trading when his lease or tenancy expires remains hedged about with strict requirements as to notices and time limits. The Act can be a minefield for the unwary tenant who walks in without the benefit of good professional advice.

What types of premises are protected by the Act? Any in which a business is being carried on, and 'business' is widely defined to include not only the usual shops, offices, factories and workshops, but professional offices. It has even been held to include schools and sporting clubs. The Act confers rights on the *occupier* of business premises, so if they are let to a sub-tenant it will be he, rather than the tenant, who will be able to claim the benefit of the protection.

What exactly are these rights? As long as the landlord takes no positive step the tenant is entitled to stay on in the premises even though tenancy has expired, on the same terms and at the same rent as before. The Act also gives him the right to apply to the court for a new tenancy at a fair market rent.

It is up to the landlord to take the first step if he wants to get the property back or to raise the rent to the current market level. He must serve a notice specifying a date, not less than 12 months in the future, for the tenancy to end. The date named can be the date on which the lease or tenancy agreement expires, or any time after its expiry.

The notice must ask the tenant to let the landlord know within two months whether he intends to apply for a new lease. The landlord must indicate in the notice whether he intends to oppose the tenant's application and, if so, on what grounds.

There are seven grounds on which an application can be opposed, but the most important are that the landlord genuinely wants to occupy the premises, or has some definite scheme for redevelopment. Vague plans are not likely to recommend themselves to the court: it will be looking for 'a clear intention, fixed and settled,' as the Court of Appeal put it in one case. Nor is the court likely to refuse a new tenancy if the landlord's plans can be carried out without dislodging the tenant, if, for instance the tenant is willing to allow the landlord's workmen access through his premises.

A landlord who has bought an already tenanted property faces a further restriction: he must have owned it for five years before he can successfully resist a claim for a new tenancy because he wants to occupy it himself.

Most new tenancies are hammered out by agreement between the landlord's and the tenant's advisers. Of 10,000 applications to the court each year, only 500 or so go to a full hearing. But the right will be lost if the tenant does not apply to the court between two and four months after the landlord's notice is served.

There is a danger of being lulled into a false sense of security if negotiations seem to be going reasonably well, but once four months have passed, if the new tenancy hasn't been sewn up and no court application made, the right is irretrievably lost. The time limits in the Act are applied absolutely rigidly by the court, which has no discretion to waive them, however much it may sympathise with the tenant.

In one recent case, court proceedings were well under way when it was discovered that the landlord had never received the tenant's counter-notice, the statement of his intention to apply for a new tenancy, which must be served within two months of the landlord's notice. It had been sent by ordinary post, and had never been delivered. Although the court had every sympathy for the tenant, they were unable to give him a new tenancy.

It is a common misconception that the terms of the new lease will be exactly the same as the old, apart from the rent. The landlord and tenant can agree any changes they like, and in default of agreement a judge can put in any clause he thinks reasonable in the circumstances. In practice, though, the terms will be the same unless there is good reason to alter them.

Variations which have been granted by the court include a shorter term where the property was ripe for development, though plans were not sufficiently formulated for the landlord to obtain possession; a rent review clause where there was none before; and a change made to legalise an existing use of the property which contravened the old lease.

Once the terms have been agreed, the most important item – the new rent – has to be negotiated.

Finally, what about the tenant whose lease has expired and whose landlord hasn't taken any steps? If he wants more security before making alterations or putting capital into the business, he is not obliged to sit tight waiting for his landlord to make the first move. The Act allows him to serve a notice on the landlord requesting a new tenancy.

Selectaplan Ltd.

**Planning To Acquire Your Own Business,
Expand, Or Have Cash-Flow Problems?**

Contact us to help you raise the money you
need, point out the tax advantages of
borrowing, and show you how best to set up
your business now.

17 Nottingham Street,
London W1M 3RD
Tel. (01) 486-4887/8.

2.6 Looking after the workers

Peter Hildrew

The responsibilities of an employer are numerous, complicated, open to varying interpretations and constantly changing. It is safer to be aware of the jungle ahead than to plunge in unprepared. Large companies employ battalions of personnel officers to shepherd them through the undergrowth but the small operator has to muddle along with little time available and a fistful of leaflets for guidance.

There was a chorus of protest as new laws came through thick and fast during the period of the last Labour government. If small firms offered the main hope for new jobs, so the argument ran, government should be making it easier to employ people rather than more difficult. This can be weighed against the view from the opposite side of the fence: that in small firms, where trade union organisation may be weak or non-existent, the worker is all the more likely to need the protection of the law.

In the hope of disentangling fact from supposition, the government mounted a survey on the impact of employment legislation on small firms, and the results – reported in the Department of Employment *Gazette*, July 1979 – map out the sensitive areas. The employment protection laws themselves ranked only thirteenth in the problems of running a small business.

But securing good, experienced and hard-working staff ranked third (after money and orders); coping with PAYE and National Insurance came eighth; and finding staff at all, ninth. Employment measures causing most problems were: unfair dismissal (difficulty in sacking people); maternity leave; redundancy provisions; health and safety requirements; and pay for temporary lay-offs.

There are two essential leaflets which are basic to taking on an employee: the *Employer's Guide to PAYE* (from tax offices) and the *Employer's Guide to National Insurance* (from social security offices). The tax collector for the business area will be only too happy to explain the income tax to be deducted, to whom it should be paid and when and to supply the necessary record cards. National Insurance contributions from both employer and employee are collected at the same time. These time-consuming procedures just have to be mastered.

Employees are entitled to an itemised pay statement, explaining their pay and deductions. A contract of employment exists as soon as an employee commences work, whether the job is permanent, temporary, casual or part-time and whether the contract is written, oral or implied. Rights to a minimum period of notice begin after four weeks (one week initially, then a week per year of service from two to 12 years).

The Department of Employment's guide for employers, *Individual Rights of Employees*, lists many of the points to watch and includes a useful code of practice on disciplinary procedures, issued by ACAS. The Equal Pay Act, for instance, lays down that men and women must be treated equally in both terms and conditions of employment if they are engaged in 'like work' or work rated as equivalent under a job evaluation study.

Partly in the hope of helping small firms, the government changed the law on unfair dismissal: from 1 October 1979 employees had to complete 52 weeks' service instead of 26 before they can lodge an unfair dismissal complaint to the industrial tribunal seeking compensation or (rarely) reinstatement. Dismissal can then only be fair if there is a substantial reason for it, such as capability in the job, conduct, or redundancy. Dismissal for trade union membership or activities is unfair.

The law on redundancy has also been changed with effect from 30 November, reducing from 60 to 30 days the period required for prior notification to the Department of Employment and consultation with unions on redundancies of 10 to 99 workers. If fewer than 10 are involved, there is no defined period, but the reasonable consultation procedures (Section 99, Employment Protection Act 1975) still apply where there is a recognised trade union.

Tribunals are frequently asked to adjudicate as to whether an employee really was redundant to the business or was dismissed unfairly for some other reason. Employees being made redundant are entitled to time off to look for another job. The law also protects reasonable time off for trade union duties where a union is recognised, and for public duties such as serving on a local council.

Employers have a duty to ensure the health, safety and welfare at work of all their employees 'so far as is reasonably practicable' and employees have a duty to cooperate with necessary measures. Health and safety covers a vast area from loose floor boards and the temperature of the room to machine guards or the handling of hazardous chemicals.

If in doubt – ask. Besides laying down what employers must do, the state also offers a wide range of advice and assistance to cover most situations. The Employment Medical Advisory Service will discuss occupational health hazards and the Factory Inspectorate will advise on the best practicable means of ensuring safety. The Department of Employment publishes another leaflet, *Services to Employers*, and it will help find and train staff. It can still offer a Small Firms Employment Subsidy of £20 per week for each extra worker taken on in manufacturing firms in Development and Special Development Areas.

Last but never least, ACAS does far more than try to sort out industrial disputes: it will advise on the whole field of industrial relations, contracts of employment and personnel management, and will try to settle complaints before they ever get to a tribunal.

2.7 The need for records

Douglas Donleavy

Some recent research into the causes of bankruptcy among small firms shows that, while poor sales, bad initial choice of site, misguided spending and sheer bad luck were all factors that occurred very often in the history of failure, one element dominated all of these – a general absence of reliable records.

One creditor that generally pursues its debtors all the way to bankruptcy is the Inland Revenue, and the major reason why small firms get into trouble with their tax bill is absence of records. Without records, the small businessman has only, at best, a vague idea of his profit. The Inland Revenue presents him with an assessment and he finds himself without the paper evidence necessary to argue against his tax bill. He is saddled with a demand, the basis of which he does not really understand and which he is unable or unwilling to pay. Lack of records also means that he has been unable to plan his cash flow to ensure he has enough saved to meet the tax demand and any other sudden expenditure. As a result, a promising business may be aborted and its owner driven into bankruptcy, all for the lack of a few simple records.

Readers may doubt that records are simple. An illusion often encountered these days is that enterprise is stifled by a bureaucratic government's unappeasable appetite for complicated forms that nobody needs and nobody reads. This has some validity in the case of government statistical forms and VAT returns, but this article is concerned with the firm too small to be involved in either of these. The Inland Revenue forms are not difficult and generally involve no more than the appendage of a set of annual accounts. Annual accounts, however, cannot be prepared without books of account.

It would be understandable for the new businessman to protest that he went into business for himself, not for the taxman, and that he is damned if he is going to spend a couple of hours a week writing up books just to please the Revenue. However, it is failure to keep books that will almost always guarantee a higher tax bill than is really fair to the taxpayer. The Revenue fights with paper, and the taxpayer must do likewise. It is quite futile to hope that you are too small to come to the attention of your tax office and quite hopeless to believe that a nice line in patter and excuses is any substitute for proper records.

It is not only the tax bill that can be controlled by good record keeping. The businessman who wishes to survive, let alone grow, must know how he is doing on a weekly, even a daily, basis. This means he must know two very important things about his business at all times: first, the amount of cash he has to spend, and, second, the true profit or loss he makes from his sales.

It is important to realise that making a profit does not necessarily mean having any spare cash and that having a lot of money in the bank does not mean a big profit has been made. The Inland Revenue is interested in the profit or loss, and the bank in both the profit and the cash, while the businessman is interested in success (a matter of profit) and survival (a matter of cash).

Now to the records themselves. First and foremost is the cash book. On the left hand pages are written all the cash received in the form of cheques; on the right all payments made by cheque. Every week the receipts are added up and the total weekly payments deducted from them to give a cash at bank balance. This should agree with the bank's records and, if it does not, the reason for the difference has to be found so a correct view can emerge. If the cash book is written in every time a cheque is received or paid out, the effort soon becomes a habit rather than a burden.

Many small businesses deal in notes and coins rather than cheques and for such transactions a petty cash book is necessary. Money in on the left-hand pages; money out on the right. If possible, retain vouchers for every entry in the book to prove the accuracy of each entry if it becomes necessary. At least once a week add up the receipts and payments to obtain a balance of cash in hand and check that it agrees with the actual amount counted from the till or the cash box. This routine will quickly reveal any carelessness with petty cash and provide an early warning system of alien fingers in the till!

If sales and purchases are made on credit, a sales and purchases ledger will both be necessary. Both of these have one page for each firm with whom credit deals are transacted. In the purchase ledger, suppliers are recorded in alphabetical order of name. Address and phone numbers are written under the name, and on the right-hand side are listed the date, nature and amount of each item bought on credit. On the left-hand side are recorded all the payments made to the supplier for the items on the right.

Every month, the left-hand total is deducted from the right to show how much the supplier is owed. If the supplier sends statements, these should agree with the purchase ledger account. In the sales ledger, customers are listed in a similar way to the suppliers in the purchase ledger but sales on credit to them appear on the left while their payments appear on the right.

The above records represent the absolute minimum for any business. In addition, limited companies must keep a record in a capital ledger of any land, buildings, machinery, furniture and vehicles owned (all entered on the left) showing the cost of such items at the time of purchase.

All expenses are posted from the cash books and purchase ledgers to the left-hand side of the nominal ledger. Income from sales, rent, dividends, etc, is posted to the right. There is a separate page in the ledger for each type of expense or income: one for rent, one for wages, one for sales, etc. It is important to keep expenses on the left and income on the right if the books are to balance.

Every month each page in the nominal and capital ledgers is totalled, taking care to keep right-hand totals separate from left-hand ones. The balances in the sales ledger and purchase ledgers are also totalled as are the totals in the cash books. These are then listed on a sheet of paper called a trial balance whose left hand totals should add up to the final total of the right hand totals. If so, the books balance and the businessman can be confident of his records.

A comparison of expenses with sales will show the profit for the month. The cash book totals will show the cash in hand. The sales and purchase ledgers will show how much the business owes and how much it is owed in turn.

A small sacrifice of time and effort in keeping simple books is well worth the return in terms of knowing where the business stands. Additional benefits are: saving the cost of employing a bookkeeper, confidence in facing the Inland Revenue and control of one's own business destiny based on accurate data instead of on some mythical 'flair' or 'gut-feel' that cuts no ice with the official receiver. Indeed, it can be said that no businessman is in control of his business fate unless he is in control of his business records.

2.8 Starting a cooperative

Steven Richards

Although the cooperative movement began in Britain some 136 years ago, the development of service and producer cooperatives (in which the workers own the business themselves) is only just starting to take off in this country. The idea that the workforce which helps create the wealth of a company should share in its success is not new, but in the past four years there has been a growing interest in the concept of producer cooperatives helping to solve the unemployment problem by giving a jab in the arm for new enterprise development.

All well and good, but there is remarkably little information around on just what a worker cooperative is, how it operates and why it provides a possible alternative to traditional businesses. And that, quite possibly, is the reason why so few of these new cooperative businesses have so far been established, despite the creation of a government-sponsored Cooperative Development Agency, and of numerous voluntary cooperative development groups around the country.

In simple terms, a producer, service, or worker cooperative (whatever the terminology currently in vogue) is a business in which the people who work in it also own it, and work together for the common good. This basic transformation in thinking which requires would-be cooperators to consider themselves as 'we together' instead of 'us' (the workers) and 'them' (the management) is the first, and possibly the greatest hurdle.

The purest form of cooperative demands that all those in the business should have a personal financial stake, that each should share in its running, and, in effect, that they all make up the board or ruling council. Even the person appointed to manage the business, control the finances, and oversee the marketing and production schedules, should have an equal say in the direction of the cooperative – equal, that is, with those actually producing the product or providing the service.

Clearly in smaller cooperatives – there must be seven people involved for the business to be registered as a cooperative under the Industrial and Provident Societies Act – the lines of communication are relatively short and there will most likely be an overlap of job functions anyway. The larger the grouping, however, the more necessary is a separate manager and marketer for the concern, and then some form of differential might arise on pay. But, in most cooperatives, the difference in wages of the 'leader' and of those providing other labour, will be small or non-existent. This aspect, coupled with the idea of taking direction from those on the shop-floor, may well be difficult for many aspiring cooperative managers.

Yet the idea of a few skilled people coming together to do their own thing is attractive, and the choice of structure between a traditional private company and a cooperative might be decided more out of consideration of total capital requirements than of

31

social ideals.

Finance is, of course, the problem which faces any new business, but all the evidence available seems to suggest that cash, or the lack of it, is not the main problem. A feature of a cooperative is that everyone involved should pay a membership fee as a shareholding. This might be as little as £1 in some cases. No matter what the size of the shareholding, though, there is only one vote in the running of the business for each member. And that factor tends to encourage cooperatives to seek equal shareholdings sufficient to provide the financial base for the business.

In northern Spain, where a group of industrial cooperatives at Mondragon has been successfully developing for a number of years, each founder member is required to contribute a substantial capital sum to help launch the business. It may not be enough to pay for all the costs of the new enterprise, but it will be of sufficient size (now usually £2000) for each member to feel bound to the fortunes of the cooperative and firmly interested in its progress. After all, the theory goes, if you have a sizeable financial stake in the business, you will want to make it grow, to ensure that high productivity is maintained and that money is not spent unnecessarily and to exercise your right to have a say in the development of the business. The need to strike – for more pay, better conditions, a shorter working week, etc – is removed since you have a direct say in all those things as a member. And you would be striking against yourself.

The Cooperative Bank has taken this possibility of greater working stability as a principle factor and encouraged it to make available start-up finance for the establishment of new industrial and service cooperatives. The Bank is prepared to match, pound for pound, the money raised by the members of the business as their personal stake and has set up a maximum limit of £25,000 as its initial contribution. This is in addition to any overdraft facilities for working capital.

The Industrial Common Ownership Finance at Northampton has a substantial amount of money available through government support to help with the establishment of cooperative-type ventures. This can also include Industrial Common Ownership (ICOM) businesses which differ slightly from traditional cooperatives in that their model rules allow each member to contribute only £1 as a share stake, and the balance to be raised from others (government, banks, etc) outside the business as loans.

Problems can also occur as cooperatives expand and need to take on extra people. Ideally, they will become members and not employees and will also contribute a capital sum at least equal to the amount paid by each founding member. But, as in Spain, newcomers can be accommodated and encouraged by allowing them to build up their contribution either wholly through deductions from earnings or through staggered lump-sum payments.

The founding group may not have all the necessary experience to launch the business, the members perhaps lacking marketing skills or accounting ability. One means of helping would-be cooperatives to overcome these problems has been the creation of 'talent banks' – lists of people in an area who are prepared to make available their experience and knowledge as managers, marketing men, engineers, and so on, either free or for a small fee. So far there are only a few such lists: one is operated by the Scottish Cooperative Development Association in Glasgow, another by the Northern Region Cooperatives Development Association in Newcastle and ICOM has made progress in this way too, via its main office at Roundhay, Leeds.

Surprisingly, the central Cooperative Development Agency has made few moves in this direction. But there is a growing group of men and women at its headquarters in London, working to convince national groups of the value of industrial cooperatives, and there is also a section looking at individual projects. Anyone wanting to start a cooperative can contact the CDA (telephone: 01-211 3000) for advice and to put specific ideas to them for assistance; so far very few people have done this and there would appear to be an opportunity to get individual attention in these early stages.

The CDA has published an information brochure on the theme of 'mutual aid, self-help and the quality of life', and a very detailed document on 'how to convert a company into an industrial co-operative', designed to appeal to small family businesses which have a succession problem and which might, instead of closing, be handed over to the workers to keep the business going.

Elsewhere in the country, in west Glamorgan, the north-east and Scotland, for example, local cooperative development groups have published their own brochures giving some detail about small cooperative ventures which have been formed in their areas and giving contact points for further information.

There are cooperatives making blouses, steel fabrication structures and iron gates, and engaged in traditional crafts, printing, publishing, building and whole foods, but so far there is little collective experience and only a little guidance.

Central to the development of cooperatives, as with any business, is the need for good, viable product or service ideas. Despite all that is said, money is not the main problem; cash is available from many sources, including banks, local authorities (under the Local Government Act and the Inner Urban Areas Act), various government employment schemes and from Europe. The big shortage is in marketable ideas, and the establishment of a cooperative will not overcome that barrier. Having overcome the ideas hurdle, producer cooperatives are still very much·in the pioneering stage and would-be founders should take advantage of the few areas of practical advice and experience.

2.9 Telephone for cash

Robert Boyd

Cash flow is a major factor in the daily life of every small businessman, and rising bankruptcy and liquidation rates have emphasised its importance. However, ideas for actually speeding up the realisation of money locked up in debts are in relatively short supply. One technique that can be used with advantage is that of 'telephone cash collection'.

This method involves systematically telephoning for payment instead of sending first and second reminder letters, seven day warnings and so on. It requires a similar skill to telephone selling, the main difference being the attitude that the telephone collection clerk has to the call. He, or more often she, is concluding the business transaction rather than starting it. She is collecting money due and is entitled to speak with authority to anyone at the debtor company to achieve this. Because of this strong position senior staff can be reached more easily and any likely problems in collection discovered early.

The key to effective debt collection by telephone is preparation. Records to be referred to must be clear and accurate. Muddle and delay while on a call is not only costly but spoils a positive first impression. The caller should always try to keep the initiative, but this is impossible if constant requests to 'hang on a minute, will you' are made.

The main information that should be available is how much money is owing in total, how much is being asked for now, and how this latter total is made up in terms of invoices and credit notes. The sales ledger must be right up to date on the cash received side. It is embarrassing to demand a cheque for invoices that were paid a few days before.

The sales ledger is best kept in a form showing all outstanding invoices separately. Any that are missing from the customers' ledger can then be easily identified. Preferably, invoices for each month should be together.

An 'aged' list of unpaid invoices for each customer is the ideal document to work from. If the present sales ledger system does not provide data in this form, an analysis of invoices into one, two and three months old and over can readily be prepared by hand.

Having verified what is due for payment the next important matter is to decide who to talk to. In most cases the customer's purchase ledger clerks will be the first stage. They will be able to say whether the caller's invoices have been passed for payment and if so when the cheque will be paid. Queries will also be identified at this stage. However, the object of the telephone call is to get payment from the debtor earlier than he would normally wish to do so. Real progress will only be made, therefore, if a promise of payment is obtained from someone who can guarantee that a cheque will be drawn, signed, and actually posted as a result of the telephone call.

This person will normally be the accountant and his name and that of the managing director should be requested in the course of the conversation with the purchase ledger clerk. This has the added benefit of letting the clerk know that the caller means business and that unfulfilled promises will be followed up.

The result of the call should, if possible, be a specific promise to send a cheque on an agreed date. There is little point in making a series of calls to be told each time that 'I will look into it' or 'A cheque will be in the post soon.' Promises received must be followed up if the cheque is not received on or soon after the date promised.

The telephone collection method works best if a careful record of results is made. The main points of a conversation should be compared with the subsequent receipt or otherwise of a cheque. This leads to the early recognition of the main techniques of avoiding payment.

Good relationships built up with the staff of regular but slow payers helps towards earlier payment. Evasive answers or broken promises help identify the major risks quickly. Combined with legal processes and, if applicable, the cutting off of supplies, the telephone collection technique can be very effective.

2.10 Slow payers

Robert Boyd

Large companies are being increasingly criticised for their slow payment to small suppliers. Reports on research by, among others, the London Enterprise Agency and the Association of Independent Businesses show there is some justification for the complaint and the chief general manager of the Co-operative Bank has emphasised the interdependence of large and small firms.

A recent check on payments made by a number of well-known companies showed that the average time taken from date of invoice to payment varied from five weeks to more than twelve weeks. Most companies paid after about eight weeks but some invoices took much longer. Even when compelled to give such extended credit it may be impossible for the small business to cut off supplies or go on to a pro forma invoice basis without doing permanent damage to its main markets.

However, whether or not large companies can be convinced that they should do more to help their smaller relatives, it is often possible for the latter to get cheques sooner by examining the payment process stage by stage.

All companies of any size are handling hundreds, and often thousands, of pieces of paper every day. To control this flood of orders, delivery notes, invoices, cheques and other documents they have laid down rigid systems for processing them efficiently.

Their methods of purchasing from and payment to small suppliers are no exception. Once a purchase invoice, for example, has got into the system then its progress is relatively automatic. Whether this movement from input to payment is a matter of weeks or months the invoices of the small company will not normally be treated any differently from hundreds of others unless they require special attention for some reason. They are in the best position for payment if they pass without delay through each stage from receipt of invoice on to the ledger and finally to payment.

The comparatively unsophisticated organisation of the small firm is competing for payment with the highly organised invoicing and cash collection departments of larger companies.

The latter have examined every link in the chain from sales invoice to payment both in their own organisation and in the customer's. The small supplier must look at this process with equal care if he is to have any chance of receiving payment as soon as his larger competitors.

The main aim is to get the invoice on to the customer's purchase ledger before it closes for that month. Surprisingly, perhaps, many large companies close their ledgers before the end of the month concerned. That is, if it is their policy to pay October invoices in early December, then for their purposes October may only be invoices received up to October 25 or even earlier. Any invoices received after that date are classed as November and paid in early January.

Companies vary so much in their purchase ledger timetables that it is difficult to generalise. What is certain is that a few days' delay in sending off invoices, particularly round about the customer's close off date, can result in those invoices being paid four or five weeks late. The purchase ledger clerk, purchase manager or accountant of each important but slow paying company should, therefore, be asked for details of their timetable.

If it is clearly explained that the reason for the call is to find out how their system works so that your invoices will be paid quicker, the cause of the delay will soon be found.

It may be that your invoices, though paid late, are not paid any later than other suppliers. but it may be the case that your invoices are getting on to a later payment run than necessary and action can be taken to rectify the situation. The lessons learnt on a few such calls can often be applied generally.

It is obvious that invoices must be raised and despatched promptly. If, because of rising postage rates, a policy has been adopted of holding invoices until several have accumulated if should be reconsidered if it might lead to that customer's ledger being missed for the month. In some cases first class post may be advisable.

All efforts to get invoices to customers quickly are wasted if queries cause them to be treated as exceptions at the receiving end. Needless to say invoices must be correctly addressed, priced, extended and totalled, but one common cause of delay is order numbers. The need for these varies from the essential to merely desirable.

In the first case an invoice without an order number will be returned. This highlights the matter which can be noted for future business. In the latter case the invoice will be circulated round the organisation until it reaches the person who ordered or received the goods or services. The invoice is delayed in getting on to the ledger, but to the supplier there is no apparent reason why he gets paid an extra month late.

Customers' staff placing orders, perhaps on the telephone, do not always tell the supplier he should be given an order number. It may, in any case, have to be obtained from a central purchasing department and arrive after the invoice has been sent. It is, perhaps, best for the supplier to insist that the name and department of the person placing the order is put on the sales invoice when an order number is not received.

The date on the invoice should normally be the date of despatch and not that of invoice preparation if later. This is particularly important if goods are despatched in one month and invoiced, perhaps the next day, in the following month.

The majority of firms close their purchase ledgers three to ten days after the month end and their 'cut off' or finishing date for that month will usually be the last day of the month.

One company, finding a fall in its cash collection rate, discovered that a computer operator had accidentally dated a batch of invoices with the next month instead of the current one. The customers had, therefore, held these invoices back until the following month's ledger.

Some queries on matters such as shortages, returns and price cannot be avoided.

But other errors that could cause a hold-up in payment will be found if all invoices of a significant amount are checked for essential detail before posting.

Examination of one's own and customers' procedures in the way described can pay substantial dividends in speeding cash flow.

2.11 Early payment

Robert Boyd

Keeping sales ledger debtors to a minimum is vitally important to the expansion, and sometimes even the survival, of small firms. Streamlining the method of raising invoices will, by itself, often lead to a significant increase in cash flow by getting the invoices on to the customers sales ledger earlier. It is also helpful to take a close look at how companies, especially the larger ones, organise their monthly payments to supplier.

The problem for the small company is how to obtain payment earlier, and it should be tackled in the most direct way by asking the customer's accounts staff how it can be achieved. This discussion gives a useful understanding of how their internal systems work, and the importance of computers soon becomes obvious from references to 'next weeks's computer run' or 'the month end cheque print-out'. The detailed working of every computer system is unique, as sellers of packaged programs soon discover, but certain common methods stand out.

One technique is for the computer to print out a cheque and remittance advice on a certain date or in a certain 'pay week' or 'pay month'. This is entered manually or, alternatively, can be calculated by the computer. Among the factors taken into account when deciding the pay week are the invoice date or company's own month end date, available discounts, terms stated on the purchase order and, most important of all, the number of weeks credit the company takes as a matter of policy. The credit taken from different suppliers may vary because of pay week decisions made by the purchasing or accounts department. It should be noted, therefore, that invoices can be 'brought forward' for earlier payment by the customers staff. In this case the original week number is changed by inputting one which causes the cheque to be produced earlier.

If a pay week type of system is not used, cheques and/or remittance advices will be prepared in advance, often at a computer bureau. The flexibility of the pay week system is then obtained in a variety of ways. Cheques may be held for some time before posting and if the dates on cheques are recorded in the sales cash book some interesting patterns can be revealed. On the other hand cheques may be made out without a date, this being stamped on at the time of desptach. At the extreme, of course, some companies will only post off cheques as final demands and cut-off notices are received.

Larger companies will not normally hold individual cheques in this way or apply onerous terms to particular classes of supplier. The inconvenience is too great and cheques will be released in bulk in some systematic manner. The Ford Motor Company, for example, pays on a four weekly cycle based on the initial letter of the supplier company name. As long as the information required by Ford is on the invoice this procedure is said to result in payment within normal montly terms.

Many companies, mainly small to medium ones, will not raise a cheque until a statement has been received and reconciled with their purchase ledger. The statement should, therefore, be sent off within 10 days or so of the month end and show all invoices despatched. Even if these are not all due, a sizeable sum owing on the bottom line can concentrate the customer's mind on paying those that are due. The reconciliation of statements is time-consuming work, however, and many larger companies ignore them altogether, but this cannot be relied upon unless the supplier is specifically asked not to send them.

Attention tends to be concentrated on the slow paying customers when deciding how to improve cash flow from debtors, but it should not be forgotten that an improvement can also be made by speeding up the better payers. As these are usually the more organised companies it is also easier to find out the information they require to get the fastest payment from them. As long as ultimate payment is not really in doubt, the expense of getting a debt paid a few weeks earlier by a slow payer may be uneconomic. The measures taken to reduce outstanding debts should, therefore, involve a review of all customers, with the greatest attention being paid to the larger ones whether they happen to be slow payers or not.

Allocation of cash resources is the function of accounts departments and, if necessary, they should be pressed vigorously for money. Contacts in the operating departments may be helpful and for large amounts an approach should be made early, preferably before the debt is overdue and certainly before it is causing serious difficulties. If delay seems certain and will cause cash flow problems it may be necessary to go above the management level directly concerned with payment. In order not to generate unnecessary ill-will it is important not to actually bypass the accountant or purchasing manager, but whenever a commitment to pay or otherwise solve the problem is broken the next level should be contacted. Time should not be wasted arguing about the broken promise because, as the request for payment gets further up the line of command, it becomes more likely that it will be made a case for special treatment.

3
Getting Organised

ROD MARGREE, Manager Barclays Bank

3.1 'I leave that to my accountant'

Numerous proprietors of small businesses have uttered those immortal words, when asked for an explanation of a particular item that appears in their company's trading and profit and loss account or balance sheet. But are they really just a set of figures produced by the accountant to satisfy the Inland Revenue and the bank manager, and of no real benefit to the proprietor? Or can they be used to analyse the performance of the company or firm and thus act as an aid to decision-making in relation to future trading plans? The use of balance sheets and accounts as a 'tool' of management is of paramount importance to the proprietor, whereas the 'satisfaction' of the bank manager and the tax inspector is, in a sense, purely a by-product. There are, however, certain factors which should be borne in mind when analysing annual accounts:

1. A balance sheet details the asset and liability structure of a business at a given point in time, and the position reflected a day later may be very different.
2. The figures may not reflect the current market valuation of certain items (eg a factory) or may be dependent on subjective judgements. However, consistency of approach will enable reasonable assessments to be made.
3. The effect of inflation on the purchasing power of the pound should be borne in mind when comparing this year's performance with last year's.
4. A balance sheet does not reflect satisfactorily all of the strengths and weaknesses of a business. Figures do not appear which effectively value the skills of its managers and other employees or, indeed, its market position.

Various techniques can be used to aid management in the interpretation of annual accounts. The approaches adopted within these techniques can also vary and it is obviously not possible within the confines of this article to produce an exhaustive appraisal. We, therefore, propose to look at various aspects of the technique known as 'ratio analysis' relating it to a hypothetical manufacturing company's accounts for 1976 and 1977 (Tables 3.1 and 3.2).

If the figures in these accounts for 1977 are looked at in isolation they give only a broad indication as to the health of the business. However, when collated with other figures as a ratio, a fuller

'A' Company Limited

The balance sheets

	1976 (£)	1977 (£)
FIXED ASSETS		
Leasehold property	10,000	9000
Plant and machinery	25,000	28,000
Fixtures and fittings	3000	4000
	38,000	41,000
Add		
CURRENT ASSETS		
Cash	1000	—
Debtors	52,000	78,000
Stock	62,000	100,000
	115,000	178,000
Total assets	153,000	219,000
Less		
CURRENT LIABILITIES		
Creditors	30,000	50,000
Bank	40,000	71,000
	70,000	121,000
Net assets	83,000	98,000
FINANCED BY		
Share capital	10,000	10,000
Profit and loss reserves	73,000	88,000
	83,000	98,000

Table 3.1   *The accounts*

	1976	1977
	(£)	(£)
Sales	250,000	300,000
Less		
Purchases (stock-adjusted)	(125,000)	(150,000)
Direct labour	(35,000)	(60,000)
Gross profit	90,000	90,000
Less		
Overheads	65,000	75,000
Net profit (pre-tax)	25,000	15,000

Table 3.2 *The profit and loss accounts**

picture will emerge. Following a comparison with similar figures for 1976 a trend will be reflected which may necessitate corrective action. There are various key ratios which can be used to assess profitability and liquidity, but they should be used with caution, given the limitations of the figures.

The profitability ratios

GROSS PROFIT PERCENTAGE

This is calculated by dividing the gross profit achieved in the period into sales and expressing the factor as a percentage. By relating this ratio to our hypothetical company it can be seen that in 1976 a gross profit percentage of 36 per cent was achieved, whereas in 1977 it declined to 30 per cent. It is important to identify the causes of this decline. By analysing the material content of sales for both periods, using a similar approach to that adopted in calculating the gross profit percentage, it can be seen that this is constant at a figure of 50 per cent. However the labour content of sales has increased from 14 per cent to 20 per cent. The underlying causes of the fall-off in gross profitability and increase in labour content per pound of sales value can be numerous. The following may be applicable:

1. A decline in productivity.
2. Increases in wage rates not passed on to the customer.
3. A deliberate policy of price cutting to achieve a larger share of the market.

*The implications of Corporation Tax have been ignored

4. Other competitive influences.
5. A change in the product mix.
6. Quantity discounts.

A decline in gross profitability is not necessarily bad. It can result from a change in pricing strategy with a view to expansion or, indeed, to ensure the survival of the company. However, if declining productivity is the cause, corrective action is obviously required if the company is to improve its performance in the future.

NET PROFIT PERCENTAGE

The method of calculation is similar to that outlined in the previous section. When applied to the example, a net profit percentage of 10 per cent is reflected in 1976, whereas 1977 shows a decline to 5 per cent. Arguably it is even more relevant, given that profits are a major source of finance for a company, that profit in money terms has declined from £25,000 to £15,000, despite an increase in sales of some £50,000. To fully assess the reasons for the fall in net profitability it is necessary to express overheads as a percentage of sales. In fact some improvement is reflected: from 26 per cent in 1976 to 25 per cent in 1977. Thus, it would appear that the directors of our company are controlling costs in this area. It follows, therefore, that the fall in net profitability of the company is largely the result of the decline in gross margins. However, in the converse situation, where gross profitability is constant and net margins are falling, steps would have to be taken to control the escalation of overhead costs if continued growth in net profit terms is to be achieved.

The liquidity ratios

COST OF SALES STOCK

This ratio is calculated by dividing the stock figure shown in the balance sheet into cost of sales. Cost of sales is arrived at by deducting gross profit from the annual sales total. This approach to identifying annual stock turn is generally valid unless there is an element of seasonality in the trading activity. In those circumstances it would be more appropriate to use an average stock figure in this analysis. Assuming that the hypothetical company is not affected by seasonal trends the application of the cost of sales/stock ratio indicates the following annual stock turns: in 1976, 2.58:1, and in 1977, 2.10:1. The investment in stock has also increased by some £38,000 to £100,000. If the stock turn in 1976 had been maintained in 1977, the investment would have increased by some £20,000. The additional investment factor can have major effects on the company in terms of profits (the interest cost) and liquidity. The survival of a company depends upon its ability to generate cash and an over-investment in stock can be a decisive factor in this equation.

SALES/DEBTORS
It is usual to express the debtor figure in terms of a number of days' sales. Thus the ratio is calculated:

$$\frac{\text{Debtors}}{\text{Sales}} \times 365 \text{ days}$$

The seasonality factor mentioned in the previous section must be borne in mind. However, given the assumption made in relation to the example, it can be seen that debtors in 1976 were outstanding on average for 76 days, whereas in 1977 the position worsened to 95 days. This obviously had an effect on cash and, indeed, on profits in terms of the interest cost on the increased investment. An additional factor to be considered is the effectiveness of the debtor control function in the company.

Conclusion
Without going into many complexities, this article has tried to show the way in which balance sheets and accounts can give important information on how a company is performing. The difference between profit and cash should always be borne in mind. A company can be very profitable, but may nevertheless have a liquidity problem: a bulging warehouse does not pay the wages or creditors at the end of the week! In sections 3.5, 3.6, 3.7 and 3.8, we will expand on this aspect, when discussing in more detail the fields of debtor control, stock management, and profit and cash planning.

3.2 Borrowing from a bank: presenting your case

The banks place great store by the banker/customer relationship, and rightly so. However, on occasions, a lack of understanding of each other's problems can arise. This is probably caused partially by a language barrier (ie the use of trade terminology by both bankers and customers), and also as a result of both parties having insufficient knowledge of how each other's business really operates. This situation is unsatisfactory from both the banker's and the small businessman's point of view, as it could result in a bank declining to provide finance for what may be a perfectly reasonable business venture. What can then be done to improve this situation?

The banks are in business primarily to lend money (subject to certain Bank of England constraints) and thus have, in a sense, a commodity 'for sale'. But have we, as bankers, given sufficient guidance to our customers as to how to 'buy' this commodity? This is a question that only our small business customers can objectively answer, but it is probably fair to say that communications in this area can be improved.

As a contribution towards this communications barrier, we attempt within this article to suggest ways in which a small businessman should present his case to his bank manager, with a view to obtaining finance for his business.

A banker, when presented with an application by a customer for finance, asks a few very simple questions:

1. What is the nature of the business?
2. What relationship will the bank's money and other borrowed monies bear to the proprietor's own stake (share capital and reserves) in this business, and how will the bank's money be used?
3. How competent are the people managing the business?
4. What are the plans for repayment and what will be the bank's position if the plans do not come to fruition? In order that these questions may be answered, the small businessman should be prepared to provide his bank manager with the appropriate information. This falls into three categories, each of which is considered below.

Historical information
Although the future trading potential of the business is the vital factor in determining whether a bank will make a loan, the bank manager will wish to review the past trading record. The information required will include:

1. Details of the history of the company which will cover the areas of activity and trading record.
2. Audited balance sheets and accounts for the past three to five years, which should include the full profit and loss account statement.
3. Details of the borrowing record of the business.

Do you run your own business?

WILLIAMS & GLYN'S BUSINESS INFORMATION SERVICE

CASH FLOW CONTROL

WILLIAMS & GLYN'S BANK LIMITED

WILLIAMS & GLYN'S BUSINESS INFORMATION SERVICE

WORKING CAPITAL

WILLIAMS & GLYN'S BANK LIMITED

WILLIAMS & GLYN'S BUSINESS INFORMATION SERVICE

BORROWING FOR BUSINESS

WILLIAMS & GLYN'S BANK LIMITED

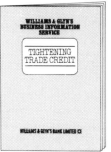

WILLIAMS & GLYN'S BUSINESS INFORMATION SERVICE

TIGHTENING TRADE CREDIT

WILLIAMS & GLYN'S BANK LIMITED

WILLIAMS & GLYN'S BANK ✖✖
Our business is helping _your_ business

Williams & Glyn's Business Information Service offers 4 Free publications specially designed to help anyone running a small to medium-sized business.

Williams & Glyn's Business Information Service is introducing a new series of booklets dealing concisely and clearly with subjects that are supremely important to anyone running their own business. The first four titles are listed in the coupon below, and other titles will follow and be announced from time to time. We should also be very pleased to receive suggestions from anyone involved in small to medium-sized business for further useful titles in this series.

Williams & Glyn's Business Information Service.
Williams & Glyn's Bank Limited,
New London Bridge House, London SE1 9SX.

Please tick booklet(s) required.

☐ CASH FLOW CONTROL
   (Plus a working chart)

☐ WORKING CAPITAL

☐ TIGHTENING TRADE CREDIT

☐ BORROWING FOR BUSINESS

NAME

TITLE

COMPANY

ADDRESS

GG1

47

Generally, much of this information will already be available to the bank manager. However, if this were not the case, arrangements should be made to provide it.

The present situation
Within this category, the small businessman should be prepared to provide the bank manager with the following information:

1. The audited or alternatively the unaudited accounts for the most recently completed financial year.
2. Details of the present ownership and management of the company.
3. Details of the resources of the company in terms of premises, plant and machinery and the labour force.
4. The current nature of the products of the company and details of the marketing strategy which is being applied.
5. Up-to-date management information which will reveal the current levels of profitability, details of the investment in debtors and stock, and liability to creditors.

Future plans
Armed with the information outlined in the two previous sections, the bank manager will have a picture of the business in terms of its past performance and current trading position. To complete this picture, attention must be turned to the most important factor in the equation: the future plans of the business and thus the reasons for bank finance. In order that the plans can be fully assessed, it is usual for these to be quantified in the form of budgets for capital expenditure, sales, profit and cash. The bank manager will, therefore, be assisted in the assessment of the proposition if the following are provided:

1. Budgets for capital expenditure, sales, cost of sales, overheads and profit for say the next 12 months.
2. A cash flow forecast which, in effect, interprets the trading and capital expenditure budgets in cash terms and thus helps to identify the projected borrowing requirement.

Conclusion
The presentation of your case in the manner suggested will not necessarily guarantee the bank manager's agreement to the level of lending which is reflected in the cash flow forecast. However, it will ensure that the bank manager has a greater understanding of the business and its needs, and thus will be in a better position to offer constructive advice and assistance, with a view to enabling the

fulfilment of the plans of the small businessman.

3.3 Borrowing from a bank: how a bank manager assesses your case

In an attempt to improve the communications between the bank manager and the small businessman, we outlined in section 3.2 the ways that a case for finance for a business should be presented to the bank. Problems arise in this area mainly as a result of both parties having insufficient knowledge of how each other's businesses really operate. If this knowledge or communications gap is to be effectively bridged we should discuss the other factor in the equation: how does the bank manager assess the case for finance presented and what criteria does he apply in this appraisal?

It is difficult to give a definitive answer to these questions as, although the bank manager is concerned with factors (which by definition can only pertain to history) the most important factor to be considered is the future trading potential of the business. The bank manager, therefore, has to test the assumptions made in the compilation of the future trading plans in such areas as the market potential of the products and profitability levels, etc. The conclusions which are drawn will be based on the bank manager's judgement of the probability of the successful fulfilment of the plans. It can be seen, therefore, that the decision to lend or not to lend is not based upon any easy scientific formula. The areas in which judgements are made fall within five main categories, which are outlined below.

Management

This is a vitally important area both in terms of the people and the function. The bank manager will wish to be assured that the management comprises persons of integrity, who are responsive to and aware of the need for change and have the appropriate skills in terms of marketing, production, finance and personnel. In addition, he will assess the quality of the management information and control systems. This includes such areas as budgeting, cash flow forecasting, profit and loss reporting, purchasing, costing and pricing. The bank manager's assessment in this area will be a major influencing factor in his decision as to whether to lend.

Products

The bank manager will also wish to discuss with the small business-man the nature of the company's products and their position in the marketplace generally. The questions which he will ask include:

(a) Is demand for the products declining, static, or rising?
(b) Are the products competitively priced?
(c) Is the quality of the products appropriate in relation to the market that is sought?
(d) What are the implications of any change in product mix on volume and profit?
(e) Are the existing and proposed sales levels well spread in terms of customer mix?

Prospects

In this category, consideration will be given to the influences of technological and environmental change which may affect the future of the business. This will be coupled with an assessment of the availability of the resources necessary for the successful fulfilment of the various sales and profit targets of the business. An appraisal will, therefore, be made of the position regarding the supply of raw materials and labour, and of the adequacy of premises, plant and machinery.

The capital base

In general terms the capital base comprises share capital, capital reserves and revenue reserves (the profit and loss account), less any intangible assets such as goodwill. In this section, we cannot outline in detail the position regarding deferred taxation, but, depending upon various factors, this reserve is often included as part of the capital base of the business.

Having ascertained arithmetically the size of the capital base, a review will then be undertaken of the nature and quality of the asset structure of the business. This is important as certain assets could either be under- or overvalued, and this would obviously affect the size of the capital base. Alternatively the business may have a relatively high investment in fixed assets which may affect the working capital position. It is difficult to generalise in this latter area, as any assessment of the asset structure, and indeed of the business itself, must be related to the type of industry in which it operates.

It is usual for bankers to relate the size of the capital base of the business to the level of borrowed money required. This will include both bank facilities and finance available from other sources. This is known as the gearing relationship. As a 'rule of thumb', the bank manager will tend to look for not more than a 1:1 relationship between the capital base and the level of borrowed monies. However this should not be seen as a definitive guideline, and in some cases they may wish to see the gearing relationship at a lower level than 1:1. Equally, however, where a business has strong management, good products and a growing market, good budgetary control, and above average profitability levels (both historic and projected) giving adequate interest cover, it would not be unusual to see a gearing relationship somewhat in excess of 1:1 being acceptable.

Working capital surplus
The working capital of the business is ascertained by deducting the current liabilities (creditors and bank overdraft, etc) from the current assets (stock and debtors, etc). An assessment of the nature of the working capital surplus is undertaken by using ratio analysis. This will reflect underlying trends in terms of investment in debtors and stock and the bank manager may well wish to review the controls in these areas. For example:

1. Are the debts being collected at a reasonable rate or are there monies outstanding in excess of the normal terms of trade?
2. Is stock turn satisfactory or is a proportion of the stockholding unsaleable?

This is an important area as the continuing circulation of current assets is the life-blood of the business. Any check on the circulation will affect the liquidity of the business and thus its ability to survive.

Conclusion
As a result of making an appraisal of the case presented to him in these five equally important categories, the bank manager will be able to assess the degree of risk that the bank runs in lending money to the business. If the risk is considered reasonable, the bank manager will be prepared to lend, though his assessment in this area may occasionally result in security being requested.

3.4 Is an overdraft always relevant?

In sections 3.2 and 3.3 we discussed the ways in which a case for finance for a small business should be presented to and is assessed by the bank manager. However we have not yet commented on a key question that should be considered: what type of finance best meets the needs of the business? Many small businessmen, having identified a need for an injection of finance from a bank, tend to ask their bank manager to provide them with an overdraft facility. But is an overdraft always relevant? For example, let us look at a small engineering company, the directors of which have approached their bank for an overdraft facility of £40,000 to finance the acquisition of some new plant and equipment costing £20,000 and the growth in investment in debtors and stock which will occur as a result of their planned expansion programme. We shall assume that the bank has agreed to provide the requested finance at a level of £40,000. Thus the question to be resolved purely relates to the type of finance that is appropriate.

In this hypothetical case there are two distinct purposes for which finance is required: (1) the financing of the acquisition of fixed assets and (2) the financing of an increase in current assets. Overdraft finance is generally of a short-term nature and its primary purpose is to assist in the financing of current assets such as stock and debtors. It follows, therefore, that this type of facility generally does not have a part to play in the financing of long-term or fixed assets. In our example the company wish to acquire items of plant costing £20,000 which will probably have an economic life of, say, six or seven years. It would seem to a bank manager, therefore, that the financing of these assets should be 'matched', thereby linking the payment for the assets to their ability to generate extra profits and cash for the business. In this case, it may well be appropriate for the bank to provide an overdraft facility of £20,000 to finance the anticipated increase in debtors and stock and in addition to make available a medium-term loan of £20,000 repayable by the company over, say, five years.

We have attempted, by using this example, to emphasise that overdraft facilities are not always appropriate. It is not possible within the limitations of this section to produce a definitive list of the forms of finance that a bank can provide to fit the varying needs of the small corporate customer. However, we will attempt briefly to cover the more common types of finance that are available to small businessmen.

Overdraft

This type of facility is well-known and is commonly made available to assist in the financing of the purchase of raw materials, the manufacture into finished goods and, following sale, the financing of the investment in debtors. Repayment is thus achieved on receipt of funds from debtors. An overdraft is thus in many ways a 'revolving' type of facility forming part of the ever-moving current asset and current liability structure of the business. Facilities of this type are usually reviewable at least once every twelve months. They may be provided on a secured or unsecured basis, depending on the circumstances. The interest rate payable is negotiable and is linked to the Bank base rate.

Medium-term facilities

Medium-term credit may be made available for the acquisition of fixed assets such as factories and plant and machinery, for a period of up to 10 years (exceptionally up to 15 years). The finance is generally provided on a secured basis, but it is an extremely flexible form of facility. Drawings and repayments can be tailored to meet individual requirements. For example, a medium-term loan repayable over a five-year period may be provided to acquire an item of plant. However, the increased profits and cash anticipated from this expansion in productive capacity may well not be reflected until two years after acquisition. The bank can gear the repayment programme to the revenue expectancy, ie nominal repayments in years one and two with the major portion of the loan being repaid in years three to five. Finance agreed on a medium-term basis gives the small businessman the assurance of a line of credit which will not be withdrawn unless default occurs. Interest rates which are generally marginally higher than those charged for short-term monies are either linked to base rates or money market rates.

Leasing facilities

These facilities are, in many ways, an alternative to medium-term credit. They can be used in connection with various assets such as machinery, computers, motor vehicles, etc. Leasing facilities are an additional source of funds which do not affect the gearing of the business and do not tie up valuable working capital. The rentals are fixed at the beginning of the leasing period and, thus, are not affected by changes in interest rates. The finance is provided on the whole of the leased asset and the corporation taxation implications of first year's allowances are taken into account when calculating the rental payments, which are in addition fully allowable as a revenue expense. However the 'lease or buy' decision is one which should not be taken without seeking advice from your accountant and bank manager.

Export Credits Guarantee Department (ECGD) backed finance

There are various types of finance backed by the Export Credits Guarantee Department which the bank will provide. However, the most common types relevant to the small business are short-term finance for exports on either bills or notes or open account. A bank will purchase, without recourse, accepted bills of exchange or promissory notes, covering exports secured by ECGD Comprehensive Bank Guarantee where goods are shipped with credit of up to two years from the date of shipment. Against similar security a bank will also advance up to 100 per cent of the value of the goods against proof of export on open account. The finance is made available for goods shipped 'cash against documents' or open-account terms up to 180 days. With both types of facility a substantial improvement can be made in the situation of the business as regards working capital. It is also an extremely inexpensive form of finance, the current interest rate being ⅝ per cent over the prevailing base rate – somewhat cheaper than normal overdraft facilities!

3.5 Controlling debtors

In section 3.1, when the use of ratio analysis as a management tool was discussed, the question of investment in debtors was briefly mentioned. This area is vitally important, as the survival of any business depends on its ability to generate cash. For example, when a sale is made on credit, a profit may well have been earned in accounting terms. However, the cash may not be received from the debtor for a considerable period of time. Thus, if debtors are not well controlled and are allowed to increase at a disproportionately faster rate than the growth rate in sales, it is possible that a cash shortage will occur despite evidence of profitable trading. How can this situation be avoided? The bank manager may be able to assist by increasing the company's overdraft facility, but is this the right answer from the small businessman's point of view? Further finance from the bank will result in an increase in the overheads of the business and it is possible that only a temporary solution has been found which does not resolve the underlying problem – poor debtor control.

How can improvements be effected in this area? It seems that certain basic questions have to be answered by the small business-man prior to action being taken. What is the size of the investment in debtors? How is it financed? How can the investment be reduced without harming the firm's ability to meet its objectives? To aid the small businessman in this assessment and in taking suitable action we will outline the various aspects of debtor control that should be examined.

The significance of debtors

The businessman should be aware of the following factors:

1. What is the cost to the business of granting credit? The costs involved can include interest charges, administrative overheads, legal costs, etc.
2. What are the true costs of granting discounts for early payment to customers? It may be worth giving discounts if liquidity is a problem but it should be remembered that a 2.5 per cent discount for payment within 30 days when the normal terms of trade are 60 days is equivalent to an annual charge of 30 per cent (2.5 x 365/30 = 30.4).
3. What return on sales do you achieve in your business? If for example a 3 per cent return is achieved, it is evident that a £3000 bad debt will nullify the profit on £100,000 of sales. On the other hand, if bad debts are not incurred, are business opportunities being missed?
4. How many days on average does it take to collect one day's sales? This is a useful ratio and changes over a period will give an indication as to the effectiveness of the debt collection system.
5. It is a fact that growth in credit sales volume will necessitate an increase in the working capital requirement. Has the amount been assessed?

Recognition of the implications of these questions is vital to the understanding of the significance of the investment. However, to complete the picture, it is equally important that the detailed procedure of day-to-day control of debtors is fully appreciated.

The management of debtors

It is obviously vital that the creditworthiness of all new customers is assessed. The sources of information which can be used include banks, the trade generally, credit registers, etc. However, it is equally important to check periodically on the creditworthiness of your existing customers. A change in their payment pattern may well suggest that inquiries should be made. In this respect it is always useful to give accounts credit limits in order that any change in trading activity can be readily identified.

Assuming that the credit risk is acceptable and that limits have been established for all of the customers, it is vital that a good collection system is in operation. The approach which should be adopted in this respect is fairly simple:

1. Send the invoice as soon as possible, and at the very latest at the time of despatch of the goods. Very few customers pay on invoice, and none pay before it!
2. Send the statements appertaining to the previous month's invoices as soon as possible after the month end; at the latest by the third or the fourth of the month following. Statements are often not sent out until the middle of the following month and this generally results in an extension of the time taken to pay by the customer.
3. State clearly the terms of sale, settlement, etc on all statements and invoices as this can avoid 'delaying tactics' by your customers.
4. Ensure that at the end of the month a list of debtors outstanding is produced, aged on a monthly basis. This document will facilitate the identification of overdue debtors and enable appropriate action to be taken, ie telephone calls, letters (a series of three letters should be devised, by which each is progressively tougher). Do not be afraid to chase overdue debts. Many businessmen consider that to chase debts from important customers will result in a loss of future business. This fear is more imagined than real, and it is probably fair to say that the companies who 'shout the loudest' tend to be paid and respected for it.
5. Ensure that no further goods are despatched to those customers who appear on the 'overdue list'.
6. Consider the possibility of obtaining credit insurance.

When a debt becomes doubtful it is important to ensure that any action taken is cost-effective. If for example the debt is £20, it may well be that the administrative and legal costs involved in recovery will be greater than the original debt. However, when larger sums are involved and it has been established that the debtor is worth pursuing, the employment of debt collectors or solicitors should be considered.

These procedures may appear to be time-consuming, but the implementation of such a system of debtor control may well be highly beneficial to the company in terms of reducing the level of investment in debtors and thereby improving liquidity and profitability.

3.6 Managing stockholding

Another major current asset which in most businesses requires similar attention to debtor control is stock. Stockholding in a manufacturing operation generally comprises raw materials, work-in-progress and finished goods, although in certain cases such items as spare parts for machines or tooling are included in the stock figure. These latter items are of a capital nature and care should be taken in instances where they are included, as this will result in misleading information being presented if say annual stock-turn is analysed.

Investment in stock can absorb relatively substantial amounts of working capital and it is obviously of paramount importance to the achievement of the twin objectives of most businessmen in terms of profit and cash that stockholding is maintained at an optimum level. Stock management is therefore an important management function. However it should not be confused with storekeeping, which is the physical control of stock. Nevertheless effective stock management cannot be undertaken unless adequate controls are exercised in the stockroom and on the factory floor. These controls should include:

1. The checking of deliveries into stock against the original order.
2. The maintenance of records detailing stock movement, stock levels, etc.
3. The issue of raw materials to the factory, the control of work-in-progress and the monitoring of the level of finished goods as compared with the original job card and issue of raw materials or components, etc.
4. Ensuring that all goods despatched are properly invoiced.
5. Stocktaking on a regular basis to ensure that 'actual' stock agrees with the 'book' stock.

It is also important to the effective operation of the stock management function that a satisfactory method of valuation is devised. It should be noted that any inconsistency in the valuation method used from one trading period to another will affect profitability.

Assuming that the business has a satisfactory information base in this area of stockholding, the management of the business will be in a position to make investment decisions in line with their objectives. However it is not unusual to encounter certain problems when formulating a stock management policy. There is often a conflict between the various aims of managers of different aspects of the business.

1. The sales manager will generally require a relatively high level of stock of finished goods in order that he and his colleagues can meet demand from stock immediately.
2. The production manager will require sufficient stocks of raw materials, components, etc to ensure that production efficiency is maximised, ie minimal levels of idle time, etc.
3. The purchasing manager's aim may be to 'bulk buy' so that maximum discounts can be obtained, or alternatively to buy forward given the expectation that prices of raw materials will rise.
4. The finance manager's aim will generally be to minimise investment in stock in view of the costs involved and to free working capital.

It is the job of the managing director of the business (who in many small companies will perform most, if not all, of the functions outlined) to balance these individual objectives and formulate a policy which, despite the inherent difficulties, will facilitate as far as is humanly possible the achievement of:

1. A first class service to customers.
2. Efficient production.
3. Investment in stock at an optimum level.

The liquidity and profitability factors which are undoubtedly uppermost in the minds of most businessmen are interrelated. Action to improve the liquidity situation will invariably improve the profitability of the business. The costs of holding stock can be high. These may include the costs of damage, theft, deterioration, the rent charge, wages and insurance. In addition there are two other important costs:

1. The finance cost, which is highly relevant during a period of high interest rates.
2. The opportunity cost: if stocks include substantial amounts of obsolete or slow moving goods, the business may be losing opportunities to sell other lines profitably.

It is important to establish whether the investment in stock is excessive. A useful ratio which can be used here is cost of sales during a period compared to the average stock level. This will give a picture in broad terms but will tend to be misleading if the trading activity is highly seasonal. If this is the case an appropriate adjustment should be made. However, for the purposes of this article, we shall assume that we have a company whose stock-turn ratio suggests that some seven and a half months stock is in hand, valued at £150,000. The managing director, after further investigation, decides that his target stock level should be five months' stock, an investment of £100,000. Achievement of this target will benefit cash to the extent of £50,000 and if it is assumed that stockholding costs are running at 20 per cent (not unreasonable today given high interest rates), the improvement in profits could be in the region of £10,000. It is a salutary thought that if this company was achieving a profitability factor of 5 per cent on sales, the action taken in respect of stockholding could have a similar effect on profits as an increase in sales of £200,000.

Stock management can be highly complex, but in many small businesses it involves making some basic decisions, ie how much, in what quantities and when, to order. This involves in certain cases the establishment of safety stock levels, the analysis of lead times, which will involve the identification of minimum and maximum stock levels in line with usage. It may not be possible to develop this approach across the entire range of stock items in view of the costs involved: the costs should not outweigh the benefits! It may be appropriate, therefore, to single out the most significant items of stockholding, and Pareto's 'Law' can be of assistance in this respect. This is sometimes known as the 80/20 rule; it suggests that 80 per cent of the value of the total holdings is made up by 20 per cent of the items in stock. This is, of course, a generalisation and the percentages may vary. However, it has relevance in most businesses and often strict control over the top 80 per cent in value terms of the stockholding will be highly cost-effective. In addition to the top 80 per cent in value terms, high value/low volume items and any low value items necessary to smooth production should also be strictly controlled.

There are, of course, more sophisticated ways of controlling and managing stock, but an understanding of the various methods outlined in this article, coupled with well defined objectives and plans for the business, should facilitate the achievement of optimum stock levels.

3.7 The relevance of planning in a small business

'It is impossible to plan in this business' is a cry that one often hears from the small businessman, and yet he will later go on to suggest that he intends to purchase new plant costing say £30,000. These two statements are manifestly contradictory. By indicating his intention to purchase new machinery the businessman is, perhaps subconsciously, planning for the future. This is not to imply that the average businessman takes investment decisions lightly, but that on some occasions this type of decision is taken solely to resolve today's problem, without perhaps considering its full implications in the future.

'Planning', as somebody remarked, 'is a hazardous business, especially when it involves the future.' There is no divine right by which a company repeats its successes of yesterday. As major decisions taken today will influence the future success of the business, it is apparent that most small businesses would benefit from a more systematic approach to planning. In the case of the businessman wishing to purchase new plant, he was, despite his protestations to the contrary, planning for the future, so why not do it systematically? Certain assumptions were being made regarding the future pattern of trading, and considerable benefit could be derived from making these assumptions explicit and testing them systematically and continuously against what occurs.

In summary, what is the case for planning, in a small business? The pros outweigh the cons, though the doubters would suggest that 'we have managed without planning so far, so why start now?' or, alternatively 'the future is uncertain anyway, so why waste time and effort looking ahead?' These arguments are entirely subjective and are outweighed by the positive factors:

1. If a form of unconscious planning is undertaken anyway, why not do it in a formalised manner?
2. We live in a changing world and a company has to react to that change if it is to survive and be successful.
3. The introduction of a planning system can boost the morale of management and staff alike, producing a feeling that 'we know where we are going' and giving the business a renewed sense of direction. As the effectiveness of management and staff are the key to corporate success, this is a vital factor.

4. A planning system can integrate the management effort by defining their individual areas of responsibility and functions to be performed towards the achievement of the overall corporate objectives.

If the case for the need for planning in a small business is accepted, an outline of the way in which planning should be introduced into a small business is necessary. Initially, the small businessman must define his (and thus the company's) objectives. Objective setting is the responsibility of top management; it cannot be delegated. It can also be a difficult task and it may be appropriate to attempt to identify the constraints that operate within the business. This inevitably involves an assessment of strengths and weaknesses of the company. As a first step in this analysis, a review of company performance over the past few years should be undertaken, coupled with an assessment of the business's potential, using the existing resources. It would be appropriate to consider such aspects as productive, administrative, management and sales capacities in relation to premises, plant and people. Analysis here tends to give advance warning of the possible need to acquire new premises or plant, recruit further management or labour, etc to facilitate the achievement of the corporate objectives. Moreover, it is necessary to review the marketplace in which the company operates, bearing in mind the effects of pricing and any technological change which may influence the life of the products.

This approach may seem a little grandiose, but if realistic objectives are to be set it is self-evident that the constraints operating should be clearly identified. For example, there is little point in a businessman deciding that he wishes to increase sales to £750,000 in the next financial year if the constraints operating in terms of premises and plant restrict the productive capacity of the business to £500,000 per annum in sales terms. Similarly, if the market for the company's products is declining, it would seem unlikely that a sales objective could be set to increase volume by 50 per cent during the next trading period unless the initial sales base was insignificant in relation to the size of the market. These two examples are over-simplifications, but they emphasise the need for general planning.

Following this appraisal it should be possible to set realistic, quantified objectives in terms of sales and profit in the short and medium term. As company success in the final analysis is dependent on profitability and liquidity, it would seem relevant for the objectives, as defined, to be formulated into a capital expenditure budget and operating budgets for sales profit and cash for an initial trading period, bearing in mind such factors as productivity and product mix. A further major constraint may be cash, and, if the availability of this vital ingredient is restricted for any reason, it may be necessary to reappraise the targets for sales, profit and capital expenditure in the short term.

Assuming that the appropriate levels of cash are available, the various budgets and forecasts may be evolved into forms of action plan for the individual members of the management team within the business. This ensures a measure of involvement by these managers in the achievement of the overall corporate objectives, coupled with that other vital factor – accountability. It is of paramount importance that company performance is monitored and compared with the various budgets and forecasts in order that variances can be identified, thereby enabling corrective action to be taken, as appropriate. It may be necessary to make mid-course adjustments in the various targets in the light of performance. This suggests a further important factor: that corporate objectives should always be flexible.

3.8 Budgeting for profit

Budgeting is an activity which is undertaken by most people in their private lives, and yet one constantly meets arguments from small businessmen that it is not relevant to the management of their companies. This resistance is difficult to understand. If the technique is relevant to the management of a household, it must surely have even greater significance in the operation of a business. The family budget is easier to plan, as in most cases income is fairly fixed, as are many of the items of expenditure. In a business, many of the overhead costs are fixed (some will vary with sales volume), but income (ie sales revenue) cannot generally be quantified as easily. It is the area of sales forecasting that appears to cause the most difficulty to businessmen and may to some extent explain their reluctance to use budgetary techniques.

The analogy with family budgeting is too simplistic, but the budgetary techniques used in the management of a small business need not be unduly complicated. A budget is in essence a projected profit and loss account for say the next six or 12 months' trading activity. It is based on certain assumptions, but reflects the plans of the management for the future of the business following the identification of their objectives, which have been determined after an analysis of the available resources and the constraints which operate.

In most small businesses the budgetary control system would include the following:

1. An operating budget. This budget quantifies the planned trading activity in terms of sales, cost of sales, overheads and thus profit (or loss).
2. A capital expenditure budget. This is basically a list of the proposed capital expenditure in the budgetary period. Expenditure in this area is financed from profits in the short or medium term and thus is not included in the operating budget. However, acquisition of capital items has an important effect on cash flow and expenditure on capital should be included in the cash budget.
3. A cash budget. The cash budget or cash flow forecast attempts to identify the implications of the operating and capital expenditure budgets upon the available cash resources of the business. The liquidity of a business is an important area and is given fuller treatment in section 3.9.
4. Management information. It is obviously vital to the fulfilment of any plans that the company's performance is regularly measured and compared with the original budget. For example, variances that occur may necessitate a change in policy or activity if the plans are to be fulfilled (see Section 3.10).

There are many advantages of introducing this type of approach into the management of a business. Although it will not guarantee the success of the business, it should make failure less likely! Budgetary control aids decision-making and facilitates the control of expenditure. It acts as a motivator to members of the management team, as they see the budget figures as targets to achieve or indeed to exceed. Moreover, budgeting can be used as an important delegatory tool in the armoury of the small businessman. Responsibility can be given to middle management for specific areas of the business activity using the budgetary control system to measure his performance. Finally, the budgetary process gives the businessman the bonus of knowing where he is going as well as where he has been.

We may now outline briefly the way in which operating budgets can be prepared. An operating budget is made up of several interrelated budgets and, for the purposes of this article, we shall assume that we are dealing with a small manufacturing operation. The various budgets which have to be prepared are now considered.

The sales budget

It would normally be appropriate to forecast sales for, say, six or 12 months ahead on a month-by-month basis. Ideally, the forecast should be made in unit terms and converted into monetary terms at a later stage. However, this is not always possible. Sales forecasting is considered by some businessmen to be a difficult area, but the following can provide a useful base for projections:

1. *Analysis of past trends.* Historic performance is a useful guide as to the future. An analysis of the individual sales performance of various products may reflect important trends which may affect future sales levels. The seasonality of sales should also be borne in mind.
2. *Trends in the marketplace.* Is the market expanding or contracting? Is competition increasing? What effect will price increases have upon demand, if any? These are important questions, the answers to which will have an important bearing on the future of the business.
3. *The forward order book.* This can give important information as to anticipated sales levels in the short term.
4. *Reports from the sales force.* Salesmen spend their time dealing with customers and should be in a position to make a useful contribution as to future sales levels.
5. *Reports from major customers.* An inquiry to major customers as to their likely future requirements can be rewarding. Indeed it may facilitate relatively accurate forecasting for the major part of the sales budget.

Cost of sales budget

To establish the monthly cost of materials necessary to support budgeted sales, the number of units to be sold each month should be multiplied by the unit cost. If this is impracticable it would not seem unreasonable to base material costs on the historic material usage relationship allowing for any factors which may cause this relationship to change. Budgeting in this area should take into account such factors as changes in stock levels, manufacturing lead times, etc.

Wages costs pertaining to the manufacturing process should be included in this budget. The projection should take into account planned increases in the wage rate, employers' National Insurance contribution, and productivity factors. In some cases it is appropriate to include certain manufacturing overheads in the compilation of the cost of sales budget.

Overhead budget

Preparation of this budget is generally relatively straightforward. Historic information derived from previous financial accounts can give a useful guide as to trends. However the budget for the next six or 12 months should take into account any known changes in the overhead structure as well as cost escalation resultant from inflation.

Armed with these budgets the small businessman will be able to calculate the level of profit which may be derived in the trading period, ie sales minus cost of sales plus overheads. It should be remembered, however, that certain components of these budgets are based on assumptions, and thus monitoring of performance is paramount if financial control of the business is to be maintained.

3.9 Budgeting for cash

The concept of cash budgeting, or cash flow forecasting as it is otherwise known, is not new. Many large companies have been using the technique as a tool of management for many years. It is, perhaps, only during the past five or 10 years that cash flow forecasting in smaller businesses has gained some momentum. However, there still exists more than a measure of resistance as to its use and its validity in the context of operating a small business is often denied. This is unfortunate. Company success and, in some cases, survival is dependent on the achievement of a mix of two main factors, namely profitability and liquidity. Although profitability is obviously a vital ingredient, it is equally important that liquidity is maintained. The most common reason for the demise of a business is that it is unable to meet its commitments as they fall due. Obviously many factors can contribute to the onset of such a crisis, but liquidation or bankruptcy inevitably follow when the business runs out of cash.

A cash flow forecast is based on a set of well-defined assumptions and inevitably the 'actual' cash flows will not always correlate precisely with the original projection. This discrepancy occurs because the cash plan is developed from the various budgets for sales, cost of sales, overheads and profit, which are themselves based on assumptions and the views of the management as to the future. However, given that a case is made for business planning in order that the corporate objectives can be achieved by maximising the use of the available resources, it follows that the planning process should incorporate the management of cash, arguably the scarcest of resources.

A cash flow forecast should enable the businessman to answer the following questions:

1. Can the plans which I have for my business for, say, the next six or 12 months be achieved within the available cash resources?
2. What effect will any planned capital expenditure have on the cash position?
3. At what time will further finance be required from the bank and what type of facilities will be needed?

The technique of cash flow forecasting, used intelligently and updated regularly, can, together with the other planning 'tools', provide information vital to the effective management and control of a business.

The formulation of a cash flow forecast is, for most businesses, a relatively simple operation, provided that adequate base information – the various operating and capital expenditure budgets – is available. Some businesmen attempt to produce cash flow forecasts without preparing these two original budgets, but this method has the inherent risk of inaccuracies. The cash flow forecast is, therefore, a restatement in cash terms of the original budgets, taking into account the timing differences and excluding the non-cash items of revenue and expenditure.

The process of producing a cash flow forecast usually follows the pattern outlined below.

Production of operating and capital expenditure budgets

These budgets will have been produced in monetary terms on a month-by-month basis. For example, sales will have been projected on a monthly basis according to the anticipated timing of invoicing. Similarly, the purchase of raw materials will have been planned to facilitate the achievement of the production cycle and the stockholding policy of the business. Direct labour costs may have varied month-by-month in line with the peaks and troughs in production, but it is quite probable that the overhead budget has been produced on a six-monthly or annual basis. The cash flow forecast will therefore interpret these budgets in terms of the receipts and payments of cash.

Production of the cash flow forecast

SALES

To project the timing of receipt of debtor monies as per a particular month of sales, it is necessary to look historically at the collection times which are being achieved. The implications of VAT must also be considered. For example, if all sales are to the home market, the budgeted sales figure must be increased by 15 per cent for the purposes of the cash flow forecast.* If these factors are not recognised there will be an in-built inaccuracy in the forecast. Following the review of credit allowed, it should be possible to identify average debt collection times. For example:

1. Fifty per cent of debtors collected in the month following invoice – ie 30 days.
2. Twenty-five per cent within 60 days and the remainder within 90 days.

It would perhaps be helpful if we outlined these points by way of a brief example (see Tables 3.3 and 3.4). We shall assume that we are dealing with a small company whose sales are all achieved on the home market. The budget relates to six months' trading.

Month	1	2	3	4	5	6
Sales (000s)	20	25	30	35	20	25
Add VAT at 15%						
Sales (including VAT)	23	28.75	34.5	40.25	23	28.75

Table 3.3 *Operating budget*

The cash flow forecast is for months four to six inclusive and the timing of receipts from debtors is in line with the earlier assumptions.

	50%	25%	25%	Total
Month 4	(3) 17.25	(2) 7.19	(1) 5.75	30.19
Month 5	(4) 20.13	(3) 8.56	(2) 7.19	35.88
Month 6	(5) 11.5	(4) 10.06	(3) 8.63	30.19

Table 3.4 *Making a cash flow forecast*

Nb: The figures in brackets indicate the month in which the sales were invoiced.

*This does not apply to sales overseas as exports are zero rated.

PURCHASES
A similar approach should be adopted to that described for sales, taking into account the implications of VAT and the average period of credit taken.

DIRECT LABOUR
The costs, including the employer's contribution, should be planned for payment in the month for which they are budgeted in the operating plan. This avoids complications in terms of the forecast, although it is accepted that most companies tend to take a short period of credit from the Inland Revenue.

OVERHEADS
Analysis of the cash book, etc will facilitate identification of the usual payment times for these costs. For example, rent is usually payable quarterly and rates on a half-yearly basis. It should also be remembered that although depreciation is a revenue item it does not affect cash. It should, therefore, be excluded in terms of the cash budget.

CAPITAL AND OTHER EXPENDITURE
If an item of plant or a motor vehicle is being purchased during the period in question, the cash outlay involved should be detailed in the month in which acquisition and payment are planned. In the event that medium term financing is to be arranged, either from a bank or a finance house, it would be appropriate to enter the cash injection from these sources on the receipts side of the forecast. The appropriate reduction programme in respect of these loans should be inserted thereafter. In terms of capital expenditure, do not forget to budget for payment of corporation tax, etc.

Conclusion
At this stage the businessman will have produced various schedules of cash receipts and payments, which should be compiled into a single document. The monthly cash inflows and outflows should be calculated and related to the cash book balance on a monthly basis. The document thus produced will provide the businessman with a plan of the cash requirement of the company for the predetermined period which will, if used with the other budgetary systems, greatly aid the planning and control of the business. It should be remembered that, if cash budgeting is to be a useful management tool on a continuing basis, regular monitoring of actual cash flows is necessary. Any discrepancies between forecasts and actual flows should be analysed and remedial action taken to ensure that liquidity and profitability are maintained.

3.10 The relevance of management information systems in a small business

Informed managers are better managers. It is fair to say that we all wish to be better managers, bearing in mind that good management is the key to 'corporate success'. However, one still finds businessmen who attempt to achieve this goal with one hand tied behind their back. In other words, these managers do not have the benefit of regular information on the performance of their businesses. It is often suggested by such managers that as they are involved with the day-to-day running of the business they have their fingers on the pulse and therefore do not need, as they call it, sophisticated accounting systems. Alternatively, or perhaps as well, one hears the view expressed that to produce such information would cost too much. It is difficult to accept either of these arguments. While not decrying for one minute the necessity for a manager to have 'his finger on the pulse', if, in addition, he has relevant information to hand on a regular basis, this would inevitably improve the management of the business. As for cost, the introduction of certain simple management reports do not necessarily involve increased costs, but may require a reassessment being undertaken as to the use that is made of management time.

What then are the basic ingredients of a good management information system? First, the information should be up to date. There is little point in having management information produced today which pertained to company performance of some three or six months previously. The situation may well have changed in the interim and thus current decisions made based upon out of date information may be totally inappropriate. Second, the information produced should be simple, easy to read, and highlight the factors relevant to the management of the business concerned. In some companies masses of information is produced for the directors but has not been used as the complexity of it belied its usefulness. One should not lose sight of the basic purpose of a management information system. Its function is to facilitate the monitoring of business performance, enabling management to review current trading and to aid decision-making. This review should, ideally, incorporate a reassessment of the constraints that operate in the business environment and their effect upon future trading performance, such as availability of labour and cash, and the overall state of the market with which the business operates. This is not an easy task and it is vital, therefore, that the key information factors involved are identified and the appropriate systems introduced to aid management if corporate success is to be achieved and sustained.

Corporate success depends on the achievement of adequate or planned levels of profitability and liquidity, and thus any basic management information system should be designed to monitor performance in the following important areas.

Profitability

The production of a profit and loss report on a regular basis is probably the most important ingredient of any management information system. The degree of regularity required must be decided by individual managers. In some businesses monthly figures are produced. However, in many small businesses, quarterly reports are probably appropriate.

The compilation of a profit and loss report is the end result of producing various constitutent reports (see Table 3.5).

(a) **Cost of sales report**		(b) **Overhead analysis**	
Opening stock	£	Rent and rates	£
add purchases	£	Insurance	£
add wages	£	Salaries	£
	£	Insurance	£
less closing stock	£	etc	£
Cost of sales	£	Total overheads	£

(c) **Profit and loss report**	
Sales	£
less	
Cost of sales	£
Gross profit	£
less	
Overheads	£
Net profit (pre-tax)	£

Table 3.5 *Compiling a profit and loss report*

The task of producing these reports is not difficult, but there are one or two areas which can cause some concern. The first is the question of stock valuation. This is an all important area. A full stocktake in a business with a substantial number of stock items can be time-consuming, and, if undertaken on a regular basis, disruptive, costly and thus counter-productive. In this type of case it may be possible to use an application of the concept of Pareto's Law or the 80/20 rule (see section 3.6). When applied by management account-ants in the context of stock valuation, it is suggested that 80 per cent of the value of the total holdings is made up by 20 per cent of the whole, in unit terms. This is obviously a generalisation, but in many cases, by applying a variation of this law, it is possible to produce a sensible stock valuation. To arrive at a stock figure using this method, it is necessary to carry out a physical check of the more expensive items held and to calculate a total value by adding an appropriate percentage for the remainder. Another method which can be used, if this approach or a full stocktake is not considered feasible, is that of calculating closing stock values by use of an historic gross profit percentage. However, this is only suitable in a business which has a fairly constant trading pattern and where there is no marked seasonality or discount structure in the sales activity.

The second area which can produce some difficulty is that of overheads. For example, certain overheads are paid on an annual basis and if the entire cost was charged to a particular quarter's profit and loss account, wide variations in performance could be reflected. Thus, if, for example, the year's insurance cost was paid in the first trading quarter, it would be appropriate to only charge 25 per cent of the cost to profit and loss account; the remainder should be charged in equal instalments over the three remaining quarters.

Having overcome these problems it should be possible to com-pile the various reports outlined previously. Ideally they should be expanded to include comparison to budget on a periodic and cumulative annual basis to facilitate the analysis of any variances.

Liquidity

The achievement of adequate levels of liquidity is vital to the survival and success of any business, and the businessman has an important responsibility in this area. In the preceding sections we advocated the use of cash flow forecasting techniques and good management of stock and debtors. Whereas the latter are generally matters of day-to-day control, cash flow forecasts (if produced) tend to be put in the drawer and forgotten after presentation to the bank manager. However, if the premise of the importance of profitability and liquidity is accepted, it becomes apparent that the comparison of actual cash flows with the budget can be an extremely relevant management report. Any variances which are identified should be analysed and a revised cash flow forecast produced as part of the constant short-term replanning process that is essential to the well-being of any business.

4
Sources of Finance

4.1 Introduction

Clive Woodcock

The experience of the small businessman looking for finance can often seem similar to that of a shipwrecked sailor all at sea in an open boat but unable to quench his thirst in spite of being surrounded by water.

As the small business industry has gathered pace in recent years the number and range of schemes to provide financial assistance to the potential or expanding small firm has increased tremendously, possibly replacing the information gap by a bewilderment gap as the prospective entrepeneur assumes a glazed look in the face of the clamour of offers.

As a result the situation still exists where the banks and other financial institutions plaintively cry that they have all the money needed to regenerate the small business sector if only the viable propositions would make themselves known. At the same time it is not difficult to find potential small businessmen with viable schemes who have experienced a remarkably long search for the capital they need.

There are a variety of reasons for this happening, not the least being the fact that the small businessman very often goes to the wrong sources of finance. He may, for example, go to a clearing bank for long-term finance – though some banks now have vehicles for providing longer-term funds – or he may put a proposal to a relatively small financial institution which requires a very large injection of cash.

Some of the banks have taken on engineers and production specialists from outside the banking world or have trained their own managers through their business advisory services in an attempt to improve their abilities to assess the propositions which come before them.

They have also developed a number of schemes with the

specific needs of the small firm in mind, the Barclays Business Start plan being an example of the more imaginative approach now being adopted, as well as setting up subsidiaries which offer different types of funds, giving the individual manager the opportunity to act as a kind of clearing house, passing on appropriate borrowers to those subsidiaries.

Considerable amounts of money are still available from government sources in the form of grants, loans and reliefs, though the present government has made some cuts in funds and, more important, has restricted the areas covered by special development, development and intermediate status.

A small firm can still obtain as much as 90 per cent or more of the money it needs from outside sources, depending on where it is located, particularly if the offers now being made by local authorities anxious to attract job creation projects to their areas are taken into account.

What is needed to obtain this money is a high degree of stamina and determination in working through the bureaucratic maze as it is not unknown for potential firms either to give up in exasperation or simply decide that all the work involved in getting the money outweighs the value of receiving it.

A wide variety of organisations have sprung up in recent years, however, to try to guide the prospective entrepreneur through these complexities. These include the London Enterprise Agency, the St Helens Trust, Enterprise North in Durham, Action Resource Centres, and similar organisations to the LEA in places like Birmingham and Manchester.

Interest in finance from the European Economic Community has also been growing and the two main vehicles for disbursing these funds, the European Coal and Steel Community and the European Investment Bank, have been developing schemes tailored to the needs of the smaller firm at interest rates in the region of 10 per cent.

Finance from these sources is restricted to projects in either coal or steel closure areas or those in assisted areas but are nevertheless a valuable additional source of funds. The European Investment Bank provides cash in assisted areas and has appointed the Department of Industry in England and the equivalent bodies in other parts of the country as its agent to make loans of between £17,000 and £2.5 million.

The EIB also recently announced a scheme for loans of between £15,000 and £50,000 which will be administered for it by the Industrial and Commercial Finance Corporation. The

ECSC provides loans and grants for ventures in areas where coal mines or steel plants have closed, a need which unfortunately shows little sign of diminishing. One of the most useful agencies in both increasing awareness of these two sources of finance and in offering help with feasibility studies and applications has been the British Steel Corporation's job creation subsidiary, BSC (Industry).

The government itself has tried to open up the flow of funds from the institutions which have increasingly absorbed savings which in the past often went into financing small firms. In order to overcome the sometimes prohibitive costs of investigating and monitoring small investments it has sponsored links between financial institutions and its Small Firms Counselling Service which does much of the assessment, weeding out the no-hopers and helping to prepare plans, and administration, with the result that only viable propositions are passed through to the institutions. The first such scheme was with the Post Office Staff Superannuation Fund and others have followed.

Tax incentives for small firms have been introduced on a limited scale, some of them extensions of those which had already existed under the previous government and there are still demands for tax concessions for those who invest in small firms.

One way of doing this would be through the Small Firms Investment Companies, suggested by the Wilson Committee on Financial Institutions. The SFICs would take in money from investors and the funds invested in smaller firms, with the investors receiving tax concessions.

Venture capital projects have also been developed by the private sector with considerable research into the needs of the smaller business and organisations such as Rainford Venture Capital, backed by Pilkington glass firm, are actively seeking out potential new businesses.

A communications gap, however, always takes a long time to bridge and that between the providers of finance and the small firm sector is no exception. Even if the financial system were in perfect working order there would always be someone to find fault, particularly those with loud voices and unviable schemes.

It will also always be debatable as to whether the right kind of finance is provided at the right price and again it may be that there will never be a right price as interest rates in the future seem likely to stay at levels higher than those to which everyone has been accustomed in the not too distant past.

Blaming the providers of finance for not providing the right funds at the right price or the small businessman for going to the wrong source or failing to see the benefits of equity participation, for example, serves little purpose. Helping to put the two sides in touch is of far greater value and the object of this section is to do that by describing many of the schemes which are available and indicating some of the circumstances in which they can be of value to the potential or existing small business.

4.2 The 'loan guarantee scheme'

Clive Woodcock

The loan guarantee scheme for small firms for which the small business representative organisations have fought for several years finally materialised in the 1981 Budget, though in a form which has so far pleased very few.

The scheme is based on the premise that some worth while projects fail to find sufficient finance because the track record of the borrower or his unwillingness or inability to provide guarantees are not regarded as adequate by the financial institutions. In an attempt to test whether such a financing gap actually exists the government is making guarantees available to a number of financial institutions to encourage additional lending.

It is planned that the scheme will run for three years, subject to an overall maximum commitment of £50 million in each year and is being administered by the Department of Industry. The scheme actually came into formal operation on 1 June 1981, and Barclays Bank won the race to provide the first loan guaranteed under the scheme.

Individual term loans are available of up to £75,000 for periods of between two and seven years; the government guarantee applies to 80 per cent of the loan, the remainder of the risk being taken by the lending institution. Borrowers pay a full commercial charge for the loan, part as an interest payment to the lender and part as a guarantee premium to the Department of Industry. The premium is set at 3 per cent, with the object of covering the cost of claims under the guarantee provision.

The scheme is aimed at most sectors of the economy and firms operating in manufacturing, construction and retailing distribution can benefit from its provisions. Excluded from the benefits of guaranteed loans are banking, education and training, estate agents, postal and telecommunications services and public houses. There is in fact no precise definition of just what constitutes a small firm, though under the scheme any obviously large firm is likely to be refused. Where guarantees are required from borrowers, personal property will not be accepted as security but business assets will qualify.

All the major English and Scottish clearing banks are participating in the scheme, together with the Industrial and Commercial Finance Corporation. These will probably be joined by the Co-operative Bank, which came out publicly in favour of a government-backed loan guarantee scheme at a very early stage while the other clearing banks were having their arms twisted to agree.

The rates of interest proposed by the participants have already come in for heavy criticism from small business representative organisations. The most competitive rates come from National Westminster and Lloyds and the most expensive from ICFC, which is jointly owned by the Bank of England and the major clearing banks and specialises in small business finance. Midland and Barclays impose a charge of 2.5 per cent over base rate, which with the government's 3 per cent premium — equivalent to 2.4 per cent over the whole period of a loan — makes a total of 17.5 per cent.

National Westminster is charging 2.25 per cent over base rate and Lloyds 2 per cent while Williams and Glyn's offers a flexible rate of between 2 and 2.5 per cent. All banks charge a 1 per cent arrangement fee. For Barclays, Lloyds and Midland this will be up to a maximum of £500, while National Westminster will charge up to £100 and Williams and Glyn's will remain flexible.

ICFC is the only lender to provide loans at fixed rates, the rate being 20 per cent including the premium. Its standard arrangement fee of 1.5 per cent for the first £50,000 and 1 per cent thereafter will be charged. The strongest criticism so far has come from the Union of Independent Companies, the representative organisation which has been the most vigorous proponent of the loan guarantee scheme. They claim that the effective charge by the banks for the unguaranteed portion of the loans is anywhere between 7.5 per cent and 10 per cent over base rate and also that the government's 3 per cent premium is far too cautious. They point out that no comparable scheme overseas has suffered losses on that scale. The UIC is planning to monitor the performance of the various lenders in operating the loan guarantee scheme and rate them according to their performance.

There is widespread disappointment at the excessive caution

displayed by the scheme as a whole. It largely overlooks the needs of those firms in the 100 to 200 employee range, those just at the point where they could be taking off to become the medium-sized and larger firms of the future, an omission which could result in many of them coming to grief and leaving a void in the industrial structure almost impossible to fill. The vulnerability of that important area of the already heavily pressurised manufacturing sector is reflected in statistics showing the number of manufacturers in that size band in the UK as being around 3000, an alarmingly low figure.

Profitability of smaller companies tends to be more volatile than that of larger ones, making it more difficult to finance future growth — or even current survival — out of retained earnings. It is just such an area of small business which could have benefited most from a bolder loan guarantee scheme and it was not unreasonable to expect that having reversed its previous opposition to such ideas the government would go the whole way and produce an imaginative, comprehensive scheme rather than the excessively cautious scheme which has emerged.

It is not as though a full-blown scheme would have been likely to prove an expensive drain on the public purse. The present version is expected to be self-financing and there is no reason why a full scheme would not have been, especially in view of the experience in other countries. This has shown loss rates, for example, in Germany of about 1 per cent and of some 2 per cent in Japan, where the birth and death rates for small firms are higher than elsewhere. In Canada — whose scheme the British one most resembles — it has been less than 0.5 per cent, though in the United States, where there are some special factors, it has been considerably higher.

A scheme which offered guarantees on loans of up to £250,000 to existing companies could have had substantial benefits for the company employing, say 100 people, its coffers low because of pressures of the recession and the owner unwilling or unable to offer the level of personal guarantees which might be needed, but with full potential for growth. A guaranteed loan at that stage of its life could easily be the platform from which major expansion could flow.

As it stands at the maximum rate only 700 loans a year can be provided and even at a £20,000 rate only 2500 firms would benefit, which is not many if small firms are supposed to spring up all over the country. The government has, however, now said that the £50 million a year limit could be raised if demand and experience justify it. But it does seem a pity that, having swallowed its previous opposition to the idea and twisted the arms of the major clearing banks to agree to operate it in the face of their distinct lack of enthusiasm, the government did not feel able to go ahead with a full-scale scheme.

The other major innovation which has been introduced is the business start-up scheme under which an investor will be able to obtain relief against income tax on up to £10,000 invested in any one year, provided the investment is held for five years in a genuine new business enterprise. The scheme is unique not just in this country but among the UK's major trading partners, and the government describes it as a striking new incentive to channel investment into new businesses. The government believes that this could mean up to £200 million being poured into small firms, costing the State up to £50 million a year in lost revenue.

The scheme was originally hedged round with so many restrictions designed to prevent it being abused that it was rendered almost totally ineffective. The government did, however, listen to the criticism and has introduced amendments which will help the scheme to achieve a considerable degree of success.

It is of some value to look first at the government's original intentions and then to detail the changes made. Initially, the trades which qualified for the tax incentives were narrowly defined and concentrated on manufacturing and its support trades. A person who wanted to claim tax relief was restricted to holding not more than 30 per cent of the capital in a company and was not entitled to acquire more than 30 per cent of the share or loan capital, 30 per cent of the voting power, or 30 per cent of the assets if the firm was to be wound up. Thus, if a firm was going through a difficult period after two or three years, an individual who had taken advantage of the incentive may have been reluctant to give additional assistance in case the relief was withdrawn. A further restriction was that the person claiming relief could not be an employee of the company and, although he might be a director, he could not receive payment for his services, only travelling and other expenses.

The original legislation stated that no more than 30 per cent of a company's capital could be subscribed under the scheme, leaving the remaining 70 per cent to be subscribed by people who were not claiming relief under the scheme. This provision would have almost completely undermined the objective of the scheme, ie to raise finance for high-risk ventures which could not be attracted from conventional sources. Any new trader who could raise 70 per cent of the capital he needed would probably not have too much trouble borrowing the balance of 30 per cent, and small businessmen would be unlikely to want to share part of the equity if the difference could be raised through borrowing.

The changes made by the government do not alter the basic mechanism of allowing investors in new companies to set off £10,000 against their taxable income, rather in the way that mortgage tax relief operates. The main change is the widening of the range of trades which qualify to include virtually the whole range of manufacturing, construction and service firms, other than financial, accounting and legal services. This amendment will bring into the scheme what are described as the ordinary trades of wholesaling and retailing. A schedule has been produced listing factors which indicate when a trade is an 'ordinary' trade as distinct from a mere speculation or financial investment in goods. There was a need to define wholesale and retail distribution in a way which allowed ordinary trades of this kind to be included without extending the incentive to speculators in commodities such as gold and whisky. The new definition includes the High Street shop and the wholesaler who actually takes delivery of the goods in which he is dealing, but excludes, for example, the wholesale steel stockholder who is able to buy steel, with the ultimate customer already lined up, so that he does not actually take delivery of the steel. It also excludes people who are dealing and buying in the same market, such as a firm dealing with a single company, a situation in which there is no real risk investment.

The new ruling means that the firm which starts out as a distributor and then moves upstream by making a better or more competitive product will now qualify under the scheme.

Another important change is that the scheme is being adapted to the provisions of 'approved investment funds'. These bring together a substantial number of potential investors — acting as a nominee on their behalf — and spread their investments over a number of separate business start-ups. Investment in these funds will not be subject to the £500 minimum limit to the amount of investment in any one company in any one year on which an individual may claim relief. This change will be of particular value to the middling and smaller investor who may want to spread his risk and to take advantage of skilled management in selecting and managing his portfolio. This new clause goes much of the way towards the Small Firms Investment Companies, the establishment of which was recommended by the Wilson Committee on Financial Institutions and which could be a very effective way of actually getting money to small firms. The reason for the effectiveness of this type of organisation is that such funds are at least an identifiable source.

Offering tax incentives to individuals in the way originally intended had a very considerable weakness: how to ensure that all those individuals clutching their £10,000 were going to meet the enthusiastic entrepreneurs with their viable business schemes who needed the money. One of the main problems in the past has been the lack of a point of contact. There was a danger before the concession on approved investment funds that the scheme would fail because of that factor alone.

There are now organisations which try to overcome this problem. The London Enterprise Agency operates what it calls its 'marriage bureau'; the Institute of Directors produces a monthly publication which acts as a clearing house to match up investors with companies seeking risk capital for amounts up to £25,000, and there are a number of other private operations with the same objective in mind. More of these are needed to complement the rather haphazard system of an accountant or solicitor having a client who has the money and by chance also knowing an entrepreneur looking for finance.

A further change is the increase — from 30 to 50 per cent — in the amount of capital in a company which can be relieved of tax. Moreover, relief is now to be allowed within the first five years of a new business rather than three years. There has also been a reduction in the circumstances in which relief can be withdrawn after being granted. The restriction on qualifying trades will run for only three years compared with five years previously and interest will be charged only from the withdrawal of relief.

Other changes allow for the use of subsidiaries, different classes of shares and the use by a company of fixed rate preference shares. Brothers and sisters can now be investors, though parents and grandparents remain excluded, and investors will be able to accept fees in a professional capacity. The amount of capital gains tax on future disposal has been reduced. There was previously a prohibition on the deduction as part of the acquisition cost for capital gains tax purposes of any sum on which start-up relief had been given and not withdrawn. This could have resulted in a charge of capital gains tax on a sale of the shares at a loss. The amendment allows one-half of such sums as a deduction in calculating a gain on the disposal of the shares, but where this deduction would produce a loss it is restricted so that the result is no gain or loss.

The idea of the business start-ups incentives was a good and imaginative one but looked like being emasculated by restrictions. Fortunately, the government has been receptive to criticism and has made changes which have rescued its own proposals from oblivion. The scheme now has a reasonably good chance of being a valuable contribution to the financing of small firms.

Unfortunately, as presently constituted the same cannot be said of the loan guarantee scheme, and it is highly questionable whether its potential will be realised.

4.3 The tax system can help spread wealth*

Joe Horner

Our much-maligned tax system can on occasions be helpful to small businesses by encouraging wealthy people to support them when they fail to attract finance from traditional sources.

The subject is of interest both to aspiring new traders and to wealthy people so we will look at the mechanism of the tax system and explain the principles which allow this situation to occur.

A would like to start a new business. He has an idea; he has the ability; and he believes that he can make a successful living. Unfortunately he cannot be absolutely certain that the business will be an immediate success. He realises that it may take time to build up and during that time he needs money with which to support his family. He has no capital and he may find it hard to put his faith in himself into figures that will convince, say, a bank manager that he should lend sufficient money to start the business. Moreover, A himself, although confident that his idea is good, is realistic enough to know

---

*Since this article was written the top rate of taxation on earned income has been reduced to 60 per cent, but this has not removed the potential support of high income earners for small businesses and has been partially offset by increased tax relief on this type of 'venture' investment.

that things can go wrong and that, if the business fails, he will be left with a large debt.

B is a person with an income of over £35,000. He could easily provide the £10,000 or so which could give A the working capital and personal living funds which he needs, but he does want to lend it to A. He also realises that plans can go wrong and that he could end up being owed money by A which A has little chance of repaying. If A is successful in the business and pays interest of, say, 12½ per cent to B, the latter's tax rate of 98 per cent means that out of £1250 interest he will keep only £25. By lending money B would risk losing a lot and stand to gain only a little. Even if a very high rate of interest was charged it would not be attractive to B.

What might be attractive, however, would be for B to run the business and to employ A to manage it for him. A could be paid a salary and have a commission or bonus arrangement based on results and there could be an agreement that, if the business was successful, A would later be given an opportunity to become a partner and eventually take over the business as his own.

The advantage to A in this arrangement would be that he would be assured of an income while he was trying to build up the business, and he would also be an employed person for National Insurance contributions, so that if plans did go awry and the business should fail he would have a full contribution record and would be entitled to unemployment benefit.

As B would be trading on his own account the risk involved if the venture failed would be partly underwritten by the Inland Revenue. If in the first year the business lost, say, £5000 B could choose to set this against his other income and his tax liability would be reduced by £4150 (83 per cent of £5000). He would still lose £850 of his own money but the tax system would have operated to reduce the risk in the venture. Of course, B may choose not to set his loss against other income but to carry it forward and save tax when the business eventually comes into profit. On the other hand, it is possible that the tax relief may be arranged to be even more than 83 per cent.

To make the venture attractive to B, however, it might be necessary not only to reduce the risk of loss, but also to increase the prospect of profit. The system also allows for this to happen. For a start, income when it comes will be earned income so that he will be able to retain 17 per cent of it instead of the 2 per cent he could retain out of investment income. He should, however, be careful to ensure that when A comes in as a partner he does not abandon all his own active participation and become merely a sleeping partner, or there will be a danger of the profit then being classed as investment income.

More important than the difference between earned and unearned income, however, is the possible advantage that might accrue to B out of the method of assessing business profits.

The amount assessed for most tax years is not the real profit made, but is related to the profit of an earlier period. In the early days the profit for some period is assessed more than once and, later, some profit escapes assessment. In the normal course of events the total amounts assessed over a period of years will be less than the true profit made.

If a business starts in a low key and then builds up success, this advantage is almost certain. If the business is successful at the outset and then starts to fail, the opposite may happen and the total assessments may be more than the total profits.

However, if the business does become successful early on, it is usually possible to ensure that the assessments can be restricted to the true profits.

In section 4.4 we will show in figures how these laws may operate to allow B to enjoy some income tax-free. Tax-free income is, of course, far more valuable to him than taxable income.

4.4 Raising the after tax stakes[*]

Joe Horner

We have examined the case of A who wanted to start a new business but who could not raise the necessary capital and B who had plenty of capital but whose marginal tax rate was so high that he was not interested in having any more income. We suggested that it might be a good idea for B to start the business and to employ A to do most of the management for an initial period until it was successfully established with a view to A becoming a partner when it was clear that the business was profitable.

A would have the security of being an employee while the business was building up and, if the venture should be unsuccessful, B could set losses against his highly taxed income so that he would

---

*This example uses 1978 tax figures, but upper-income tax rates are still high enough to encourage people to invest in new ventures to ease the tax burden.

4.4 Raising the after tax stakes [*]

in fact be taking a much smaller risk than a person who financed the venture with loan money would do.

We now show how, as well as minimising the risk B would be taking, the tax system might give him the opportunity to receive a bigger after tax return on his investment than he would receive from an investment which produced interest. The advantage arises partly because of the difference between the taxation of earned and unearned income and partly because the method of assessing business profits taxes some profit twice and some profit not at all.

In the following example we have assumed that a business commenced on the first day of fiscal year of 1978-79 and that accounts are then always prepared to the last day of the fiscal year. In such a case the normal method of assessment would be for the first two years to be assessed on the actual profit made but for the third and subsequent years to be assessed on the profit of the preceding year. This means that the profit of the second year would be assessed for the second year and also would be assessed again for the third year.

We have assumed that in the first two years the business is not fully established and that, after paying A his wages, there is little profit left for B. However, in the third year the corner is turned and B does have a reasonable profit.

Because it is clear that the business has now got on its feet, B takes in A as a partner from 6 April 1981. The profits from then on are much higher because the wages A earns are no longer an expense of the business. Because he still contributes most of the activity A takes five-sixths of the profit from 6 April 1981.

Let us assume that the trading results for the first five years are as follows:

1978-79	B's profit	100
1979-80	B's profit	400
1980-81	B's profit	1500
1981-82	partnership profit	9600
	(B's share	1600)
1982-83	partnership profit	10,500
	(B's share	1750)
B's total share of profit in five years		5350

Assuming that A and B elect to treat the entry of A into the partnership as a continuation of the business and not as a new business, B's assessments plus his share of partnership assessments will be as follows:

		£
1978-79		400
1979-80		400
1980-81		400
1981-82 (one-sixth of 1500)		250
1982-83 (one-sixth of 9600)		1600
B's total assessments for the five years		2750

Assuming that the maximum earned income tax rate stays at 83 per cent the full tax that B will pay over the five years on income totalling £5350 will be £2282.50 leaving him with a net income over the period of £3067.50

If B had merely lent the £10,000 to A at an interest rate of, say, 15 per cent he would have received interest of £1500 a year on which, because it was not earned income, he would have paid tax of £1470 a year. His net income for the five years would therefore have been only £150.

Moreover, if the money had been lent at 15 per cent, A would have had to find a total of £7500 to pay as interest. On the above basis A receives, either as wages or as share of profit, all the profit except £5350.

Different figures and different accounting dates will produce different results, but provided that the general picture is one of lower profits at the outset with an improvement after a few years the principle will be the same.

We return to this topic of business accounting periods in section 4.3 because there is a cloud on the horizon. We should at this point emphasise that entering into a new business or a partnership may be a good thing for tax purposes, but it also has a lot of other implications and experienced professional advice should be sought before a venture starts.

4.5 Setting tax losses against income

Joe Horner

We have been looking at the role of the tax system in encouraging the formation of new businesses. We have explained that a person with a high tax rate might decide to start a new business because of two features of tax law. First, if the business was unsuccessful he could set the losses against his other income and reduce his tax bill so that the actual loss would be much reduced. Second, if the business was successful, income earned from this type of activity would very often suffer much less tax than an equal amount of income received from a different source.

The advantage of the lower taxation arises principally from the basis on which businesses are taxed. The system which has applied for many years ensures that few businesses pay tax on the true amount of profit that they make. A few unfortunates pay tax on more than they earn but the great majority, over a period of years, pay tax on less than the full amount of profit.

For many businesses the benefit is not very great but in extreme cases half of the profit can escape assessment. This rather odd situation has been tolerated because it enables the Inland Revenue to make assessments much earlier than would be possible if they had to wait each year to find out the true amount of profit earned.

There is, however, a cloud on the horizon: the recent report of the Public Accounts Committee. The subjects of the basis of assessment and of partnership assessments were discussed and the Inland Revenue quoted a survey of a small number of cases in which the gap between profits earned and profits assessed was very wide.

The Committee was surprised to learn that the scope for this 'fallout' of income existed and that some large partnerships had apparently organised their affairs to take advantage of it. They felt that a system should be devised to ensure that overall assessments should equal overall income.

The general public and the business community should be concerned that the matter came as a surprise to the Committee. The system has been in operation for many years and no secret was ever made about it. If the members of the Committee were unaware of it we may wonder how many of the other oddities and anomalies in the tax system (both for and against the individual taxpayer) they do not realise exist.

A change in the system is now a strong possibility. There are many different ways in which the change may be made. It is to be hoped that the legislators bear three points in mind when considering the change.

First, this anomaly does act as an incentive to highly taxed people to develop new businesses and to create job opportunities. If people are going to seek ways of avoiding the highest tax rates (and they most assuredly are) it is better that they do so by doing something which is economically desirable than by doing some of the economically destructive things which are traditional tax planning. In this respect the tax fallout might be compared with the Regional Development Grant scheme or the exemption from tax of save-as-you-earn interest.

Second, there are many anomalies in the tax system which act unfairly to many businesses and the fallout is no more than a counterbalance to these. If this aspect is to be changed it would be only fair to correct some of the others as well.

Third, if a change is to be made it should be done in such a way as to apply to new businesses only and not to existing businesses if the atmosphere of distrust of the government is not to be accentuated.

Prior to the introduction of corporation tax in 1965 the system of some profits being taxed more than once and some profits escaping tax applied to companies as well as to individuals.

When Corporation Tax was introduced the compensating fallout was withdrawn with no attempt to give any relief for the additional profits already assessed, except for a few companies which finished trading within the next few years. This was really a dishonest act by the government and it seems likely that the bitterness created has been partly responsible for the common attitude that no taxpayer owes any moral debt to the state.

The shareholders of the companies had had no part in framing the law. They had entered a system which was an illogical amalgamation of benefits and penalties. They had endured the penalties and then found that the government cancelled the benefits. If a similar thing happens again with individuals it can do nothing but harm to the reputation of the government, and to the relationship between taxpayer and taxing authority.

4.6 European funds

Clive Woodcock

Small firms in the United Kingdom have not in the past made as much use of the sources of finance available from the European Economic Community as perhaps they could have done, largely because of a lack of awareness of what is available but also because the European institutions themselves have not publicised their facilities extensively.

This is changing considerably now, however, and the European Coal and Steel Community, which provides funds for projects in areas where coal mines and steel plants are closing, is stepping up the range of schemes it has for financing the smaller firm.

The European Investment Bank, the EEC's bank for long-term finance, has in the past been associated more with the financing of public works and infrastructure development but it is now emphasising more and more its facilities for the private sector, especially small firms.

Loans from the ECSC are the main source of relatively low cost finance for industrialists investing in coal and steel closure areas; it offers funds for investment projects offering employment prospects suitable for redundant steelworkers and coal miners. Assistance is given only for investment projects and not for general cash requirements or working capital.

The maximum loan is for 50 per cent of the cost of the fixed asset investment and loans can be negotiated for periods of up to 20 years although the government's exchange risk guarantee on the loans is at present available for eight years only.

Interest rates depend on world interest rate levels and currently are around 11 per cent. This can be reduced by a rebate of 3 per cent a year for the first five years of the loan for industrial projects of recognised priority status. The average interest rate for the life of the loans can, therefore, come down to 9 per cent. This interest rebate is only available on part of the loan equal to approximately £12,500 per job suitable for ex-steel or coal workers and is unique to coal or steel closure areas. Capital repayments do not start until after the end of the fourth year.

An organisation which can give considerable help in obtaining funds from ECSC is British Steel's job creation subsidiary, BSC (Industry), especially as it can provide assistance in producing a feasibility study of the project.

Loans of under £500,000 are handled by the Industrial and Commercial Finance Corporation (ICFC) as agents for the ECSC but larger loans are handled directly with the ECSC. ICFC has so far been allocated a total of £50 million from the ECSC and of this about £33 million has gone to 165 companies.

ECSC is working on a scheme designed for small firms where loans of £50,000 or less are required. The government is expected to provide exchange risk cover for this scheme and the effective interest rate should be around 10.5 per cent. About £20 million is being allocated for the scheme over a period of two to three years.

This money will be lent through banks and other institutions, acting as agents of ECSC, and could be disbursed in packages made up partly of Community finance at low rates and partly of bank finance at commercial rates.

The European Investment Bank recently announced a scheme aimed at the smaller firm, offering £5 million worth of finance with the prospect of more to come if the ventures create or safeguard jobs in assisted areas.

The EIB finance is being made available through a global loan to Finance for Industry, whose subsidiary, ICFC, will make sub-loans of £15,000 to £50,000 to support a wide range of investments, including tourism, chosen in agreement with the EIB. The funds will be made available in foreign currencies, enabling ICFC to lend for up to eight years, including a two-year grace period on capital repayments, at interest rates lower than those for comparable finance in sterling.

The government will provide exchange risk cover at a premium of 1 per cent, which will result in a basic cost to the borrower of 11 per cent, plus any additions by ICFC itself, which could bring the total rate to 12 or 13 per cent.

This new global loan is complementary to existing facilities to help small and medium scale ventures in assisted areas, which are operated through the regional offices of the Department of Industry in England, the Scottish Economic Planning Department, the Welsh Office Industry Department, and the Northern Ireland Commerce Department, all of whom use EIB funds to make loans, usually in larger amounts, up to a limit of £2.5 million.

Finance above £2.5 million can be arranged directly with the EIB, which has a liaison office in London. The Department of

Industry has so far been involved in 128 loans involving £50 million of EIB funds.

The scheme for small sums with ICFC may be the first of a series of such global loans and it is possible that other institutional outlets for these funds will be sought. The amount available is virtually open-ended and the total will be increased as and when it is needed, depending mainly on the level of response.

The Department of Industry and its equivalents in other regions of the United Kingdom act as the bank's agents in making loans for amounts ranging from £17,000 to £2.5 million. These loans are restricted to projects qualifying for selective assistance under Section 7 of the Industry Act or its Northern Ireland equivalent. The appraisal of applications, which should be made to regional offices of the Department of Industry or the equivalents elsewhere in the UK, is carried out at the same time as the processing of requests for selective assistance.

Agency loans are for a period of seven years, including an initial two-year deferment of capital repayments, at a fixed rate which at present is around 10 per cent. The government covers the exchange risk and provides the guarantee required by the EIB in return for a counter-security provided by the borrower.

The government's charge for these facilities is 1 per cent or 2 per cent for direct loans, thus giving a total cost to the borrower of 11 per cent in special development areas and Northern Ireland, or 12 per cent in development and intermediate areas, for a loan effectively in sterling.

Addresses

European Investment Bank
UK Liaison Office
23 Queen Anne's Gate
London SW1H 9BU
Tel: 01-222 2933

BSC (Industry) Ltd
42 Grosvenor Gardens
London SW1W OEB
Tel: 01-235 1212

Department of Industry: Industrial Development Departments

Scottish Economic Planning Department
Industrial Development Division
Alhambra House
45 Waterloo Street
Glasgow G2 6AT
Tel: 041-248 2855

Welsh Office Industry Department
Government Buildings
Gabalfa
Cardiff CF4 4YL
Tel: 0222-62131

Northern Regional Office
Stanegate House
Groat Market
Newcastle-upon-Tyne NE1 1YN
Tel: 0632-24722

North West Regional Office
Sunley Building
Piccadilly Plaza
Manchester M1 4BA
Tel: 061-236 2171

Yorkshire and Humberside Regional Office
Priestley House
1 Park Row
Leeds LS1 5LF
Tel: 0532-443171

East Midlands Regional Office
Severns House
20 Middle Pavement
Nottingham NG1 7DW
Tel: 0602-56181

West Midlands Regional Office
Ladywood House
Stephenson Street
Birmingham B2 4DT
Tel: 021-632 4111

South West Industrial Dvelopment Office
Phoenix House
Notte Street
Plymouth PL1 2HF
Tel: 0752-21891

Northern Ireland
Department of Commerce
Chichester House
64 Chichester Street
Belfast BT1 4JX
Tel: 0232-34488

4.7 Venture capital

Clive Woodcock

There are as many definitions of what constitutes venture capital as there are now companies and institutions which set out to provide it and the development capital with which it is frequently confused.

At first glance it may be difficult to see the difference between venture and development capital but there is indeed a difference. An assessment of which is which actually depends on the stage of development at which a company finds itself rather than the form in which the finance — equity capital or long-term debt — is supplied.

On that basis it is possible to define venture capital as that required for all start-ups as well as that needed by firms up to about four years old to develop a financial base on which it can exploit the full potential of its products in the market place.

Development capital on the other hand represents the finance needed by well-established business with good trading prospects and a track record of several years of profitable trading and pre-tax profits of £50,000 a year and upwards to fund expansion and growth.

Both kinds of capital are now available from many financial institutions and companies established specially for the purpose.

Although there has probably been some growth in the past four years in the number of sources of venture capital it is probably true to say that the stronger trend towards the provision of development capital has shown no sign of slowing. Table 4.1 summarises some of the major development capital options open to small businessmen.

The banks, pension funds, insurance companies, institutions such as ICFC, and a range of private companies, some backed by large public companies, have been very much involved in efforts to encourage small firms. For example, Rainford Venture Capital, backed by Pilkington's, seeks to back new and young businesses that could grow within three to five years into multi-million pound enterprises in which Rainford would have a minority equity holding. The investments range from £50,000 to £250,000. Rainford is initially investing only in St Helens, where the Pilkington head office is located, and the other partners in the project include ICFC, Prudential Assurance, British Petroleum and the Community of St Helens Trust. It has £2 million available for equity funding over a two to three-year period, though the amount and geographical scope may be broadened.

A feature of Rainford's activities is the management of its entrepreneur search and venture development programme by Venture Founders, the subsidiary of an American venture capital company, which has developed a number of techniques which it claims reduces risks in evaluating, financing and launching new enterprises.

Both Venture Founders and ICFC are involved in a project in Scotland in partnership with the Highlands and Islands Development Board and the Bank of Scotland. The aim again is to set up job-creating firms but this time in the Scottish Highlands. The purpose of the project is to provide financial backing of up to £300,000 for entrepreneurs with ideas but limited cash or no track record. The finance for the project comes from a fund established by the three partners.

ICFC is a major provider of venture capital and has been particularly involved in the growing trend towards management buy-outs, which could be said to combine both venture and development capital.

These are situations where the senior management of a company, usually the subsidiary of a larger group, buy it from the parent. It happens in circumstances where perhaps the parent wishes to divest itself of interests which no longer fit in with its business or sometimes where a subsidiary has persistently failed to turn in the kind of performance required by the parent.

It frequently happens that even firms which have in the past been loss makers become profitable performers when they become independent enterprises with the senior managers as owners of the business. In addition to ICFC companies such as Candover, Midland Bank Industrial Finance and others are now involved in financing management buy-outs.

Another company, Capital Partners International, was set up to channel European investors' money into promising British enterprise. It provides sums from £10,000 to £250,000, usually in the form of an equity stake though it does also offer loans. A seat on the board is often required and its equity stake can be in the region of 30 to 40 per cent or even more.

One of the clearing banks, Williams and Glyn's, now has its venture capital subsidiary, National and Commercial Development Capital, managed for it by a specialist company, Development Capital Ltd. This company also manages the Small Business Capital Fund for the Co-operative Insurance Society, as well as operating for other institutions.

The Midland Bank's Industrial Equity Holdings group includes Midland Bank Venture Capital, which provides equity finance of £5000 to £50,000 to recently established companies. In order to appraise investment proposals and monitor progress thereafter Midland has recruited engineers, production managers and other specialists from outside banking.

Barclays has set up Barclays Development Capital which makes equity investments of £100,000 or more in firms with a net value of between £250,000 and £10 million. Like the Midland it does not take holdings of more than 49 per cent and the normal range is 10 to 30 per cent.

National Westminster has a Capital Loan Scheme involving the provision of fixed rate, unsecured subordinated term loans of £10,000 to £50,000 for financing new or growing ventures over periods of up to 10 years. A capital loan gives the bank the option to subscribe to a minority of the company's shares, usually less than 25 per cent.

If the option is exercised a Nat West subsidiary, Growth Options, holds the shares. It can take a seat on the board of the borrowing company but does not usually do so.

Several pension funds are now actively promoting their services as providers of venture capital, usually requiring an equity stake in the business and frequently, though not always, wanting a director on the board.

Lender	Ownership	Size of investment (£)	Term	Rate	Equity stake	Board seat
AP Bank, 7 Bishopsgate, London EC2 Tel: 01-638 4711	Norwich Union Insurance	250,000+	5-7 years amortising	Tied to base rate	No	No
Abingworth, 26 St James's Street, London SW1 Tel: 01-839 6745	City institutions incl Barclays Bank	100,000 – 400,000	Long-term equity only	Dividends	Yes 15-40%	Yes
Barclays Merchant Bank, Dashwood House, Old Broad St, London EC2 Tel: 01-600 9234	Barclays Bank	50,000+	Up to 10 years	Usually variable tied to LIBOR	Not usually	No
British Steel Corporation (Industry), 33 Grosvenor Place, London SW1 Tel: 01-235 1212	Exists to encourage firms to come into areas of declining steel employment with factory space and advice, not loans or equity					
Charterhouse Development Capital, 25 Milk Street, London EC2V 8JE Tel: 01-248 399	Charterhouse Group Institutions	50,000 – 5 million	Open-ended	Dividends	Minority 15-30%	Yes
County Bank, 11 Old Broad Street, London EC2 Tel: 01-638 6000	National Westminster Bank	Minimum 100,000	Up to 10 years	Interbank, +1-3%	Not necessarily	Not necessarily
Development Capital Investments, 88 Baker Street, London W1 Tel: 01-486 5021	Electa Investment Trust	200,000 – 750,000	4-8 years	Commercial return	25-49%	Yes
Equity Capital for Industry, Leith House, Gresham St, London EC2 Tel: 01-606 8513	City institutions	250,000 – 5 million	Medium/long term	To reflect delay in obtaining commercial return	About 25% (never control)	Perhaps
Estate Duties Investment Trust, 91 Waterloo Road, London SE1 Tel: 01-928 7822	See ICFC					
Gresham Trust, Barrington House, Gresham Street, London EC2 Tel: 01-606 6474	Gresham Investment Trust	Up to 250,000	Permanent capital	Dividends	Up to 33% (never control)	Yes
Hambros Bank, 41 Bishopsgate, London EC2 Tel: 01-588 2851		Finance usually from clearers	About 5 years	Dividends	10-40%	Depends on size of investment
Industrial & Commercial Finance Corporation, 91 Waterloo Rd, London SE1 Tel: 01-928 7822	Bank of England and clearing banks	5000 – 2 millions	7-20 years	Fixed	Sometimes	Rarely
James Finley Corporation, West Nile St., Glasgow Tel: 041-204 1321	James Finlay Group	Up to 250,000 on own account	Flexible	Flexible	Not necessary but interested	Yes

Name and address	Backed by	Amount	Term	Return	Equity stake	Board
Midland Montagu Industrial Finance, Moor House, London Wall, London EC2 Tel: 01-638 8861	Midland Bank	50,000 – 250,000 +	Open-ended Long-term equity only	Dividends + interest based on MLR	Always but never control	Yes
Moracrest Investments, Moor House, London Wall, London EC2 Tel: 01-628 8409	British Gas Central Pension Fund, Midland Bank, Prudential	200,000 – 500,000		Dividends	10-40%	Yes
National Coal Board Pension Fund, Hobart House, Grosvenor Place, London SW1 Tel: 01-235 2020 ...		150,000 – 2 millions	Up to 20 years	By arrangement	Usually	Only if above 10% equity share
National & Commercial Development Capital, 34 Nicholas Lane, London EC4 Tel: 01-623 2632	National Commercial Banking group	100,000 – 500,000	5-7 years	Variable	10-40%	Yes
National Enterprise Board, 12-18 Grosvenor Gardens, London SW1 Tel: 01-730 9600	also Scottish and Welsh Development Agencies					
National Research Development Corporation, Kingsgate House, 66 Victoria St, London SW1 Tel: 01-828 3400	Public Corporation	10,000	Open-ended	Levy on project turnover	No	No
Noble Grossart Investments, 48 Queen Street Edinburgh Tel: 031-226 7011	Scottish investment institutions	100,000 – 700,000	Variable	By arrangement	20-40%	Yes
Rainford Venture Capital, Prescot Road, St Helens, Merseyside	Pilkington Brothers, Prudential Assurance, Community of St Helens Trust and others	50,000+	Primarily equity. Loans where appropriate to agreed term	No short term return	Yes, but preferably not control	Probably
Small Business Capital Fund, 88 Baker Street London W1 Tel: 01-486 5021	Co-operative Insurance Society	50,000 – 250,000, usually as equity plus subordinated debenture	Usually 4-8 years	Dividends required	25-49%	Yes
Technical Development Capital, 91 Waterloo Rd, London SE1 Tel: 01-928 7822	See ICFC					

Table 4.1 *Sources of finance*

VENTURE CAPITAL FOR GROWTH COMPANIES

Our multi-million pound fund provides financial backing to business owners committed to starting or expanding high growth companies. If your expansion is restricted by limited capital please contact:

RAINFORD VENTURE CAPITAL LIMITED
Rainford Hall, Crank Road,
St. Helens, Merseyside WA11 7RP

Telephone: St. Helens (0744) 37227

Addresses

Industrial and Commercial Finance
Corporation (ICFC)
91 Waterloo Road
London SE1
Tel: 01-928 7822

Technical Development Capital Ltd
91 Wateroo Road
London SE1
Tel: 01-928 7822

Candover Investments
24 Old Broad Street
London W1X 3DA
Tel: 01-409 1888

Midland Bank Industrial Finance
Scottish Life House
36 Poultry
London EC2R 8AJ
Tel: 01-638 8861

Gresham Trust
Barrington House
Gresham Street
London EC2
Tel: 01-606 6474

Barclays Merchant Bank
Dashwood House
69 Old Broad Street
London EC2P 2EE
Tel: 01-600 9234

National Research Development
Corporation
Kingsgate House
66-74 Victoria Street,
London SW1E 6SL
Tel: 01-828 3400

Capital Partners International
Westland House
17 Curzon Street
London W1
Tel: 01-629 9928

Development Capital Ltd
88 Baker Street
London W1
Tel: 01-486 5021

Rainford Venture Capital Ltd
Rainford Hall
Crank Road
St Helens
Merseyside WA11 7RP
Tel: 0744-37227

4.8 Starting up

Clive Woodcock

Cash for starting a business can come from an almost bewildering range of sources with the scale of the enterprise envisaged usually being an important determining factor. Most small firms, however, begin life as a one- or two-man operation with the most common sources of finance being the savings — or increasingly these days, redundancy money — of the potential entrepreneur and loans from their banks.

There is invariably a need for personal resources of one kind or another because banks are unlikely to advance funds in situations where there is not some sharing of risks between them and the prospective businessman. The banks claim that they no longer apply rigidly the rule that commitments should be on a ration of 1:1 of personal resources and bank advances. Some banks even go so far as to say that they will advance funds without personal security if the businessman comes forward with a viable business plan, though the likelihood of this happening in many cases is probably not high.

There are financial institutions which have a policy of providing funds without the personal guarantees which the entrepreneur can find so onerous. The main one of these is actually owned by the clearing banks, Industrial and Commercial Finance Corporation, and its subsidiary, Technical Development Capital, which concentrates on technologically based firms.

ICFC provides finance from £5000 upwards either in the form of equity or loan or a combination of both and does not take a seat on the board, leaving the management of the company to the owner, though it does offer advisory service if they are required. ICFC has been financing a rapidly increasing number of start-ups with relatively small sums of money.

Some local authorities are now becoming involved in start-up finance while other local enterprise organisations, such as the Community of St Helens Trust, often have funds available.

But the banks with their network of 13,000 branches provide by far the largest proportion of start-up finance for small firms and in fact are often the independent businessman's only point of contact with the financial system.

It is *essential* to work out a viable business plan before approaching any potential source of finance as this will indicate not only that the promoter has a serious purpose but has also given thought to how the business will develop once it has got off the ground.

Help and advice on how to prepare a plan is available from a variety of sources, and there are many organisations which can give detailed assistance. These range from the Department of Industry's Small Firms Service to local organisations such as the St Helens Trust and the business advisory services run by two of the clearing banks, Barclays and Lloyds.

Support by the banks for small firms is still largely in the traditional form of overdrafts and term loans but many innovations have been introduced in recent years with many special schemes being developed for the start-up or newly established firm.

Overdraft will obviously be a major source of finance at the start of a business, provided the bank manager is prepared to agree to one, though the businessman should be clear that their purpose is to cover short-term needs such as financing of stock and work in progress.

It is generally inappropriate to try to use them to finance capital spending, though it is certainly not uncommon for this to happen, and when signs of such practices appear the bank manager will quickly try to steer the firm in the direction of the other loan schemes.

Some 50 per cent of bank lending to small firms is now in the form of term loans repaid over one to ten-year periods and these can be tailored to the particular circumstances and needs of the borrower. Their flexibility is one of the reasons for their growing popularity, and such loans will probably eventually form the bulk of bank involvement with the small firm sector, particularly as there is no sign of the small businessman's reluctance to part with equity stakes in his firm diminishing.

Term lending has by tradition been at fluctuating rates of interest but there are now many variations on the theme, with banks giving the borrower opportunities to take loans at either fixed rates of interest or fluctuating rates or even as a combination of fixed rate and variable rate.

Examples of these schemes are the 'Asset Loans' and the 'Enterprise Loans' announced by Lloyds Bank. Asset Loans are available in sums of £5000 to £25,000 over a period of five years at fixed rates of interest to cover up to 100 per cent of the cost of capital projects, such as buying or altering premises, and the purchase of machinery or vehicles.

The Enterprise Loan scheme is for business development on a larger scale and is available in sums ranging from £25,000 to £250,000 at rates of 3 to 5 per cent over base rate, depending on the performance of the business and the bank's appraisal of the risk involved. Repayment is over a 10-year period. In both cases the bank says that although loans are normally secured it may be prepared to lend without security.

Barclays has introduced an innovatory scheme called the Business Start Loan. This is mainly intended to provide finance for new companies but is also available to established firms wanting to launch a new project or product.

Loans of £5000 to £50,000 will be provided over five years and no repayment of capital will be required until the end of the term. Loans are available for up to 100 per cent of total expenditure for fixed assets, research and development costs and anticipated losses in the first two years. No security is required outside a company's assets.

The novel feature is that payments to the bank are made as a royalty linked to the borrowing company's sales, which is fundamentally different from charges for other forms of bank finance. The royalty charged differs for each loan but, calculated from sales projections supplied by the prospective borrower, it is designed to provide a return to Barclays of 12 per cent on the principal sum in the third year of the loan.

By linking the payments on Business Start loans to a company's sales the royalty is treated by the Inland Revenue as a distribution of profits and enables Barclays to offer the loans more cheaply than normal bank finance. The attractions of this kind of loan are obvious as it does not call for personal security and avoids the burden of repayments in the early years.

Midland Bank has supplemented its traditional medium-term loans with a long-term loan scheme for amounts of £20,000 to £500,000 to be repaid over periods of 10 to 20 years. The borrower has a choice of either fixed or variable rates of interest and can opt for an interest-only repayment period of up to two years. The Midland also provides venture loans of up to £250,000 repayable over periods of up to 10 years.

Special lending schemes are available from National Westminster and Williams and Glyn's. Nat West provides fixed rate Business Development loans of £2000 to £100,000 for periods of up to 10 years, and Williams and Glyn's Business Borrowing Plan gives small firms the opportunity to borrow up to £50,000 repayable over five years at either fixed or floating rates. If a customer wants to borrow more or to repay over a longer period, the balance can be provided on a variable rate basis.

The smaller clearing banks, the Co-operative Bank and the Trustee Savings Banks, have not gone in for special schemes for small firms in any substantial way but both are extremely keen to develop their business in this sector. The Co-operative Bank is, indeed, the only one of the clearing banks to come out in favour of a loan guarantee scheme.

4.9 Regional aid

Clive Woodcock

It is possible for a company setting up in a special development area, particularly if it is one in which there are steel plant closures, to finance nearly 90 per cent of the fixed assets costs of a project by grants and low-cost loans.

A high degree of determination is needed to battle through all the processes involved in a firm actually getting its hands on the money but the effort can be very worth while, and there is now a rapidly growing number of organisations prepared to offer a guiding hand through the maze. These range from the job creation subsidiary of the British Steel Corporation, BSC (Industry) to the four-man operation on Merseyside, the Community of St Helens Trust. Others include the Action Resource Centres (ARC), Enterprise North at Durham, Birmingham Venture, the London Enterprise Agency, In Business at Birkenhead, and the Chambers of Commerce around the country, some of which are very good.

The Small Firms Centres can also be useful in providing guidance. Virtually all of the assistance is handled through the Department of Industry and applications for the various kinds of aid which are available should be made to its regional office or London headquarters. The Department will provide up-to-date information on what is on offer.

The schemes of assistance to industry fall broadly into two categories: those which depend on the location of the project and those which are related to the sector of industry or type of activity involved. Aid which depends on location has undergone revision under the present government with help being concentrated on areas where the government believed unemployment or structural weakness to be most severe.

There are still three categories of assisted areas — special development area, development area and intermediate area — but the government has restricted the area covered by these, and the new limited areas take effect from 1 August 1982.

Special arrangements cover the conditions under which grants for building, plant and equipment can be made in the period before that date. Selective assistance can be obtained by firms planning to make investments which will create or safeguard jobs in the assisted areas.

101

Regional development grants in the chosen areas provide substantial support for new and existing businesses with grants of 22 per cent in special development areas and 15 per cent in an ordinary development area. The grant is designed to cover part of the cost of new buildings, plant and machinery. In some areas factories are also available for rent-free periods.

The Department of Industry also provides help in the training of new personnel in manufacturing industry which in some cases can amount to 40 per cent of the eligible costs of the basic wage of the trainee, instructor and essential materials. A matching contribution of up to 40 per cent is also available from the European Social Fund, applications for which will also be handled through the Department of Industry.

Outside the manufacturing sector the DoI can provide grants of between £2000 and £6000 for firms in the office or service industries while employees moving with their firm into the areas for expansion can qualify for a grant of £1500 to assist with removal expenses. Selective assistance is also available in the construction and tourist-related sector.

Firms in Northern Ireland are offered separate aid which ranges from industrial development grants of between 30 to 50 per cent to start-up grants. Grants of up to a maximum of £250,000 are also available for research and development.

The unemployment caused in areas where steel plants are being closed by the British Steel Corporation attracted a package of government measure to try to alleviate the effects. These are being administered through the corporation's job creation subsidiary, BSC (Industry).

Several of the incentives are available to any firms wanting to locate in special development or development areas but include the provision of workshop facilities on BSC sites, assistance with land or property deals, lease of plant and equipment on attractive terms, and support with research and development and also consultancy and feasibility studies, which can be of considerable help in obtaining finance from many sources.

The assistance of BSC (Industry) can be valuable in drafting applications for low-cost loans from the European Economic Community organisations, such as the European Coal and Steel Community, the European Investment Bank, and the European Social Fund. Details of these facilities are described elsewhere.

Sections 7 and 8 of the Industry Act 1972 provide for selective financial assistance subject to the project satisfying certain criteria. This could be in the form of phased cash grants against

SMALL BUSINESSES
find the
RIGHT ENVIRONMENT
in
CORNWALL

* Government financial aid
* An existing community
  of small businesses
* An industrial development
  & liaison service
  that understands your needs

for free brochure and information contact:

Peter Davey
Industrial Development Officer
County Hall
Truro
Cornwall TR1 3AY

Tel: Truro 74282 ext. 68

INVEST IN CORNWALL'S
INDUSTRIAL TRADITION

(EXPORTERS SINCE 500 B.C.)

THE FIRST RAILWAY LOCOMOTIVE – TREVITHICK 1804

103

capital spending, loan repayment guarantees, and exchange risk guarantees for ECSC and EIB loans.

The criteria for negotiable assistance under section 7 are: that the investment would not go ahead in the same nature, scale or timing without such assistance, that is, financial needs must be demonstrated; the project must offer benefits to the UK economy, such as import substitution, increased exports, productivity gains; and the project would not be located in a steel closure area unless the incentives were offered.

Section 8 of the Act covers sectoral assistance and to qualify a project must offer technology new to the UK, development of new processes or techniques, or industrial development desirable to the UK.

Tax allowances on capital spending also have to be taken into account. Regional development grants are not a taxable receipt and are therefore free of tax. The full cost of machinery and plant may be set off against tax, and on industrial buildings 54 per cent of the construction cost can be written off in the first year and thereafter at the rate of 4 per cent on the original cost each year. For buildings under 2500 square feet costs can be written off completely in the first year.

4.10 Leasing

Margaret Dibben

The dreaded words 'cash flow' send a chill down the spines of small businessmen. Getting hold of the finance they need to start a business is only the beginning of their headaches. The squeeze of paying out bills weekly while creditors take 90 days to settle has been the downfall of many companies.

So, rather than tie up massive amounts of money in capital equipment, plant and machinery, many finance directors opt for leasing, hire purchase or renting equipment. Thus, instead of paying for a purchase all at once, they can spread the cost over a period of years. Last year £2.3 billion worth of equipment was leased from members of the Equipment Leasing Association.

Almost any item a business needs can be acquired this way. The fastest growing sector for leasing last year was plant and machinery where the market doubled to £830 million in 1980.

Car leasing fell of sharply last year as the recession forced many fleet operators to extend existing leases rather than enter into new agreements.

In the area of new technology, renting equipment is becoming increasingly popular since a firm can try out a new piece of equipment before deciding whether to commit the cash to buying it. Neither does it have to sign a long-term agreement.

The choice between leasing or renting is fairly straightforward as different criteria govern the decision in the first place. Leasing is a form of purchase, although the equipment belongs to the leasing company, with a commitment to regular payments over a set period of years. By renting you only pay for the equipment while you are using it, which can in some instances be for periods as short as one day, and there is no responsibility for repair if the machine breaks down.

Another choice is to pay by hire purchase instalments. If your company is making sufficient taxable profit against which to offset capital allowances, this is the best course. But if not the leasing company operates by claiming the allowance and the small company can still benefit. When the lessor has collected the tax allowance, he passes the benefit on to the lessee.

The main difference between leasing and HP is at the end of an agreement. Under the HP contract, the buyer owns the equipment he has been paying for, but the lessee does not. However, the usual practice is for the leasing company to allow him to sell the machinery and keep, say, 90 per cent of the proceeds. The leasing company has no use for the second-hand equipment.

The clearing banks, through subsidiaries, are the largest lessors and deal with more than 50 per cent of the business done in the UK. After the bank manager, the next people who can help are the merchant banks, international banks and finance houses. There are some corporate lessors but they are not large and, as profits are falling, the business is declining.

Leasing brokers will arrange a deal but, as with brokers in any area, not all are as scrupulous as the majority, and the lessor should make comparisons and work out for himself exactly what he is committing to payment. Another growing trend is for a salesman to produce a vendor leasing agreement from his brief-case when he clinches a deal to sell equipment. A leasing package produced this way may be a good deal but again anyone considering leasing should talk to his bank manager or accountant before signing a contract.

The rates charged differ from company to company, and even

within the same company depending on the time of year. Because the leasing company makes its its money by offsetting the cost of the equipment against tax, the closer to the end of the financial year and thus to paying the corporation tax, the better deal it can offer.

Once the business has entered into a leasing agreement, there is no restriction on the use of the machinery. It just pays an agreed stream of calculated payments over a given period, say five years. The length of the contract is usually spread over the expected life of the equipment. No deposit is needed.

The demand for renting equipment has been growing at between 20 to 30 per cent a year for the last 10 years. Regardless of any financial advantage, the main reason for renting is to find an urgent solution to an emergency. A piece of equipment breaks down or a sudden rush of work overloads capacity, and a company is compelled to rent the necessary equipment.

But there are positive advantages. Renting gives a small business maximum flexibility, and the businessman only pays as he uses the equipment. If he contracts to rent for one week but needs the machinery longer, he can keep it. If he thinks he will need it for six months but business drops off after two, he can cancel without penalty. If the machinery breaks down, it is the responsibility of the rental company to repair and replace it. He can regularly replace the equipment with new up-to-date items when they come out, try out a piece of new technology to see if it suits his needs or even if he is eventually buying, fill in if there is a prolonged delivery period after he has ordered a piece of equipment.

4.11 State agencies
Clive Woodcock

There are now several government-backed agencies in various parts of the country which offer either finance for small firms or advice on how to obtain it from other sources or both.

Although the National Enterprise Board has been reduced in scope from its former role of ambulance service for ailing giants such as British Leyland, it is now able to concentrate more on the task of helping the development of the smaller and medium-sized enterprises which was always a substantial, though under-publicised, part of its business.

In theory there is no upper or lower limit to the size of company which qualifies for NEB assistance, but in practice it has usually helped the rather more substantial smaller firm, dealing in hundreds of thousands of pounds rather then tens of thousands, but there is no reason why any firm with a well-prepared plan, an essential for an approach to any organisation, should not try its chances.

The board is required to look for an adequate return on all the investments it makes on its own initiative and also has to give special attention to areas of high unemployment and high technology sectors in making investment decisions. Its finance is usually made on the basis of a combination of an equity stake and loan finance.

The NEB has regional directors in Liverpool and Newcastle and has also entered into joint ventures in the regions, such as that with the Midland Bank with Newtown Securities in the North-east.

The writ of the NEB is of course confined to England as is that of the Council for Small Industries in Rural Areas (CoSIRA). The aim of CoSIRA is to regenerate depopulated and disadvantaged rural areas, and its facilities are available to firms in manufacturing industry, equipment servicing, or tourism employing not more than 20 skilled people, though there is no restriction on numbers of unskilled workers involved. The firms must be located in a rural area or a town of not more than 10,000 population.

Among the assistance it offers are commercial loans for up to 80 per cent of the cost of a project — up to a figure of £30,000. It is, however, increasingly working closely with the banks and has reached agreements with some of them under which certain sums of money are allocated each year for projects processed by CoSIRA.

In effect CoSIRA is carrying out the assessment and weeding out processes and ensuring that the projects which go forward to the banks are viable ones. For the potential entrepreneur it has the advantage of ensuring that he has a properly prepared plan and vastly increases his chances of being offered bank finance.

In Wales there are two agencies which can give valuable help to the small businessman: the Welsh Development Agency and the Development Board for Rural Wales.

The WDA can provide finance for companies either by equity

A new House-A new Factory

£30

per week in Mid Wales

We have factories available at Llandrindod Wells, Newtown, Dolgellau, Bala, Lampeter and Cardigan.

Starter Factories of 500 and 750 square feet are ideal for the expanding small company or the new business starting up.

As well as providing a new factory the Development Board for Rural Wales can help in other ways:

Business Advisory Service

Provides expert advice on all aspects of running a business.

Training Courses

New Enterprise Promotion

A programme especially devised for developing small businesses.

Getting Into Business Courses

A series of evening classes for people who want to start a business.

Seminars

Short term courses on specific topics e.g. finance, marketing.

Business Development Course

A programme to help the established company to expand.

This is an opportunity too good to miss, send the coupon today for further details.

 **Development Board for Rural Wales**

Ladywell House
Newtown
Powys SY16 1JB
Tel: (0686) 26965
Telex: 35387

Please send details
of your Starter Factories.

Name . . . .

Address . . . .

. . . .

. . . .

To: Development Board for Rural Wales,
Freepost, Newtown, Powys, SY16 1JB.

108

capital or loans at commercial rates of interest or a combinatiion of both. In 1979 the WDA agreed with the National Westminster Bank on a joint venture under which the agency would investigate business propositions and guarantee loans of up to £50,000 for businessmen who had sound projects but were unable to provide the necessary security.

The loan guarantee scheme was subsequently extended to include Lloyds and Barclays banks and attracted a great deal of interest when it was launched, but no firm business has yet resulted.

Through its own investment activities the WDA has provided guarantees for funds totalling about £1 million for nearly two dozen companies. Altogether it has more than £11 million invested in 157 companies, two-thirds of which are small firms which have had funds totalling £2 million in individual investments of up to £50,000. The agency limits its shareholding to 30 per cent of a company's equity and negotiates buy-back arrangements so that the businessman can regain full ownership if he wishes.

The agency also has wide powers to develop factories and industrial estates, reclaim derelict land, and provide advisory services to industry. It also works closely with agencies such as British Steel's job creation subsidiary, BSC (Industry) in steel closure areas.

The lively Development Board for Rural Wales operates in the rural areas of mid-Wales in much the same way as CoSIRA in England.

It was established to counter depopulation and encourage repopulation by economic and social measures. It can offer loans and factory space through its advance factory building programme — which also includes small workshop space for the very small starter — often with an initial rent holiday.

It also has a very practically orientated business advisory service and organises courses for prospective and established small businessmen.

For Scotland there are two principal agencies; the Scottish Development Agency and the Highlands and Islands Development Board. The SDA has similar powers to its counterpart in Wales, playing an important part in meeting the needs of small independent companies which are undercapitalised.

Some years ago it took over from the Small Industries Council for Rural Areas in Scotland its role for assisting small firms in rural Scotland and also runs the government's Small Firms Service in Scotland. Its small firms division is also able to offer, in addition to finance, a business advisory service, and the SDA has also organised overseas trade missions.

The Highlands and Islands Development Board has extensive powers to boost the economic development of the area through a variety of means, including promoting companies, taking shareholdings, providing advisory services, acquiring land, building factories, or granting or lending money under powers similar to section 7 of the Industry Act for activities ranging from engineering to tourism.

The board also has special powers to bring the volume of assistance beyond the normal level from public sources in exceptional cases. Finance can be as much as 70 per cent of the capital required, in addition to custom-built or advance factories with initial rent-free periods of up to two years.

The Department of Industry's Small Firms Service, available throughout the country by ringing Freefone 2444, can be useful both as a signpostings service to where finance can be obtained and for help from its counsellors in preparing a business plan with which to approach a bank.

The Small Firms Service itself cannot provide finance but it can offer a link with institutional sources by appraising investment propositions and then putting them to institutions such as the Post Office Staff Superannuation Fund. The investments that are made are on a commercial basis and there is no question of subsidised terms being available.

Many local authorities are also now offering financial help to encourage the growth of small firms in their areas, often through organisations such as the Greater Manchester Economic Development Corporation which can provide both finance and accommodation. Some local authorities have also bought and converted older premises in their areas for use by small firms as well as building nursery units.

The Industrial Common Ownership Act of 1976 gave support to certain organisations which give advice to potential new cooperatives. There are sums available for loan through Industrial Common Ownership Finance in Northampton, while one of the clearing banks, the Co-operative Bank is prepared to match, pound for pound, the money raised by members of the cooperative as their personal stake in addition to overdraft facilities for working capital.

The prospective cooperative can obtain considerable help from the Co-operative Development Agency, which, while it does not have money to lend itself, can give invaluable aid in advice, feasibility studies and preparation of business plans through which finance can be obtained from other sources.

A further source of finance from a government-backed agency is the National Research Development Corporation, which provides public funds for the development and exploitation of inventions by both large and small firms. It is a successful, profitable organisation though it does sometimes come under fire, being accused of not taking sufficient risks; it is no secret that it takes a hard-nosed commercial approach to propositions.

There are three main ways in which it provides finance. One is a joint venture deal under which the NRDC will provide up to 50 per cent of the cash flow required for a specific project. Another is the provision of working capital through recirculating loans. NRDC is also willing to provide equity and loan capital in technology base firms, the outlay ranging from £5000 to £5 million in a single project.

It also provides help for the academic researcher, although it requires the assignment of any patent rights in these cases. Small loans are available for the private investor and the organisation will provide leasing finance through its off-shoot Finovia to help to promote the development of innovations.

Towards the end of the last year NRDC set up the Small Company Innovation Fund to provide finance for start-up companies through a range of equity, loan, participating preference shares and working capital.

In Northern Ireland the Department of Commerce has extensive powers to help industry, and operates a full range of incentives, many of which are at higher rates than even those available in the special development areas in the United Kingdom reflecting the special problems of the region.

The Northern Ireland Development Agency has funds with which to assist companies through stimulating investment by way of loans or equity shareholdings. The needs of very small firms are specifically catered for by the Local Enterprise Development Unit, which has branch offices around the region and can offer a range of assistance.

Addresses

Industrial Common Ownership
Finance Ltd
4 St Giles Street
Northampton
Tel: 0604-37563

Co-operative Development Agency
20 Albert Embankment
London SE1 7JT
Tel: 01-211 4633

Development Board for Rural Wales
Ladywell House
Newtown
Powys SY16 1JB
Tel:0686-26965

Highlands and Islands Development
Board
Bridge House
Bank Street
Inverness IVI 1QR
Tel: 0463-34171

Welsh Development Agency
Treforest Industrial Estate
Pontypridd
Mid-Glamorgan CF37 5VT
Tel: 044 385-2666

Scottish Development Agency
20 Bothwell Street
Glasgow
Tel: 041-248 2700

Council for Small Industries in Rural
Areas (CoSIRA)
141 Castle Street
Salisbury
Wiltshire SP1 3TP
Tel: 0722-6255

Northern Ireland Department of
Commerce
Chichester House
64 Chichester Street
Belfast
Tel: 0232-34488

BSC (Industry) Ltd
42 Grosvenor Gardens
London SW1W OEB
Tel: 01-235 1212

Industrial Common Ownership
Movement
c/o Beechwood College
Elmete Lane
Roundhay
Leeds LS8 2LO
Tel: 0532-651235

Scottish Economic Planning
Department
Small Firms Information Centre
57 Bothwell Street
Glasgow
Tel: 041-248 6014

4.12 Equity capital
David Simpson

Standard bank borrowings are the most obvious means of funding for a company; in many instances they are neither the most suitable nor the most accessible of routes.

Banks demand a certain amount of security, despite the good neighbour propaganda of television and colour supplement advertising campaigns. Security can be material, with charges on specific assets and these terms themselves intransigently linked to other borrowings, forcing unacceptable future financing restrictions upon the company.

The security can take other forms, hitched to historic trading and/or future trading performances, with a business either unable to provide the record required or unwilling or unable to

112

The competitive alternative for long-term capital.

Buying out a fellow shareholder?

Contemplating a management buy-out from your parent company?

Seeking long-term capital for expansion?

Whatever your reason for needing long-term capital, if yours is a profitable operation, Gresham Trust could provide it.

Naturally you'll want the finance packaged in the way that best suits your needs. But how can you be sure you've got it if you haven't found out what Gresham can offer?

Gresham Trust

Gresham Trust Ltd.,
Barrington House,
Gresham Street,
London EC2V 7HE.
Tel: 01-606 6474.

meet the future targets demanded.

The main impediment to conventional bank borrowing is that a firm may be loath or unable to meet either repayment deadlines which are demanded, or, even more so, unable to meet interest payments from cash flow while still obtaining any return at all on capital, let alone a commercial return.

These problems have been exacerbated in the current economic climate. To begin with, interest rates reached new heights last year and, though they have fallen, their levels not only remain daunting but are never again likely to recede to past levels.

An additional problem is that trading margins have become imperilled for a number of reasons: the strength of sterling; overmanning in British industry; the relatively high costs of energy in this country; the disincentive toward new capital investment and modernisation which has prevailed for too long, and so on. The list is a long one.

This symptom makes the burden of interest payments all the more acute for any company, whether or not finance is forthcoming. With a government committed to restraining the growth of money supply, and operating on the belief that money supply and Public Sector Borrowing Requirement are inseparable, the situation is aggravated. Banks are under pressure to take a cautious view of lending and their judgment at present is not always amenable to the needs and circumstances of the smaller business in particular.

All of this diverts the spotlight to the case for equity capital as a means of funding for growth or development. The availability of equity funding has always been open to criticism. The Stock Exchange, a public listing, is one pathway but a pathway strewn with barriers for the small company, although some of these have recently been removed.

Almost two decades ago, the Jenkins Committee was scathing about the amount of risk capital the City and its institutions offered to business; criticism has continued with the attack repeated by the Wilson Committee.

Nonetheless, over this period there has developed an ever-increasing number of specialist institutions — now supplemented by the clearing banks which have begun to recognise this gap in their repertoire — which are geared to providing backing for companies by way of equity stakes.

The amounts of backing, and the terms vary enormously. A few years ago, little equity backing under a minimum of perhaps

£250,000 was available. This has dipped more and more, and today there are institutions which will put up as little as £10,000 into direct equity, convertible shares or loan stock in one form or another.

The advantages of equity capital are fairly self-evident. Those institutions prepared to put up direct equity backing will not put barriers on a company's immediate cash flow or set impossible repayment terms.

At the same time, there are drawbacks. Some measure of control will pass out of the hands of the founders of any business as a proportion of his holding changes hands, by the creation of new capital and there will, in some instances, be unwanted and unwarranted interference in the running of the company.

The amount of equity which passes out of a business tends to vary from about 10 per cent up to customary maximum of 50 per cent although most of those institutions supplying equity backing want to hold a minimum stake.

Some will seek boardroom representation; some a voice in future company policy and strategy. Neither of these steps is perhaps unreasonable. The lender is after all supplying risk capital unavailable from other sources and must take at least some steps to protect his investment.

With the enlarged number of options available, however, the company should shop around for the best alternatives. The options can vary to a large extent, primarily of course in the share in a company's capital which is sought in exchange for a particular loan.

Companies seeking equity finance should also beware of other pitfalls. One of these is the amount of research and financial information they will have to provide the potential investor at their own cost. The preliminary steps are cheap and easy, but only a tiny proportion of initial approaches for equity capital backing ever mature.

In the end, before the final documents are signed, some would-be investors will demand full audit reports and future forecasts or profitability which are more comprehensive — and expensive — than those needed for a full Stock Exchange listing.

The other issue which may cause a company to hesitate before creating new capital is what can or will happen to the shares that are exchanged for capital. Few investors give guarantees on what they will do with their new investment, other than a cursory assurance that it will be in the interests of the company as a whole and that no decisions will be made without prior agreement with the directors or other members.

Even with the most reputable and experienced of the lending and investing institutions in the field this sort of guarantee can prove meaningless. The situation is not improved by the existing restrictions on companies repurchasing shares which they have issued for financial backing.

Fortunately, this dilemma has been recognised by the government as part of its policy to encourage the growth of small business and private investment and steps are being taken to ease the way for share buy-backs, as an inducement to companies to take up equity capital financing opportunites.

The new provisions to widen the sope of share buy-backs are scheduled to be introduced at the committee stage of the Companies Act which had its first Parliamentary reading in February 1981. A consultative document on the subject was issued in the summer of 1980 and drew a great deal of adverse comment and at the time of writing it is unsure exactly what measures the government will ultimately introduce.

But for the private company at least, the changes are likely to be wide-ranging, allowing companies to repurchase shares issued in exchange for new capital with a minimal amount of formality and at minimum expense.

Addresses

Anthony Gibbs and Sons
3 Frederick Place
Old Jewry
London EC2
Tel: 01-588 4111

Arbuthnot Latham
37 Queen Street
London EC4
Tel: 01-236 5281

Charterhouse Japhet
25 Milk Street
London EC2V 8JE
Tel: 01-248 3999

County Bank
10-11 Old Broad Street
London EC2
Tel: 01-638 6000

Hambros Bank
41 Bishopsgate
London EC2
Tel: 01-588 2851

Hill Samuel and Co
100 Wood Street
London EC2
Tel: 01-628 8011

Gresham Trust
Barrington House
Gresham Street
London EC2
Tel: 01-606 6474

Keyser Ullmann
25 Milk Street
London EC2
Tel: 01-606 7070

Minster Trust
Minster House
Arthur Street
London EC4
Tel: 01-623 1050

Norwich General Trust
London Regional Office
Norwich Union Buildings
39 St James Street
London SW1
Tel: 01-493 8030

Wintrust
Imperial House
Dominion Street
London EC2
Tel: 01-606 9411

4.13 Exporting
Rod Chapman

A common explanation of Britain's extraordinary current account surplus — an estimated £2.3 billion in 1980 — is that companies squeezed almost to the point of extinction in the home market are scouring even more remote areas in search of new export markets.

The biggest question mark against the new export drive is how new entrants and existing exporters looking for fresh outlets should underwrite their foreign forays. And, while the risk is heightened by increasing international political ferment, the number of options open to small and medium-sized British firms also seems to be broadening.

The official Thatcherite line is that the big clearing banks should take more of the strain, easing that on the Public Sector Borrowing Requirement. But the mainstay of Britain's exporting effort remains the Export Credits Guarantee Department, a massive subsidy operation which now underwrites some 30 per cent of the country's exports.

Whatever the dogmas of successive governments, the ECGD has quietly expanded since the Second World War, before which its share of the export trade was only 8 to 10 per cent. And its empire building has been of great benefit to exporters and banks alike.

The ECGD provides facilities which guarantee the exporter against non-payment — through default on the part of the buyer, cancellation of import licences by the country of destination, restrictions on the transfer of currency, or a number of other stratagems. It also furnishes unconditional guarantee of 100 per cent repayment to the banks, enabling them to provide finance to exporters at favourable rates.

117

Its umbrella has extended in recent years to insure new overseas investment against the risks of war, expropriation, and restriction of remittances. And its cover has also helped protect exporters against part of the increases in the UK costs for large capital goods contracts with long manufacturing periods.

Nevertheless, the ECGD has been hard hit by political events such as the Iranian Revolution, and paid out a record £264 million in claims last year — double the previous year's figure. This meant that the department had to draw on its reserves, with the result that they fell for the first time in years, and the logical consequence will be a rise in premiums this year by some 5 to 10 per cent for most established exporters.

The ECGD is a member of the International Arrangement on Guidelines for Officially Supported Credit, otherwise known as the Consensus, signed by the OECD countries in 1978 to provide favourable long-term credit rates for exporters. But the level of these rates has become increasingly unrealistic by comparison with those on the open market (in some areas, such as aviation, the going ECGD rate is almost 5 per cent below the commercial rate) and there are international moves afoot to tighten up on mixed credit and aid schemes under the Consensus.

The other main official export financing scheme is the British Overseas Trade Board's Market Entry Guarantee Scheme. Introduced experimentally two years ago, this is designed to allow small and medium-sized manufacturing firms to insure part of the risk of entering a new export market. The BOTB has decided to continue the scheme, and is now carrying out a study to see whether it should be extended to non-manufacturing sectors of industry.

The Bank of England published a comprehensive guide on export finance two years ago entitled *Money for Exports*, listing both public and private sector financial and associated services for exporters. And its own in-laws, the big clearing banks, have extended their export services considerably of late.

The banks are currently negotiating with the ECGD and the Treasury on a proposal to take some £1¼ billion of ECGD low-interest credits directly on to their books — in a plea bargaining exercise which would not add to the monies available for exporters but might persuade the government to drop its windfall tax proposal.

However, they are all busy promoting their own services and ECGD-linked facilities. Lloyds Bank, for example, publishes a booklet on *Exporting for the Smaller Business,* which is matched by

Midland Bank International's *Services for Exporters* and National Westminster Bank's *ECGD and Associated Bank Finance*.

Midland has a Smaller Exporters Scheme for firms with turnovers up to £1¼ million, which involves interest payments of 1½ per cent above its base rate. It expanded the scheme last year following an enthusiastic response from small firms.

Barclays took over UDT International Finance Ltd recently, and has incorporated it into the Barclays group as Barclays Export Services to bolster its export and import financing facilities. The subsidiary is now running an advertising campaign in the national press to publicise its short and medium-term credits and other services such as finance for the export of capital goods to Comecon — always a tricky exercise.

The banks offer various methods of payment for exporters, including open accounts, buyer's cheque, banker's draft, and bills of exchange. There is also the option of overdraft finance, not always that attractive with MLR at its present rate. The 'bread and butter' deals of Britain's export trade are usually handled on open account, with credit terms of either 60 days or 60 to 180 days.

The banks have also stepped in in the last year to provide foreign currency loans. The ECGD dropped its fixed-rate refinancing of sterling landing for foreign business in April 1980, with the government's relaxation of exchange control regulations. The scheme provided for large export contracts to be financed in foreign currencies, then refinanced by the ECGD. But few leading exporters have made moves to get out of foreign currencies into sterling for large contracts, and the clearing banks have adjusted the balance of their funds accordingly.

Publications

Money for Exports
Bank of England
Economic Intelligence Department
London EC2R 8AH

ECGD Services
Export Credits Guarantee Department
Aldermanbury House
Aldermanbury
London EC2P 2EL

BOTB's Services
Overseas Trade Board
1 Victoria Street
London SW1H 0ET

Services for Exporters and Small Exports Service
Midland Bank Ltd
International Division
60 Gracechurch Street
London EC3P 3BN

Exporting for the Smaller Business
Lloyds Bank Ltd
71 Lombard Street
London EC3P 3BS

ECGD and Associated Bank Finance
National Westminster Bank
Export Finance Division
25 Old Broad Street
London EC2N 1HQ

119

4.14 Factoring

James Erlichman

If this recession has proved nothing else, it is that negative cash flow can kill with devastating speed even healthy companies — especially small businesses. But what can the small man do when, for example, he supplies to only a handful of powerful customers able to make him sing for payment while he is obliged to pay cash on the nail for his raw materials? The flow of money out of his business looks like a raging red river against the trickle of money, dammed up by debtors, which comes back in.

His rescue is engineered by the factor: the financial doctor who promises to staunch his wounds by sorting out the sales ledger, collecting debts and advancing money against them all until the good times roll.

But is the factor just an old-fashioned leech attracted to sick and dying companies? Or is he the purveyor of a modern wonder cure, which, if administered in careful doses, can revive with astonishing speed?

There is, of course, no simple answer. Much depends upon the kind of business you run, the kind of businessman you are, and the kind of factor you employ.

Factoring in the bad old days was really little more than money-lending. The factor would, in effect, buy your sales invoices (debts owed by customers) and give you up to 80 per cent of their value immediately in cash. He would then attempt to collect these debts, charge you interest on the money he had advanced, and then pay you the rest of what he had collected if anything was left after the interest due to him.

This is still the way that all factors make most of their money. The interest charged on money advanced is usually between two and three per cent above either base rate or finance house base rate.

But most reputable factors these days offer a far more comprehensive 'sales ledger administration' service which allows a business to dispense entirely with the costly and laborious job of sales and debt chasing.

With the complete service, the factor takes over each sales invoice immediately the ink is dry. The factor uses his sophisticated bank of computers to dispatch bills to your customers with miraculous speed. This technology is designed to impress

CASH FLOW ASSURED
LEDGER ADMINISTRATION
SIMPLIFIED!
CREDIT COVER PROVIDED
EXPORTING MADE EASY!

H+ HFactors

The independent factor in business

we offer a uniquely flexible approach
to Factoring which may be able to provide
one or more of the above benefits to
suitable companies.

H & H FACTORS LTD.,

Randolph House,
46-48 Wellesley Road,
Croydon CR9 3PS, Surrey
01-681 2641
A. M. Walker

Danlee Buildings,
Spring Gardens,
Manchester M2 2BZ
061-228 2344
J. M. Bagley

Penthouse Suite, Rackhay,
Queen Charlotte St.,
Bristol, BS1 4HJ
0272-20298
P. A. Finnigan

 The U.K. subsidiary of Walter E. Heller & Co., the world's largest
Factoring organisation.

your customers so much that they pay up instantly with a smile on their face.

In addition, the factor undertakes to underwrite every bad debt that he cannot collect, so you are completely protected. For these combined services the factor charges between ½ and 2½ per cent of your gross turnover.

The factor's money-lending facility has never been a bargain. Presumably, one would only ask for it as a temporary measure against cash flow difficulties if the local bank manager refused to stump up an overdraft at less onerous rates of interest.

But the sales invoicing/debt underwriting service can be a real benefit, depending, of course, on how fast you are at collecting your own debts and how much it is costing you to employ a sales invoicing team to do it.

Several things should be borne in mind. These services can be bought without borrowing money from the factor. Second, the revolution in computerised information technology may have made your own in-tray/out-tray human system hopelessly obsolete. Just as you may buy in specialised advice from accountants and lawyers so, too, you may think it sensible to buy in a computerised sales invoicing system from a factor.

Remember also that, if the factor has taken over your sales ledger completely, his incentive to perform efficiently increases. It is now in his interest to clear his computers of your accounts quickly and to collect all your debts (not just the easy ones) because your bad debts become his financial burden.

The Association of British Factors proudly announced recently that its members had reduced the average collection time of debts on their books from 67 days to 65 days in the last year. That kind of efficiency, however, can cut two ways.

Getting your money back quickly is splendid so long as your factor is not achieving this miracle by using strong-arm tactics which might ruin your carefully cultivated relationship with a valued customer. The Association, which speaks for its eight member factors, strenuously maintains that its debt collection efficiency is based strictly on thoroughness, accuracy and speed — and never on unpleasantness.

To prove its point the Association admits that its members last year were forced to write off £1.5 million in bad debts they could not collect — a rise of 117 per cent over 1979.

There is no doubt that factors, by wantonly lending money 'up front' on invoices, can damage business by connecting them to pure oxygen, when they ought to learn to breathe air. One obvious example is a business with very seasonal trade which gets addicted to quick cash from invoices only to discover that its supply dries up when it hits a bad sales period. Using invoice money to invest in new machinery can be equally disastrous if the new equipment does not produce a quick return.

It is important to remember that unlike the bank manager the factor does not lend you money on future sales, only on approved sales completed. He therefore has no vested interest in your survival and can, if unscrupulous, encourage you to borrow money you cannot afford.

But there is equally no doubt that factoring, performed reputably, can be an invaluable service to many small businesses. Certainly the factoring industry has grown dramatically, increasing its turnover tenfold to £2 billion between 1973 and 1979.

The Association of British Factors was established in 1977 as a watchdog for the industry and has accepted eight firms into membership, all of which are subsidiaries of clearing banks or other large financial institutions.

As in all industries, some perfectly respectable firms stand outside the umbrella of a voluntary association for entirely valid reasons. But membership of the ABF is certainly a good guide.

Addresses

Alex Lawrie Factors Ltd
PO Box 12
Beaumont House
Banbury
Oxfordshire OX16 7RN
Tel: 0295-4491

Arbuthnot Factors Ltd
Arbuthnot House
Breeds Place
Hastings TN34 3DG
Tel: 0424-430324

Barclays Factoring Ltd
Paddington House
PO Box 9
Basingstoke
Hants RG21 1BE

Credit Factoring International Ltd
Smith House
PO Box 50
Elmwood Avenue
Feltham
Middlesex TW13 7QD
Tel: 01-890 1390

Griffin Factors Ltd
21 Farncombe Road
Worthing
Sussex BN11 2BW

H & H Factors Ltd
Randolph House
46-8 Wellesley Road
Croydon
Surrey CR9 3PS
Tel: 01-681 2641

123

Independent Factors Ltd
98-9 Queen's Road
Brighton
Sussex BN1 3WZ
Tel: 0273-21271

International Factors Ltd
Circus House
New England Road
Brighton
Sussex BN1 4GX
Tel: 0273-21211

4.15 Tax incentives

Joe Horner

One possible source of finance for aspiring new businesses is the support of individuals who have paid income tax at the higher tax levels. It is not widely realised that some aspects of tax planning are specifically encouraged by the government. One such area is what can be called the 'safety net'.

If a new enterprise is carried on by an individual (or a partnership of individuals) and if it makes losses in its early years the individual can ask the tax inspector to set those losses against income of three years earlier and can reclaim tax on the appropriate amount of income. Thus, if a loss of £1000 is suffered in the tax year 1981-82 the individual can set it against income for 1978-79. For that year the top tax rate on earned income was 83 per cent so that if the person had paid tax on £1000 at the top rate he could reclaim £830. In some rare cases it may even be possible to set the loss against investment income which had suffered the investment income surcharge of 15 per cent in addition to the top tax rate and thus to recover £980.

In addition to the tax refund the individual will receive interest (which is non-taxable). The amount of interest will depend upon when the tax was paid and when the refund is agreed, but the overall picture is that the tax and interest mean that virtually the whole of the loss can be recovered.

If a further loss is incurred in tax year 1982-83 it can be set against income of 1979-80 when the top rate was reduced to 60 per cent (or 75 per cent on investment income). Although the total immunity to loss will therefore cease to apply, the tax plus interest will still mean that there is a large measure of protection.

It may seem excessively timid (and a poor omen for future success) to be too concerned about losses when approaching a new venture but the safety net can be very useful even for a profitable new venture. If the business needs expensive equipment on which 100 per cent first-year allowance is available the allowance may create a tax loss even if there is a trading profit. In effect, therefore, the equipment may be purchased out of past tax so that the business can get off to a good start with the increased prospect of being ultimately successful.

Of course, many people in the appropriate tax brackets do not want to be heavily involved in new enterprises but there is no need for them to commit a great deal of time. If there is a would-be new business person who has the idea and the ambition but lacks the access to capital it should be possible for the people with the safety net to employ him to run the new business for them. He would thus be assured of an income during the vulnerable early period and they would be assured of an enthusiastic manager.

If, and when, the business was shown to be profitable the relationship could be changed, if desired, so that he took a partnership rather than employment. Alternatively, the business could be transferred to a company in which he held shares.

It must be emphasised that the safety net can be used only for genuine new businesses which have a reasonable prospect of success. This particular way of dealing with business losses was introduced by Denis Healey as Chancellor in 1978 and is obviously intended to be an inducement to 'have a go' with new ideas in order to reduce unemployment and stimulate economic activity. In effect, certain people are allowed to promote new, approved activities and if they do so they will be allowed to invest money which they have parted with already.

It is hoped, of course, that the business will be successful and the safety net not necessary. If that does come about the manner in which business profits are assessed and the reduction of the highest rates of tax since 1979-80 will enable the investors to retain a reasonable share of the profit.

4.16 Going public

David Simpson

Going public has always held a great number of drawbacks for the smaller company. In the first place, the cost of an issue can be prohibitive in relation to the amount of new funding to be raised.

Cost acts as a deterrent in another way. The amount of disclosure required of the company under Stock Exchange listing requirements, both in terms of the expense involved in the many documents which must be produced, and in terms of the man hours employed in maintaining the requisite accounting systems, is formidable. Disclosure in itself is another problem. An essentially private or family firm may be reluctant to expose itself to the public eye to the extent demanded, if only for commercial reasons.

Finally, there is the reluctance of the owners of the company to divest themselves of too high a proportion of the equity and control of their business.

Some of these problems have been exacerbated with the passage of time; others have been eased. The costs of an issue for a full listing on the Stock Exchange have risen and will continue to rise in line with inflation. There are statutory advertising demands — the cost of a three-page prospectus in the Financial Times, for example, which is now more than £30,000 — and the expense of printing prospectuses.

There are, moreover, the professional fees for bankers, brokers and accountants; the cost of underwriting an issue when it is an offer for sale rather than a placing; and there is the 1 per cent capital duty on the proceeds of an issue.

It is quite possible for the cost of an issue to reach 5 per cent or considerably more of the proceeds of the issue, although the percentage tends to fall as the size of the issue rises because of the fixed cost element involved. But for the smaller firm, the cost can be high.

On top of all this, the Stock Exchange seeks a minimum five years' trading.

The main way in which the burden of going public has been lightened in recent years is that the Stock Exchange has lowered the minimum amount of capital in a company which must be offered for public subscription from 35 per cent to 25 per cent.

More pertinent to the smaller firm has been the development of the secondary markets within the orbit of the Stock Exchange. These initially developed under two rulings: 163 (2) which allowed limited dealings in the shares of some companies which were not seeking a full listing, and 163 (3), created in 1976 to allow trading in the stocks of companies involved in North Sea oil exploration and which could obviously not fulfil a five-year trading record.

126

This second rule has recently been expanded to allow trading in the shares of UK-registered energy or mineral companies engaged in overseas exploration.

But the event of most significance for the small company was the introduction last December of the Unlisted Securities Market (USM), whose structure is geared to re-encouraging private companies to come to the Stock Exchange, to the institutional private investor, for capital.

The USM minimises the qualifications for an applicant firm. Two basic criteria are required: that the company is registered as a public limited company and that it has achieved a normal three-year record of trading.

The second qualification, however, is negotiable with the Stock Exchange and may be reduced in some instances, where the company is involved in aspects of high technology, for example.

The requirements of a listing have been cut. Only 10 per cent of the company's authorised capital — and this can be reduced — need be sold to the public.

The costs of entry to the USM are also smaller, thanks to the lesser provisions for marketing the new issue. For example, no newspaper advertising is mandatory, apart from the requirement of an abridged or boxed advertisement in at least one national daily.

The favoured or permitted methods of marketing can also lead to reduced costs. The Stock Exchange prefers that new listings should be obtained by way of a placing which cuts out underwriting and advertising expenses inherent in an offer for sale.

A placing is banned only when the sum being raised does not exceed £3 million and/or the total authorised capital of the applicant does not exceed £15 million. A listing is also permitted through an 'introduction' which cuts costs even further as it eliminates the need for a separate accountant's report.

Broadly, the cost of a £500,000 USM issue would be £50,000, half the expense of a full Stock Market quotation for a similar size of issue.

The cost of an offer for sale, which has the advantage of allowing the issued shares to be spread around a wider number of investors, preventing too large a holding from falling into one set of hands, is proportionately higher because of the need for underwriting expenses to be paid.

At the bottom of the list comes the cost of an introduction

which need amount to no more than a few thousand pounds. The final charge is that all entrants to the USM are required to pay an annual listing fee of £1000.

In terms of continuing disclosure obligations once a USM listing has been obtained, some of the requirements which would be necessary for a company with a full listing have been alleviated. The most notable of these relates to the circularisation of acquisitions and disposal by the USM company.

Other principal differences are that the USM company will not be forced into full revelations of directors' service contracts, while the interim reports of the companies need be published in only one newspaper rather than two.

To obtain entry to the USM it will be necessary to obtain the services of a sponsoring broker. This, it is hoped, will encourage participation by local brokers, breaking the trend of recent years whereby most new issue business has devolved to the top national brokers.

The other theory behind the creation of the USM is that the small, and above all local, investor will be inspired to buy shares in local industries once more and indeed that it will prove preferable for the company seeking some form of equity finance to have its shares held by local investors, rather than unknown financiers or faceless institutions.

The development of the USM was prompted by the growth of secondary share markets along the lines of those prevailing in North America. Some secondary markets have already been born in the UK; the Stock Exchange recognised this development and believes it should play a leading role in it.

The leading secondary market is the over-the-counter market run by investment bankers, MJH Nightingale, which will place a minimum of about 5 per cent of the equity of a company with an approved list of institutions.

There has also been a move towards other secondary markets in recent months. One of these opening up is run by Harvard Securities, and it will buy small packages of shares in companies, selling them on its large list of private investment clients.

Addresses

Quotations Department
PO Box 119
The Stock Exchange
London EC2P 2BT
Tel: 01-558 2355 (day);
01-588 6970 (night)

The Stock Exchange
Margaret Street
Birmingham B3 3JL
Tel: 021-236 9181

The Stock Exchange
4 Norfolk Street
Manchester M2 1DS
Tel: 061-833 0931

The Stock Exchange
PO Box 141
69 St George's Place
Glasgow G2 1BU
Tel: 041-221 7060

The Stock Exchange
Northern Bank House
10 High Street
Belfast BT1 1BP
Tel: 1232-21094

The Stock Exchange
28 Anglesea Street
Dublin 2
Republic of Ireland
Tel: 0001 778808

4.17 Term loans

Maggie Brown

Medium-sized lending by the banks is the prime way for small and medium-sized companies to fund expansion plans. Further, the banks, stung by criticism that they are not doing enough for industry, have been vying with each other for the past two years in drawing up a range of special medium-term lending packages as alternatives to, or at least variations on, conventional term arrangements. So, there is a wide choice.

The starting place for anyone considering a medium-term loan therefore must be one (or several if you plan to shop around) of the 14,000 High Street clearing bank branches. In fact, about half of bank lending is now in the form of term loans, running from one to 20 years. But the vast bulk of the funds are lent out for five to seven years, and this remains the favourite and conventional medium-term period.

One further point is that the banks have been increasingly steering customers into term arrangements and away from frequently negotiated short-term credit arrangements and the overdraft. For the businessman the term loan has one major advantage. It is not at instant recall. The drawback is that it may cost more.

Two other trends are also apparent. More businesses are showing interest in borrowing on slightly longer terms. The ten-year term is reported to be increasingly gaining ground, not least because the sustained period of high interest rates has led borrowers to slow down on capital repayments, especially as profit margins have been squeezed.

Second, the move towards designing flexible finance plans, geared to customers' needs, has resulted in a tendency to liberalise the security requirements demanded by the banks, which have always fallen heaviest on smaller business. Indeed, the majority, by value, of bank loans are now unsecured. The banks are also keen to offer fixed rate loans linked to an estimate of the average minimum lending rate for the term of the loan. At present Lloyds regards 11 per cent as fair, putting fixed rate loans at around 14 per cent.

Opinions vary as to the popularity of such money. Banks clearly like the arrangement, pointing out that small businessmen like to know exactly what their commitments are too. But most borrowers still prefer a floating rate.

Other sources of medium-term finance include the US banks, which some people say have a better understanding of new technology ventures, the Industrial Commercial Finance Corporation and the finance houses, such as Lloyds and Scottish, Lombard North Central or Mercantile Credit. Lombard specialises in loans to finance hotel, shop and restaurant fixtures.

Medium-term loans are basically designed to finance investment in new assets, where the repayment, with interest, can be taken from the cash flow investment generates. So they are of crucial relevance to small firms with plans to expand. The formal term loan, usually secured against other assets, is most likely to be granted by the bank for a specific purpose, a new factory or extension, investment in new plant to diversify or modernise production or the provision of new facilities to meet a new contract.

The key to unlocking the bank's vaults is to accompany your request for capital — whether you want £5000 or £250,000 — with a well drawn up plan. 'The chap who comes in with ideas sketched on the back of an envelope just doesn't stand a chance', was how a senior adviser to one of the big four clearing banks put it.

The banks are increasingly anxious about the straightforward business logic behind expansion plans, above all, will the investment produce the required pay back in the time required. The balance sheet, profit and loss accounts, and the security to offset the loan all count. But an organised expansion plan is just as important. Both Barclays and Lloyds run business counselling services which are geared up to advise on precisely these issues.

Flexible elements can be built into the basic loan term agreement. For instance, it is a growing practice to allow a period of grace for one or even two years so that new equipment can start generating revenue. Repayments can be made to suit the customer, on a monthly, quarterly, half-yearly, or even, in the case of hotels and holiday restaurants, seasonal basis. It may even be possible to pay only interest on the loan, repaying the capital at the end of the term from, for example, the flotation of shares or a property asset sale.

Term interest rates vary according to the size and length of loan but are generally 3 to 5 per cent above the bank base rate. There is usually an additional charge of up to 1 per cent for an additional arrangement or commitment as outlined above. Any special legal costs in drawing up a loan may be passed on to the borrower too. And the fact remains that the better the bank knows you the easier and cheaper the process will be.

Finally, it is worth investigating the special schemes which the banks have drawn up. Barclays business loans offer up to £500,000 for up to 100 per cent of the cost of the asset for up to 20 years. Security is usually asked for but can be waived. Capital repayments can be deferred for two years if wanted, and the interest can be floating or fixed. Barclays also provides the most radical five year business start-up loans either for new companies or established businesses launching new products.

The outstanding feature of this scheme is that no capital need be repaid for five years, and even then, when the loan expires, the debt can be refinanced. Also, the cost of the loan is expressed as a percentage royalty on the borrower's sales, rather than as a rate of interest. So, as long as the company's sales are low, the cost of the loan will be too. Security is asked for under this scheme, but directors' own guarantees and third-party security are not required.

Midland has built on a foundation of conventional medium-term loans with a longer-term scheme of between £20,000 and £500,000 over 10 to 20 years to finance new capital projects for established firms. Security, as with most long-term finance, is required but options include a choice of fixed, or variable, interest rates, and moratoriums on capital repayments of up to two years.

National Westminster offers fixed rate business development loans of £2000 to £100,000 for repayment within 10 years. As with Lloyds which has a range of enterprise schemes, security may be sometimes waived.

The point about all these schemes is that it is now possible to negotiate flexible terms (within reason) to suit your circumstances.

5
Marketing

TOM CANNON
Professor of Business Studies, Sterling University

5.1 The small firm's route to profits and performance

Recently, the clarion call has gone out for more aggressive, more rigorous, more sustained or simply more marketing by Britain's small firms. Improved marketing, particularly by smaller manufacturers, is central to the industrial strategy. The need for small companies to emphasise marketing in developing their business is the cornerstone of the recent report on industrial innovation by the government's Advisory Council for Applied Research and Development.

Despite this, many managers of small firms question the relevance of marketing to them, given the severe limits on their resources, particularly of time and money. Large advertising budgets, expensive and time-consuming market research projects and the jargon which marketing appears to involve hold little appeal to the practical small firm manager. Problems in measuring the pay-offs from this effort reinforce the notion that marketing is a luxury, which only large and wealthy firms can afford.

However, many smaller businessmen intuitively apply the marketing concept every day. This is often done in a manner almost impossible for the large firm manager to achieve. It is because, as an approach to business, marketing is both simpler and more subtle than any of the cruder notions of large expenditures in areas such as advertising. It involves seeing the firm's goals in terms of meeting customer needs and wants. It means recognising that the better the firm matches its offering product, process or service to what the customer wants, the higher the value he will place on it. The higher this valuation, the stronger the relationship, with resulting improvements in returns for both the producer and the buyer. It is not a philanthropic gesture by firms, but an approach to improving the management of the exchanges between producer and buyer with resulting gains in performance.

The closeness that characterises relations between the managers of small enterprises and customers, whether a small plastics processor dealing with industrial buyers or tenant landlord with regulars, provides a powerful basis for the dialogue essential to effective marketing. The initial step involves recognising the importance of looking outside the firm into the marketplace for leads to further developments.

This was seen recently by Midland Furnishings. They produce a wide array of furniture, particularly wooden dining and living room furniture. Timber wall units are a major line. They used to produce these in teak and to a height of about five feet six inches. About four years ago the firm made a major effort to introduce their products into Europe. They suffered an early setback, primarily because these styles were not popular in the major European markets, and the wall unit market was dominated by other woods and different sizes. A product orientated firm would probably have abandoned its efforts to develop these markets. A sales orientated company might have worked very hard, spending large sums of money to win sales against retailed reservations and customer rejection. The response of this small, owner-managed firm was very different. Lacking the money or resources immediately to introduce new designs for these markets, the lessons from the market were built into longer-term design work. In the next major styling exercise conducted by the firm, its offerings incorporated these ideas. The intervening period has been used to explore their thinking with major UK retail buyers who encouraged their developments. In fact, changes in housing design, particularly the popularity of converting traditional domestic storage space to other uses, was creating changed customer needs. These pressures were encouraging sales of larger units in Britain. The rapid growth in demand at home for their units is now preventing a new European initiative.

This contrasts dramatically with the difficulties facing Century Belting, a small producer of transmission belts. Their prosperity had been built over many years through their strong relationships with a number of major manufacturers. An export initiative some time ago had failed because of the highly automated equipment used by European customers. Despite their considerable technical expertise and longer-term potential to adapt, the firm decided to concentrate their resources on satisfying the day-to-day needs of their current domestic customers. However, the progressive growth in inter-

European trade has forced their British customers to adapt rapidly to meet European competition. Over the last two years, a number of major accounts have sourced their new products from other suppliers as the company has worked to solve the technical problems associated with the newer systems. A number of competitors have established toeholds with Century Belting's traditional customers.

The adoption of a marketing perspective by Midland Furniture permitted them to steal a march on their competitors. There were no increases in advertising or more conventional marketing costs. They recognised that their prosperity was built on successfully meeting customers' needs both today and as they changed over time. Their networks of relationships and contacts provided their information base. Their technical skills and production capability gave them the opportunity to develop. Century Belting's difficulties contrast vividly with this. Their primary focus of attention was their current offerings and capabilities. They assumed that they were immune to change. Technical skills, production orientation and dangerous assumptions trapped them into a negative approach to buyer needs. Changes in the marketplace forced them to invest heavily in price cutting, increased services, advertising and promotion to arrest the tide which their lack of marketing insight had led them to ignore.

It is recognition that successful businesses are based on effectively meeting buyer needs that is the essence of marketing. The different areas of activity – information gathering and organisation product policy, promotion and selling, pricing and distribution – gain their real value from being built on this and the firm's willingness to implement lessons from the marketplace. The smaller firm with its stronger, more direct links to the marketplace, shorter lines of communication, flexibility and ability to act quickly and decisively has the scope to implement the reality rather than the appearance of marketing.

5.2 Information for marketing decisions

Information is the cornerstone of modern marketing. It binds the marketing system together by providing data on the needs of customers as well as building a picture of the external pressures and internal capabilities determining the firm's ability to meet the market requirements profitably over time.

The manager of the smaller firm has greater access to his customers and shorter lines of communication. These give him major advantages over the large corporation executive. He is seldom cut off from customer comments, attitudes and needs. Despite this, his intelligence gathering capability is often not used to the full. This reflects a lack of recognition of the potential value of information and a failure to plan its role in the firm.

The marketing orientated firm works hard to ensure that the gathering, organisation and use of information from the marketplace is geared to effective management decisions. The retailer hearing an assistant say 'You're the sixth person today to ask for that but we don't stock it as there's no demand', and the engineering firm convinced that it is their level of after sales service that sells their product but 'we still offer the lowest prices in the area' already have some of the data to improve their market position.

Collecting this information and organising it to answer questions, solve problems and meet customer needs is the sphere of marketing research. The array of sources ranges from the firm's own records and staff to government, private and commercial agencies and ultimately to specially commissioned studies. In fact, many managers starting off on the information gathering effort find the sheer volume of data the greatest deterrent to its use. This is why a clear brief which identifies the questions, problems and issues is vital. To specify the date needed and plan its uses effectively, the variables affecting these issues need to be identified. It calls for careful thought before the search starts. But the firm which recognises that there is a problem is halfway to solving it.

The prime source of data for the manager of a small firm is in-house information. This includes sales records, dispatch figures, stock details, details of inquiries and orders, and the material that can be gathered by salesmen, delivery staff and top management. It appears very easy to collect this information, but it is often so badly organized that the value is lost. Hard thought about what facts are required is necessary. Simplification of the material can provide massive advances in access. This can be as simple as rounding figures to tens, hundreds or even thousands while ensuring that simplification does not lead to distortion. Specific problems can be examined by deeper analysis of company records.

Oceania Motors had always emphasised high service levels and good quality in its new and used car sales. The high costs were paid for by high levels of repeat purchase of replacement vehicles by customers. A progressive deterioration in turnover forced a rethink about the overall approach. Before changing policies, the managing director checked his assumptions about levels of repeat purchase from company sales records. He was shocked to find that, during the 1970s, they had fallen from over 60 per cent of sales to less than 20 per cent. Further data analysis led to other important findings.

The most important of these was the picture from government sources of the changing population profile of the area. It emerged that their home town had changed from being largely self-sufficient in jobs to being increasingly dependent on a major city and several new towns. The middle management groups on which their business has been built increasingly worked for large city-based firms. A research report by their trade organisation pointed out the rapidly growing proportion of managers obtaining company cars. Rival car firms, based in the city, were winning this business. This information was only part of the store collected and disseminated by the government. Any executive who has felt, when filling in government forms, 'how useful it would be to know more about my competitors' is most of the way to recognising the value of government information because it is all published somewhere, albeit in a form geared to government requirements while protecting confidence.

This information is supplemented and made more relevant to specific industries by material published by such bodies as trade associations, industry research associations and commercial services. Much of this information can be purchased if firms are not members of their trade associations. Recently, industry research associations have become more marketing orientated. A number of commercial publications now exist providing detailed marketing intelligence.

Much information is available through central, university and polytechnic libraries. They often employ specialist staff to assist inquirers. One Manchester-based electrical equipment manufacturer regularly uses the information gleaned from various publications in the Manchester Central and Manchester Business School libraries to direct his activities. Some libraries, such as the City Business Library and those of certain chambers of commerce, have outstanding reputations for helping the practical businessman.

Sometimes the need may emerge for a more structured and scientific approach to information gathering. This is the sphere of market research. British firms are fortunate in having access to large numbers of highly skilled and reputable research agencies. These offer systematic and formalised investigations of both general topics and specialised areas. There are costs involved but these should be related to the value of the information and the potential pay-offs. A number of firms have found that, within their limitations, business studies students at colleges and universities have been able to assist with research.

We are now seeing an information and communication revolution. Smaller firms are well-placed to take advantage of the opportunities offered to those able to respond quickly, positively and flexibly to market conditions. However, this depends on their willingness to look outside, and build up and use a picture of the marketplace.

Sources of information

Tupper, E and Wills, G (1975) *Sources of UK Marketing Information* Ernest Benn

Marketfact (weekly) Haymarket Publishing Ltd

Government Statistics: A Brief Guide to Sources HMSO

Trade and Industry (Weekly) HMSO: London

Directory of British Associations CBD Research, 154 High Street, Beckenham, Kent

Retail Business The Economist Intelligence Unit, 27 St James Place, London SW1

Mintel Mintel Publications, 20 Buckingham Street, London WC2N 6BR

The IPC Consumer and Industrial Marketing Manual IPC Publications, The Market Research Society, 39 Hertford Street, London W1Y 8EP

The Industrial Market Research Society, Bird Street, Lichfield, Staffs

Direct access through:
The Statistics and Market Intelligence Library, 50 Ludgate Hill, London, EC4M 7HU
Tel: 01-248 5757 ex 368

or

Central Statistical Office, Great George Street, London SW1P 3AQ

5.3 Products and planning

The firm's product or process lies at the centre of most small firm managers' thinking about their companies. The ability to make some item well, to offer a special service or to meet requests to supply particular components or materials was probably the main reason for starting up the firm.

The commitment, flexibility and creativity applied to the product, service or process has a direct effect on the firm's ability to survive and prosper. In this it is increasingly important to recognise that the company's offering goes far beyond the individual, physical product offered.

The customer will order a particular item of equipment, specific tooling or moulding, a meal or a holiday, but will assume that a host of other things are included. He may expect free installation, regular maintenance of the tools, specific quality levels on the mouldings, quick service with the meal. All these affect his evaluation of the firm's offering, the prices he will willingly pay and the likelihood of repeat business. The close links between supplier and customer in small firms give managers the chance to understand these needs and design offerings capable of meeting them.

The starting point might simply be the division of the firm's customers into groups buying, roughly, the same items but wanting different things associated with them. Moulded Plastics Ltd produce a wide assortment of lines for the building industry ranging from clips and fasteners through to complex, moulded fittings. Some customers such as large builders or local authorities had extensive warehousing, professional buyers, projects under construction and skilled workers. Their need was for large consignments of standardised items at low prices. In contrast the DIY enthusiast needed items for a specific small job, available locally, simple to fit with clear instructions, all far more important than price.

Moulded Plastics eventually subdivided their clients and their needs into five groups or segments: architects, large builders, jobbing builders, local authorities and DIY. The item bought or specified was roughly the same, but there were pronounced differences in requirements for other aspects of the total product. These centred on the product itself: its colours, quality, robustness and, very important, ease of use. It quickly became apparent that serious attention had to be given to the range of associated items. Contact customers wanted considerable *depth* in product offering with, for example, many different pipe clips.

As the DIY business grew the *width* of their range expanded as wholesalers and end customers called for lines associated with the initial product. Controlling these extensions of the product became more important than spotting new opportunities.

Many firms find that the range of spares, service levels, installation, replacement and warranty policies are more important to some customers than the product. Dividing the market up provides the opportunity for this, as the customer wanting low prices may not want a high service level but others will be willing to pay more for associated services. This lesson came home very clearly to Moulded Plastics with a particular retail line which eventually required expensive packaging and branding to provide the buyer with re-assurance about quality and reliability.

Innovation and new product development are increasingly important in ensuring the long-term profitability of smaller firms. Large companies often envy the creativity, speed of response and flexibility that smaller firms can apply to this process.

Successful innovation comes from the combination of a good array of new product opportunities and rigorous selection of a small number of ideas for development. Access to new product opportunities is often easier than expected. Internal sources can be salesmen, production and research and development staff. Other fertile sources are research organisations, government dissemination programmes, new product directories, foreign markets and suppliers. Probably most important is a willingness continually to search outside, perhaps through journals and magazines.

For a country with a long history of innovation we show a surprising reluctance to look outside ourselves for licensing and other forms of technology acquisition. Both Germany and Japan 'buy in' innovation at a far higher rate than the UK. The recent report by the Advisory Council on Applied Research and Development highlighted the scope in this area, and made the important point that innovation is often far cheaper than managers expect.

The innovative ideas, new products and developments need to be carefully screened before introduction if they are to avoid joining the large pool of failed products. The first step is to evaluate all the ideas for their practicality and appropriateness to the firm. The market potential of those left can then be evaluated, with only the best progressing. Development of the remainder will probably eliminate others, leaving only a few for tests, perhaps involving selected customers. Full introduction is only worthwhile with those products successfully getting through all these stages.

Many companies embarking on a product management programme find that they are forced to think hard about marketing planning. Unfortunately, the relatively simple process of planning is saddled with an elaborate mythology which deters many firms. A good plan is a simple, practical set of guidelines for the firm's future development based on a proper understanding of its potential.

The main elements are an *audit* of resources and potential and a set of simple, concise and practicable *objectives*, perhaps noting major *alternatives*. Implementation can be seen in terms of a basic *strategy* backed up by specific *tactics*, both judged in terms of their relevance to objectives. *Evaluation* will provide an ongoing basis for learning and modification geared to *control* and *costs*. Medical Engineering Ltd draw up their marketing plan every year under these headings, revising it as necessary throughout the year. Actually writing it down is seen as an important discipline in itself, forcing managers rigorously to appraise their ideas and beliefs about the direction the firm will take.

They are in an area where expenditure and technology are moving at an increasing rate. Their products must compete with larger rivals while remaining competitively priced and efficiently produced. In this, they share the problems of most small firms whose products, the bedrock of their operations, are continually under challenge from changes internally, among customers, among rivals, and in technology. Successful management here is vital to survival.

Sources

NEW PRODUCT IDEAS
National Research and Development Corporation
Kingsgate House,
66-74 Victoria Street,
London SW1E 6SL
Tel: 01-828 3400

International New Product Centre Newsletter
PO Box 37c,
Esher,
Surrey KT10 0QN

International New Product Newsletter,
PO Box 191,
390 Stuart Street,
Boston,
Massachusetts 02117
Tel: 617-3225

Planned Innovation, NPM Information Services
Management House,
Parker Street,
London WC2B 5PT
Tel: 01-404 5414

MARKETING PLANNING
Winkler, John *Winkler on Marketing Planning* Cassell and Co Ltd

5.4 Sales promotion and advertising

Sales promotion and advertising are the most visible aspects of marketing. They provide the main mechanism for communication between seller and buyer. The representative provides a near ideal basis for the dialogue which helps the company meet customer needs while ensuring that business relationships are developed and orders won. Advertising enables the firm to reach many thousands of prospective customers and project information on and images of the company. Sometimes, such as through mail order, orders can be won directly through advertisements.

In most small firms, the salesman or owner/director actively engaged in selling leads the firm's marketing effort. Among the many facets of their work, the ultimate goal is the construction of a good array of profitable accounts. Partly for this reason sales targets are becoming increasingly important. Originally this involved simply setting targets for volume and perhaps profit contribution. Now targets are being designed to include a proportion of new accounts, direction towards key industries, even a profile of the industries or customers a representative should seek out. Despite some criticism, they provide a spur to action, at least when seen as fair by both salesman and manager. Perhaps surprisingly, the best results are often achieved by the owner/director who, leading the sales effort, sets himself these types of target. A giftware manufacturer in the south-west saw his sales increase over 50 per cent within a year of setting himself targets.

Initiatives here call for careful evaluation of current activities. Customer contact time – the potentially profitable time actually spent in front of the prospect – can easily be swamped by costly time in the car, plane or hotel. In some firms, less than 20 per cent of the salesman's time is spent in front of the prospects.

The calls themselves call for a balance between: (1) *cold canvassing*, sometimes necessary but never to be the norm; (2) *prepared calls* for new and established customers; (3) *repeat visits* with a clear idea of the relationship between customer liaison, business development and order gathering. All need underpinning by effective report back and follow through in the firm.

Too often the sales effort is wasted by inefficient order processing. In fact it has been said that 'in Britain, the problem is buying not selling'. The participants on one sales training course were shocked by the results of a simple exercise involving the attempt to buy, incognito by telephone, a stock item from their firm.

The joint owner and sales director of Hasty Footwear faced his greatest problems when the company grew large enough to employ its first full-time salesman. Recruitment and selection posed problems of job description, finding a sample of good candidates, evaluation and choice. Once the representative was appointed, the almost inevitable problem of the self-motivated entrepreneur in dealing with staff cropped up. He expected the employee's commitment to be as great as his own. In fact, he was forced to introduce a planned process of management, motivation and control, through involving the salesman in planning and setting targets, close liaison, target-related bonuses and detailed evaluation of his work. In Hasty Footwear, the director's gradual change in role led to a greater awareness of other aspects of sales promotion and advertising.

Advertising can be used in a number of ways: *awareness*, to establish *interest*, to stimulate *desire* and prompt *action* by customers to buy the product (AIDA). Specific adverts can be geared to do each of these through a mixture of creative input and the right medium. There is an enormous range of media available to the smaller businessman: from television and newspaper advertisements through to exhibitions, mail outs and brochures. As a result, the scope for achieving different results is enormous. Effective advertising management is built on four elements: clear goals, constant monitoring of performance, evaluation of results and a willingness to learn and adapt.

Most small firm managers handle their own advertising effort but there is a massive body of knowledge of and research into this area which should be tapped wherever possible. Much of this accumulated information is in the hands of the advertising agencies. They vary greatly in size from giants like Ogilvy, Benson and Matner to small local firms. Details can be obtained through the Institute of Practitioners in Advertising.

Much discussion of sales promotion and advertising suggests that they are totally separate spheres of action. In fact, they interact powerfully. The buyer who knows the salesman, his firm, its products, the company's reputation, its other customers and its record will respond to the sales visit. Advertising and other methods of preparing the ground are vital to this.

Public relations can play a major part. Many managers are overcautious in their media relations. A good relationship with journalists on the local, trade and national media, a system of issuing press releases communicating stories in a simple and pithy form, geared as much as possible to the normal style of the newspaper or magazine, can earn great benefits for any firm. Innovations, major orders and success in any sphere are worth communicating to the media, which will generally handle the topic in a very supportive way.

Sales promotion and advertising provide the firm with the opportunity to direct the process of communication between the firm and its environment. Planning, targets, constant evaluation and updating of knowledge sustained by the vital spark of creativity are the basis of pay-offs here.

5.5 The marketing dimension to price in the small firm

Almost any discussion with managers of smaller firms about buyers, customer relations or any facet of marketing will sooner or later get round to the problem of price. It is at the centre of the relationship between the supplier and his customer. It provides the former with the resources to survive and prosper, while measuring the value the latter places on the goods.

In many smaller firms the price decision has a significance far greater than for larger companies. They may lack the resources to invest in advertising, and to build brand or supplier loyalty to protect them against cut-price rivals. Large numbers of small firms supply industrial and commercial customers on a contract or tender basis. Here specifications might be tightly defined and a number of competitive tenders received. In these circumstances, pricing policies can be a constant battle to keep prices as low as is compatible with holding on to business.

This can lead to a vicious circle in which low prices can produce a steady deterioration in the firm's position as funds are starved from product development, promotion and improving customer relations. The firm can easily become vulnerable on two major fronts: product improvements by rivals meeting customer needs more effectively and price cutting by competitors with lower costs. The marketing approach to price seeks to overcome these problems.

Underlying this is the proposition that pricing is a strategic decision which over time is geared to building a business rather than winning specific orders. To some extent these are inseparable. But, although it is impossible to build a business without winning orders, some orders can contribute towards weakening a firm.

The objectives the firm wishes to achieve through the prices under specific market conditions are particularly important. Understanding these is as important as incorporating operating production and material costs into the price. This calls for systematic information gathering to build up a picture of the likely reactions in the market, among customers and competitors, to price changes.

The close links that top managers of small firms have established with many of their customers can help in this. Industrial buyers can be surprisingly helpful in providing guidance and useful information. The right approach to them, allied to a well-organised system of cross-checking and organising this material, can provide significant insights into the results of changes.

Effective use of the information derives from clearly setting the objectives of the firm's pricing policy. A company seeking increased volume sales will follow a policy totally different from one looking for a particular return per unit or a specific high-quality image for its goods.

A foundry in the Midlands faced a problem common today. Should they increase prices because of an increase in materials costs, and put its prices in line with the rest of the industry? The managing director and his two salesman raised the issue with a few of the major customers and, perhaps more importantly, some of the firms they part serviced. It soon became clear that the volume would increase so much with prices held that overall operating costs would be dramatically cut.

A furniture company based in West London found a totally different situation. Their customers saw discussions of holding or cutting prices as part of an overall cheapening exercise. For this firm, high prices were a major part of the process of reassuring customers of the overall quality of its products. Reviewing the alternative pricing policies open to the firm led to a decision to increase prices significantly in the new season, while backing it up with heavy investment in design, development and promotion.

The introduction of a new product, the company start-up or the launch into a new market bring the problems of setting prices into their sharpest focus. Costs can be determined with a fair degree of accuracy for certain volumes. There may be no competition to get clues from. Customers will have no benchmarks by which to judge responses. Here there are two basic strategies: *penetration* prices seeking to win large volume at low prices or *skimming* prices seeking to earn maximum returns from an initial high price. Although specific circumstances are the best guides to action it does appear that it is easier to correct problems caused by high prices. A firm looking to expand will generally find it easier to 'spin down', ie launch lower priced new products, than 'up'.

The decisions the firm makes about its prices affect, and are in turn affected by, all other decisions the firm makes about its offering. At its most basic the income earned will determine the resources for investment in product development, promotion and distribution initiatives. Price is probably the clearest clue the consumer has about quality, and, like all other aspects of the firm's offering, prices have to be designed to make a positive contribution to the firm's performance in the market.

Ultimately each element in the firm's offering – product, price, promotion and distribution – has to be designed to maximise both their individual and, probably more important, their joint contribution to meeting customer needs more effectively and to building a more profitable business. Small firms, with their shorter lines of communication, clearer decision-making system and greater flexibility, have the potential to exploit fully the marketing concept.

5.6 Exporting by small firms

The shock of Britain's £2.4 billion balance of trade deficit has highlighted the deteriorating trade position of Britain's manufacturing industry. Although North Sea oil can cushion the blow for the nation as a whole, small firms across the country are already feeling the effects of the real crisis in Britain's economy.

In key areas of component supply and process industries such as plastics, aluminium and other metal, the underlying weakness of the consumer industries is already affecting business. On the home market future projects are inextricably tied to the fortunes of the car, appliance and other key sectors. The only short – to medium – term opportunity for stability and growth appears to lie in exports or a selective policy of substitutes for imports in certain key areas.

Although there is no shortage of exhortation to action by all manufacturers, including small firms, the degree of real support is small in the light of the potentially crippling effects of deficits in non-oil balances of the type we have seen recently.

Much of the support that does exist is of only limited value or interest to smaller firms, whose managers do not have the time to cope with the large quantity of bumf that seems to be the inevitable corollary of action here. Even more important, many managers find that export schemes involving two or three weeks overseas are not practical when there are only one or two people running the company. There is an urgent need for export support initiatives geared specifically to the needs of smaller firms. The only recent initiative in this area, the Market Entry Scheme, is a limited and tentative step in this direction.

Ultimately, the achievement of significant exports is in the hands of the managers themselves. Government, banks, chambers of commerce and trade associations can only support their action, not be a substitute for them. The scope for effective export business development is often greater and easier to achieve than many managers believe. It is based on four elements: resource mobilisation, market selection, efficient service and organisation.

Resource mobilisation calls for the bringing together of the variety of elements that make up the firm, from its management skills through to its design and development capabilities. The most important single factor is the determination of top management to devote time and resources to building up export business. In this process the inherent flexibility and adaptability of the smaller firm provides a real advantage over larger competitors.

These resources provide the key to the next stage in the export effort – market selection. There are no good or bad markets; there are only those right or wrong for the firm given its resources, skills and knowledge. There has recently emerged a surprising degree of consensus on one issue in this area: whatever you do *concentrate*. British exporters, particularly small firms, tend to spread their export efforts over a very wide array of markets. This can undermine one of their greatest strengths, the network of contacts in the market providing insights into needs and developments to which they can respond more quickly and more appropriately than their competitors. This can be done in one, two or three markets but not in 50 or 60 markets.

Concentration can be a vital aid to the establishment of the right kind of service and marketing relationship with the market. This goes far beyond merely appointing an agent. For some firms in certain markets this may be neither necessary or appropriate. A giftware manufacturer in Yorkshire decided not to bother with an agent in Holland when he found that he could visit the British

Overseas Trade Board in Leeds, sail from Hull and visit 15 prospective retailers in Holland and an exhibition in Utrecht on a drive of less than 400 miles. At the centre of any attempt to establish an effective level of service in any market is the recognition that there is no reason to expect the foreign buyer to expect worse service than UK customers. The overall produce, price, distribution, sales and advertising effort should be designed to meet their market conditions rather than the pattern in Britain. This can only be realistically applied in a number of key markets in which the firm is determined to succeed.

Long-term success requires a well thought out export organisation. This will create a commitment to success throughout the firm ensuring that sales won in fierce competition overseas are not lost in the packing department, on the delivery bay or in the design office.

Britain's smaller firms already play a major part in exporting. There is enormous potential for further growth if real determination in the firm is matched by effective marketing and by the right type of support from government, other institutions and the head offices of those small firms which are part of larger groups.

5.7 Marketing and selling for the start-up firm

The most fundamental questions for the person starting up a new venture are: who is going to buy from it and why? It is seldom sufficient to comment that 'everyone will buy it' and 'because it is better'. The confidence implicit in these statements is probably necessary to persuade the entrepreneur to take the risks involved in starting his own business. To minimise the inevitable risks involved in this step these assumptions have to be examined in a disciplined way. The questioning involved in this ought to be directed towards two basic propositions:

1. Why should anyone buy this product or service from me?
2. If it's such a good opportunity why is someone not already doing it?

These two things – a real need among buyers and the firm's ability to meet it better than anyone else – will probably go a long way to determining the success or failure for the venture. Here, it is not enough to think solely in terms of the customers. Intermediaries, agents, distributors, wholesalers and retailers can have a major impact on this.

Asking the questions is not enough. They must be posed in the right quarters. This calls for some decisions on precisely who the product or service is catering for. No firm and virtually no product or offering appeals to everyone. Their appeal is selective. In fact, it is the ability of smaller firms to be adaptable and flexible enough to cater for the complex and varied needs of their customers that is often their greatest strength.

Once the decisions about who the customers are going to be are made, the detailed specification of the product, service or other offering can be made. The person considering starting up probably has the broad outline of what he wants to do mapped out. He will be seeking to blend this with his increasing knowledge of the target market. His firm's future will be determined in the marketplace; in judging its prospects or seeking ways to reduce his risks the market provides the most important clues.

Decisions should be made in the light of real knowledge, not on the basis of hopes or wishful thinking. Prospective customers are often willing to invest surprisingly large amounts of time and effort in helping the new firm. The man who has done his homework on the market perhaps using government or other publications in the commercial department of his nearest central library, will generally discover a real desire to assist him with up-to-date or more detailed information among buyers, whether government, large or small firms or the man in the street.

These groups will ultimately determine the success of his venture. They should be approached, talked to, involved for as long as possible before big risks are taken and large expenditures made. This direct access by the top man to customers will gradually become one of the firm's greatest assets. In some instances, entrepreneurs hold back because of fears about their ideas being stolen or copied. Although this does happen, the overall standards of business ethics in the UK are very high. These dangers are normally far less than those resulting from not having early access to prospects.

The target customers can only say what they might do under certain circumstances. The onus lies on the firm to meet their needs. These go far beyond the physical product itself. The buyer wants a specific item at a particular price with a certain level or service. One customer might want a more robust product and be willing to pay more for it. Or may be less concerned about immediate delivery of the equipment than the provision of a rapid maintenance and repair service. Another might be buying the same basic equipment but want a totally different mix. The notion that it is the combination of product, prices, distribution and service levels, advertising and sales promotion that determines the satisfaction of different types of customers is being recognised increasingly by successful entrepreneurs.

Sometimes the right mix will come intuitively; on other occasions arriving at it will involve hard work, difficult decisions and errors. For the engineer or the craftsman the problems involved in taking this approach can be severe. These and others are so involved in their product that they lose sight of the rest of the forces affecting success. Gaining some direct sales experience and accepting that a great deal of time must be spent on the road are important steps for this type of entrepreneur.

Talk of customers can create the impression that selling and marketing involves a single set of direct contacts. Often the situation is far more complex than that. The farmer or mine owner sell to the processor such as British Steel. Their output passes in turn to manufacturers such as Metal Box whose customers, like Heinz, will eventually sell to retailers or wholesalers before the product reaches the consumer. All those involved in this chain depend to some extent on the others.

The new firm may have a product with real customer appeal, but if it runs contrary to the intermediary's interest or if the customer's market is hostile or simply depressed, the venture's prospects are bleak. The depressed state of the UK domestic appliance and automotive industries directly affect their desire to invest in new ideas.

At the same time, these depressed circumstances may create their own opportunities. Established suppliers may be less able to cope with shorter production runs, low levels of customer stockholding, etc than the new firm. In general, the companies already in a market start with real advantages: better contacts and information besides their capital and equipment investment. It is the gaps that they have left in the market that can provide the most lucrative opportunities.

In some industries such as rubber processing, industrial brushes, components and many others, long production runs have become the norm. This opens up opportunities for the firm geared to short runs and special products. The circumstances creating the gaps should be closely studied. A hole may exist in the market because no one wants to be there because it is so unprofitable. A site for a shop may be available simply because others have failed on that site. Specific engineered units may not be produced because the trouble involved and the wastage rates destroy profits.

Equally, the opportunity may exist because no one else has noticed it or has been capable of satisfying it. Once into a market competition is likely to emerge. Holding on to a market is as important as winning it initially and probably far more difficult. It calls for some kind of plan defining how the market will be developed over time. The twin themes of meeting customer needs better while keeping ahead of the competition are at the centre of this.

This may call for the introduction of new services linked to the existing product. A hotelier might introduce a babysitting facility for guests. A component manufacturer may start factoring certain lines. It may involve new products. In New Technology Based Firms (NTBFs) this is to some extent critical to their very existence. In some new firms the commitment to opening up new markets provides the spur to growth.

It is the scope for this type of development which provides the spur to individuals to take the enormous steps involved in setting up their own firms. Failure by new firms is often at least in part attributable to neglect of the marketing and selling dimension to their activites. They should look to answer these basic questions:

☐ Who are my potential customers?
☐ How many of them are there and what is their potential demand?
☐ Can I reach all of them with my existing or planned resources?
☐ Who are the major intermediaries between me and the end users?
☐ Will they stock my offering?
☐ Will they give it support and display space and hold sufficient stocks for it to be viable?
☐ Who are the competitors?
☐ What are their competitive offerings?
☐ If there are no competitors, what is the reason?
☐ What am I offering that is in the customer's eyes sufficient inducement to buy?
☐ What is the mix of product, price, distribution and advertising that I am offering to my customers and what is its appeal to them?

5.8 Distribution and the small firm

In no area of marketing are the potential strengths of the small firm more clearly seen than in the use of distribution as a marketing tool. Managers of small firms frequently come back from foreign visits angry at the comments about the 'English disease' of poor delivery and service. Many have records of performance in these areas that their overseas rivals would envy. Jim Duffield of Springfield Furnishings found the prevalence of this belief an eye opener on his first foreign sales trip. In Britain the firm had used its delivery performance as a central plank of its marketing strategy.

The role of distribution in the firm's marketing effort involves many things beyond price. It is useful to subdivide the area into two spheres of action: physical distribution and channel management. Both cover major aspects of the firm's attempts to manage its relations with the market.

It is in physical distribution management – the combination of inventory, delivery, transport, warehousing and location policies – that recent evidence has suggested that smaller firms have assets that large companies need to spend a great deal of time and effort to achieve. Increasing numbers of firms, large and small, are finding it valuable to look afresh at physical distribution.

The sheer size of their investment in this area has forced some companies to review their policies. In some firms stocks (pre-production plus finished goods), vehicles, warehousing and delivery itself can account for over 40 per cent of working capital. The scale of this may not come to light because of the tendency of firms as they grow larger to fragment responsibilities and budgets in this area.

A warehouse or stores manager might be appointed; later a traffic manager and then a purchasing manager will be given responsibility for stocks. Each will try to make his area perform as effectively as possible. Unfortunately the efforts of each will have a direct impact on the performance of the other areas. All affect in different ways the overall level of customer service.

The stores manager's decision to run down stocks might make his budgets look better. But it could mean that purchasing will be buying in smaller, less economical lots. It might involve the traffic manager in increased costs as he makes multiple deliveries to customers to fill their orders. Perhaps most important it may mean that purchasing waiting time increases with some lost sales.

The overstocked firm might be able to achieve these reductions with none of these losses. Generally there is a price to be paid in other areas for savings in one department. The company might be willing to face these costs but major marketing decisions are involved. Policy formulation and implementation calls for top management involvement and needs to be seen in terms of costs to the total physical distribution system.

In-depth knowledge of the different areas and of their impact gives the manager of the smaller firm insights not usually open to his rival in the larger organisation. It is a potential advantage which should be matched with a disciplined and structured approach to the pay-offs between service level, transport, stocks, location and packaging.

The same combination of individualism and discipline probably provides the key to the successful marketing of the company's products or services to its distribution channels – the network of intermediaries between the product and his market. It is useful to view the construction of a network of middlemen or industrial users in terms of an interacting marketing chain. The firm is generally dealing with independent concerns with considerable discretion in buying.

Effectively moving the product through the channels is a combination of the producer's push and the customer's pull. Discounts, special deals or packings, longer credit, etc help to push the buyer into purchasing. But it is his customer's demand which will persuade him to rebuy. Improved deliveries, special features and other advantages welcomed by the buyer's customers or giving him the chance to satisfy customer pull have a particular appeal.

It is often said that small firms have special problems in these areas. Some retailers are reluctant to deal with small suppliers, others demand a high level of advertising support, and increasing numbers insist on their own name appearing on the product. When other manufacturers are the main channel members they may expect support in specific areas such as technical development or customer service. In these cases it may be useful to construct a picture of the channel right down to the final user of the product no matter how remote. This can provide management with a clear indication of the different points at which they can influence demand besides giving clues to future prospects and opportunities.

The ability of management to take this broader view but build into it speed of reaction and flexibility is the key to the effective use of distribution as a marketing tool. The enormous costs involved, allied to the continuing pressures for faster service and smaller unit deliveries, are posing major threats to the viability of some concerns.

Nevertheless, it represents an area in which effective action can lead to major benefits. The importance of the area has been recognised by the British Institute of Management (BIM) in the establishment of the Centre for Physical Distribution Management.

Useful address

Centre for Physical Distribution Management
Management House
Parker Street
London
WC2B 5PT.

5.9 Marketing and the smaller service firm

The growth of the service sector is probably one of the most striking features of modern commercial life. It is now estimated that over 60 per cent of the UK workforce is employed in services. Far more small firms are involved in services than in manufacture. The generally greater ease of entry and widening opportunities here will probably mean that the numbers in services will grow faster than in manufacture. It is arguable that the special strengths of small firms, particularly the intimate involvement of top management in all aspects of the firm's operation, are a great advantage in the service sector.

Despite this growth and the opportunities here, many attitudes to services are marked by a peculiar ambivalence. The impression is sometimes given that service companies are not as important nor as acceptable as manufacturers. Government support schemes frequently ignore services. Interest in the special needs of the service sector is negligible. This can be seen in the way the marketing of services is neglected and ill understood.

People are far more important in service marketing than in manufacturing. Individually they play a far more important role in designing and determining the nature of the offering itself. This is partly because services are generally designed around the needs of a specific customer, often on the spot by the supplier. The travel agent will help the customer choose his holiday on the basis of his

153

understanding of the buyer's needs, comments and financial resources. He will need to consider all these factors.

The difficulties of the service firm are made even greater in this situation by the intangible nature of their offering. The holiday is not a fixed commodity capable of being measured and judged on objective grounds. The motor trade suffers particularly from this. There can be an enormous gulf of understanding between the supplier, the garage and the customer on as basic a level as the meeting of the 'service' to the car being repaired. Faults or breakdowns totally unrelated to the original problem occurring some time after repair are put down to poor garage service.

Overcoming these problems is critical to ensuring good, repeat business. It is essential to recognise the importance of handling customers carefully, of probing to establish their real as opposed to their stated requirements and of explaining differences of understanding. Here the manager should recognise that the extent of access to staff is generally far greater in services than in manufacture. In many garages the mechanic is spoken to by clients as often as the receptionist.

The degree of contact with customers is a significant difference between most service firms and manufacturers. A small tobacconist has far more frequent direct personal contact with individual smokers than the giant Imperial Group. This can lead to negative, even hostile, attitudes towards the public or specific sectors. In some recent research among 12 to 16 year old children the scale of hostility they felt retailers had towards them was remarkable. A service firm cannot afford the luxury of these sentiments if he wants repeat custom. His actions determine his offering. There is not the compensation of other aspects of the product.

At the same time sectors of service industry do fail fully to capitalise on their opportunities. A classic example of this is the tendency of retail salesmen to spend all their time selling the product and virtually no time selling their own firm. The top manager should make it clear to his staff that their job is to promote their own company at least as much as their supplier.

This involvement of people creates massive problems of standardisation, and partly explains the high failure rate among rapidly growing service firms. Once the owner's direct control is lost, quality can slump. Before this occurs, the basic appeal and offering has to be identified and isolated. The manager is responsible for closely monitoring and responding to customer needs. Within this framework routes to standardisation can be sought. Individuality and flexibility have a role, but within the framework of objectives and controls set out by managers. Franchising has emerged as one of the best ways of maintaining quality in growth orientated services.

The perishable character of most services places a special onus on management accurately to forecast and sustain an even level of demand. Hotel rooms left vacant and unoccupied tables in restaurants are complete waste. Despite that, many small service companies make little systematic effort to estimate forthcoming demand. Even less effort is put into differential prices and advertising, modifying the offering to even out peaks and troughs in demand.

The close direct personal contact between the small service firm and its client provides an invaluable opportunity for systematic information gathering. This might simply involve giving customers a reply paid questionnaire card or getting all those involved in customer contact to review and explore customer action. A determination to use the firm's intimacy with the customer characterises the market orientated service firm.

The adoption of this approach will do much to influence the service firm's prosperity. The opportunities exist in services. We can reasonably expect the growth of the last 20 years to continue. Three things will dominate the development of services: the use of marketing, people and productivity. The last of these is particularly important. Seeking out innovative ways of resolving productivity problems in established services and using this to open them up to new markets has been the foundation of growth from Butlins to MacDonalds. Ultimately, however, the small firm with its closeness of personal control has enormous advantages in an area whose marketing is so dependent on people.

6
Planning the Office

ROGER HENDERSON, Managing Director, Space Planning Services, Hillingdon

6.1 The organised office

In the eyes of many small business owners, office planning is regarded as a subject to which only companies large enough to warrant employing their own office manager could afford to give more than passing consideration. Managers of new ventures in the first throes of development are much more likely to be caught up in the excitement of generating new leads and keeping existing clients or customers happy, and there is a strong tendency to adopt an attitude of *laisser faire* when it comes to even the most basic principles of the organised office environment. However, no business is so small that it can afford to ignore the benefits of efficiently planned accommodation.

Although there is a great deal of satisfaction to be derived from a close personal involvement in a small but growing concern, any business in such a situation will inevitably be generating more and more paperwork, will need to recruit more personnel and be making larger investments in furniture and equipment. One filing cabinet, two telephones and a pocket calculator may have been sufficient to cope with requirements in the early days, but it is a situation which is likely to become increasingly strained as the two-man band develops into a 10 or 20 piece orchestra.

Firstly, considerable thought should be given to a few basic principles of office planning, particularly in the light of a decision to acquire more space. This is probably one of the most important and significant first steps in the life of a small company and one which represents a major investment. Miscalculations or lack of thought can, and commonly do, lead to extremely expensive mistakes which can affect the rate of development for years to come. For example a decision to acquire accommodation based simply on a average space per head and cost per square foot calculation can go badly adrift.

The square foot quoted by estate agents often includes some degree of unusable space, so what initially looks like a very favourable rent may not be so attractive once this factor is taken into consideration. A brief layout or plan of the actual floor area offered is essential to ensure that there is enough space for staff and equipment.

The tendency is to take just enough space to suit the company's current requirements, but the importance of developing a plan to cope with future short and long-term needs when more staff will be taken on cannot be underestimated. This could, for example, involve the acquisition of more space than is needed and organising a sensible sub-let which provides for an option to take over the additional space after a period of time. One way or another, it is essential to allow for growth and expansion to protect the firm against the unsettling and disruptive process of moving more frequently than is necessary.

The next consideration, once premises have been found, must be their layout, fitting out and furnishing. It is again worth assessing the working needs of the staff, in terms of equipment and their inter-relationship with each other, and planning accordingly. To take a simple example, it is distracting for someone involved in the preparation of detailed figure work or reports to share a small office with a heavy telephone user; the efficiency of both is likely to be impaired. The location and siting of furniture and equipment should be given at least as much thought as most people devote to planning a new kitchen. The furniture selected should be carefully chosen to meet the needs of the user in terms of their job function and not just because it looks good and doesn't cost too much.

Few small businesses can afford the luxury, in terms of space or manning power, of a full reception area, but an assessment of the number and nature of callers received is still a worthwhile exercise. A suitably furnished waiting area to create the right first impression is necessary if visitors consist of clients and customers to whom a certain image is to be conveyed. On the other hand, that image may be tarnished if the waiting visitor is able to overhear irate telephone conversations with recalcitrant suppliers.

The choice of the right storage equipment will also make an important contribution to the smooth running of the business, and help prevent that 'drowning in paper' feeling from which many small operations (and some larger companies) suffer. A simple in-house survey of the type of material which needs to be stored, from correspondence, order forms and invoices to ledgers and reference books, will provide a specification for an appropriate system. Once the analysis has been made, advice from one or two office equipment sales people should be helpful in providing information on a simple yet flexible system to meet your needs. It is only too easy to fall back on traditional box files which are comparatively expensive, wasteful in terms of space, and rapidly become a general dumping ground for irrelevant material.

There is also a tendency for small businesses to overlook the recent advances in office automation, or to dismiss the more sophisticated equipment because of cost. No office nowadays would be without a calculator, which has become smaller and more powerful than ever before, and is now within the reach of everyone's pocket. Yet this advancement has, in fact, been mirrored in many other fields of office technology.

Automatic typewriters, the simplest form of word processors, have become much less expensive, and at around £1,000 equate with the financial outlay necessary for two ordinary electric typewriters. Even a mini-computer is now within the reach of many small firms. A computer terminal with telephone link to a Bureau has, in fact, just been installed in our own offices (where we have a staff of 30), for the purposes of cost control, manpower planning and project programming. The use of a computer to carry out these functions would have been beyond the wildest dreams of most companies of our size even five years ago.

There is one further aspect relating to the organised office, of which every business should be aware. The terms of the Health and Safety at Work Act affect all employers, and potential sources of accidents, such as trailing telephone or electrical wires or a blocked fire exit, could attract an enforcement notice, the execution of which could prove expensive.

Taken step by step, the road to a properly planned office is within the reach of any business, whatever its size. The following sections, looking in detail at the general points made here, attempt to signpost this road.

6.2 Office accommodation

Whether you need 500 or 5000 square feet of office space, the problems remain virtually the same, and the choice of the right kind of accommodation is as important to small businesses as it is to larger concerns. Office space is expensive to acquire and maintain and should be considered as much a part of the company's assets and resources as personnel or capital equipment. A successful company, whatever its size, will expect to grow and it will certainly change as it reacts to market forces and develops new ideas and methods. Unless you give as careful consideration to planning your accommodation needs as you would to marketing and sales strategy, you could find your business in a straitjacket which will inhibit its development and growth as effectively as a badly planned costing system. Shortage of space presents a barrier to recruitment when you most need more staff; overcrowding exacerbates problems of noise, leads to poor ventilation and reduces efficiency.

The short-term expediency of 'squeezing people in' may work wonderfully well if the motivation is there, as it often is with the first flush of success, and if it really is a short-term measure. However, the dynamic hub of your enterprise may quickly degenerate into a sweat-shop atmosphere with disgruntled staff spending their lunch-time scanning the small ads. There are too many office 'slums' around, both large and small, which effectively demonstrate this point.

The search for space

The first consideration is the amount of space you actually require. The legal minimum is 40 square feet per head (or 400 cubic feet where ceilings are less than 10 feet high). However, in practical terms, this is too small an allocation and is certainly not an appropriate figure on which to base your calculations.

A more realistic figure is 60 square feet for clerical workers, but this does not take into consideration space for filing and office equipment which should be added in separately. Other elements for which you should allow space include circulation and corridors, and any supporting facilities such as meeting rooms, coffee machines, library, stationery store, telephone equipment and so on.

Once you have made this kind of assessment, you should then plan your search for office space systematically, or you will waste time which is as likely to be in as short supply as money when you are starting up. Whether you take on the search yourself or instruct an estate agent to act on your behalf, the first essential is to prepare a brief in writing. Your requirement is not just 'a small office suite in West London'; it is important to be as specific as you can or want to be on the following points:

☐ Location
☐ Usable area: minimum and maximum
☐ How it is divided: open space or divided into rooms?

- ☐ Type of office: self-contained suite or multi-tenanted block?
- ☐ Standard: prestige building in prime location or a room over a butcher's shop?
- ☐ Furnished or unfurnished?
- ☐ Ready for occupation? If not, are you prepared to spend money on fitting the space out for your own purposes?
- ☐ Total cost target: rent, rates, service charge, amortisation of any premium payable.

The process of setting down this type of information will help to clarify your thoughts. If you use it as a brief to instruct a good estate agent, he will be able to provide a more informed service and he will not deluge you with details of unsuitable properties.

Assessing the space on offer

With your carefully prepared brief, you will be able to appraise the alternatives and check off the points that have been met satisfactorily. When it comes to the size of space in question, do not take paper figures quoted in the property details at their face value: floor areas measured from plans are notoriously inaccurate and even more importantly figures often include space which, in effect, is unusable. It is quite common, for example, for measurements of the so-called carpeted area in an office block to run under the 12 inch deep heating units at the perimeter, into cleaning and electrical riser cupboards, and to include all the corridor space. By taking careful on-site measurements of the areas which are truly usable, we have on many occasions been able to negotiate substantial reductions in the total rent payable on behalf of our clients, when this has been quoted at the outset on a price per square foot or square metre basis.

It is also important to analyse the way you work and what your requirements are in terms of open areas and individual rooms, and recognise that the building will exert constraints on what you can do within it. These will affect the size and shape of single offices, the acoustics, the physical environment and how services such as power and telephone can be provided where they are needed.

In fact there are many factors which may prevent you from providing the size of rooms you had originally planned. Oversized offices, access corridors, dead areas without ventilation, heating or natural light, for example, may all eat into the available space and result in cramped or badly organised accommodation. Draw up a rough layout of the available space ensuring that the constraints the building and its services might impose are not overlooked, and this will help you determine what can and cannot be achieved within the given area. Check your plan on site to make sure that what you have in mind is feasible.

Coping with expansion

There are a number of ways in which you can allow for future development and growth in terms of your accommodation without taking on more space than you can cope with financially, or finding yourself in a situation where you have to seek new premises every two or three years.

The first essential is to maintain contact with the right firm of agents and instruct them to send you information until you tell them to stop (in the spirit of James Bond with vodka martinis). Resist the temptation to shelve the search until a move is crucial; you may then be forced to take the first vaguely acceptable alternative that turns up.

You should also consider properties which offer more space than you appear to need. Take on the excess and organise a sub-let on short leases. Small packages of offices are in very short supply, so you should not encounter any problems in finding a tenant. At the end of the first term you can either renew the lease or repossess the area for your own occupation; your legal position is secure in this latter case.

Or you could consider taking on the additional space and simply leaving it empty. This will depend on the total rent you pay for the use of given space, but located almost anywhere outside Central London, it will still represent a small proportion of your total operational overheads. Do not overlook the derating factor on empty space, and the possibility that no heating, lighting or cleaning costs will be incurred.

Consideration could also be given to using the extra space as meeting or conference rooms, or as a staff recreation area or restaurant. This facility could then be rented out or the costs shared with neighbouring tenants.

Then there is the cuckoo-in-the-nest syndrome to consider. If you move into a multi-tenanted building, a close ear to the ground will often secure first option on additional space as it becomes available.

A strategy to provide additional occupation in 'steps' might also be appropriate. Assess your liability to meet the business plan within a given space. If, say, 40 per cent of your staff are out of the office at any one time, they will probably accept a squeeze in order to accommodate extra people. You need then take over extra space only when you have reached a certain target level of recruitment.

Conclusion

The management of office space, or indeed of any space for commercial or industrial use, is as important as any other aspect of management. Tackled in a thoughtful and logical way, it will undoubtedly contribute towards the overall effectiveness of your operation.

6.3 Legal requirements

It is often said that ignorance is no excuse at law, yet the rules and regulations that control our use of office space are so numerous, so complex and so phrased in legalistic jargon that even experienced administrators may find them difficult to understand. Because of their complexity they were often ignored by many small businesses who had no inclination to waste time on anything seemingly so unproductive.

With this is mind and faced with the increasing tide of accidents at work, the Health and Safety at Work Act was introduced in 1976. Its purpose was threefold: to put greater legal emphasis on accident prevention; to define accurately the onus of responsibility and to simplify previous legislation by bringing under one authority a wide range of rules and regulations introduced over many decades.

So far, because of other priorities, little in the field of simplification and standardisation has been achieved. We are still faced with all the old rules and regulations in all their complexity.

So what action should the small businessman take to ensure his business conforms to the law? He could rely solely on outside advice. Just as his lawyer and accountant give advice on their specialist disciplines, so similarly his estate agent or building surveyor will advise on requirements of the Offices, Shops and Railway Premises Act. His architect or interior designer will be able to advise him on how to meet the conditions laid down by Building Regulations or London Building Acts and the Fire Precautions Act, and his insurance broker will arrange the necessary cover to be provided under the Employers' Liability Act and the Occupiers' Liability Act.

However, this is probably not sufficient. Small businesses grow fast, demand more staff, more space, more facilities, and the investment in these is substantial. It should not be jeopardised by plans based on ignorance of statutory requirements.

The small business owner should also bear in mind that the responsibility for the health, safety and welfare of all employees is his and his alone. He cannot blame bad advice if accidents occur. The wise businessman will therefore balance outside advice with his own efforts to keep up to date on the broad outline, purpose and intent of legislation. He can then assess the effects not only on his current situation but also of the impact of rules and regulations on his future expansion plans.

What in fact are his responsibilities? The legislation states: 'He must ensure as far as is reasonably practical the health, safety and welfare of all his employees' and this is defined under five headings:

☐ Safety with office equipment and plant
☐ Safety in handling or storage of materials
☐ Provision of instruction and training
☐ Maintenance of a safe building
☐ Provision of a safe working environment within the building.

These rules are applied to every building, irrespective of location and size, where the prime use is as an office. Numbers of staff are irrelevant provided they work more than 21 hours per week. Where doubt exists, compliance in terms of reasonable practicality is seen as adhering to and following accepted national and industry based codes of practice.

So much for the spirit and intent. What is the scope of the legislation? The main points have already been referred to. Their impact on everyday office life is discussed by category below.

Administration

Paperwork and form filling is an integral part of all legislation. The Offices, Shops and Railway Premises Act details what is required. It relates to the registration of office premises, reporting of accidents, application for fire certificate and the display of an abstract of the Act itself.

Insurance

The Employers Liability Act and the Occupiers Liability Act detail the insurance cover that must be provided for both staff and visitors whilst on your premises.

Working conditions

The Offices, Shops and Railway Premises Act details quite comprehensively the minimum standards which determine density of occupation, natural light, ventilation and heating. The Act also specifies standards for welfare and amenities in terms of numbers of toilets, the provision of washing facilities, drinking water, coat storage, and the availability of first aid.

Safety and fire precautions
The Offices, Shops and Railway Premises Act and the Fire Precautions Act deal with this aspect. This legislation covers the provision and testing of fire alarms, the need for fire drills and the maintenance of and access to escape routes. The Health and Safety Act has established rules governing the fencing and guarding of machinery and requires all users to be instructed on the dangers and the precautions to be taken. Heavy work is also banned without the proper equipment.

Constructional maintenance
The majority of the rules and regulations which govern methods of construction, the choice and use of materials and the standards of workmanship required, come within the scope of Building Regulations (or, within the GLC Area, the London Building Acts). This subject is so complex and so detailed, there is little purpose in attempting any summary. Suffice it to say that they are in force to provide minimum standards of safety in design and construction, to safeguard the health and security of the public and to prevent or mitigate the incidence of fire. Their interpretation and application is thereafter best left to your consultants or to an experienced design team.

Alterations and improvements
Most alterations or additions that involve significant structural works will be carried out under the supervision of an architect or other competent specialist. Nevertheless, it is important to remember that all alterations and additions, even of a minor nature, such as changes to partitions, extra lighting runs etc not only require local authority approval but also can bring existing circumstances and conditions within the scope of regulations retrospectively.

This means that new regulations introduced do not normally have retrospective implications on buildings or surfaces already in existence. However, once you start to alter, modify or improve such buildings you can become liable to bring old work up to certain standards which are now mandatory. This is often very costly, as the type of works most often required to be updated relate to stairs, toilets and perhaps even the reinforcement of structural elements.

Conclusion

Many small businessmen may consider all this to be yet more bureaucratic interference, another administrative millstone which diverts their energies into unprofitable and often frustrating fields. They may feel that, if the information they provide is limited, so too will be the level of such interference. To do this is to misread the spirit and intent of the law and to allow its inadequacies of form and language to cloud judgement. It is a mistake which can lead to prosecution and is one which many have regretted. Consultation and negotiations with both local authorities and specialist consultants will actually speed up the whole process of design, approval and implementation, and could well save time and money. It will certainly help in the successful development and expansion of the business by providing a pleasant, safe working environment.

6.4 Fitting out office space

For the small business, taking on new office premises and fitting them out can be a daunting undertaking when it has to be done in addition to keeping things running without interruption. In considering the problem, it is difficult to generalise about a subject which, in practice, varies so much with the nature of accommodation which is to be fitted out. However, in principle, there are far more opportunities to create an interesting, even unusual, interior office environment where a small organisation is concerned; the scope for imaginative schemes does not exist to nearly such a degree with anonymous 1960s style slab buildings in which many large companies are installed.

Even if you have taken the time and trouble to find accommodation which most closely suits your needs, it will still need some adaption to get the right space configuration to meet your organisational requirements. The temptation to make do, and bend the structure of the company to fit the accommodation available is great, but the danger of short-term expediency is that more problems will occur in the long term. Shortage of space, overcrowding in shared offices and poor communications will all lead to a deteriorating physical environment which will become more apparent as the firm expands.

165

A common problem is that very often premises are taken on a short lease, making more than the minimum expenditure inappropriate. There is normally no spare capital for ambitious alterations and improvements. The furniture and equipment may, in some cases, have been begged, borrowed and bought second-hand; however much you improve its setting, it will never work as well for you as furniture selected with a specific job function in mind.

This may not apply to the same extent where the company 'image' is important. Where potential or existing clients visit the offices frequently expenditure on such items assumes a greater importance. It is undoubtedly true that staff working for a small business often have a high degree of motivation and involvement in what they are doing. However, this should not be traded on to the extent of assuming that their working environment is of no importance. There is no doubt that given good management motivation, a well-designed environment can do nothing but improve performance.

The small organisation should have a number of advantages which it can exploit. For example, in small premises with short leases, you can afford to experiment with more adventurous colour schemes which would otherwise be inadvisable. In the same way, materials can be used which would be inappropriate where a longer life was required. This can add up to having more 'fun' with design, something that can be a disastrous failure where large numbers in more permanent situations are involved.

A tight budget should not be viewed as too great a constraint to improvement; it can almost be turned to your advantage. Designing to a price is a very good discipline, which in the past has produced ingenious *ad hoc* solutions to problems to produce a strikingly original and economical result. One such example is the use of self coiling conduit lines, or floor to ceiling aluminium poles, to lead power and telephone wires to work stations to avoid expensive and disruptive floor grid modification.

In terms of specific aspects of the design and fitting out process, there are other ways in which the small company enjoys certain advantages. Large offices need an even distribution of light and fluorescent fittings are the norm.

Smaller offices, composed of individual rooms, could make use of tungsten (ie the domestic type of lighting) instead, which gives a more pleasant effect and a greater feeling of warmth. The penalties of greater heat output and power consumption have little significance on a small scale.

In the same way acoustics are less of a problem. Individual offices

Another way to help your business

If you've been tempted to think that a magazine titled **Business Matters** deals solely with high finance and international commerce, then as a small business you've been missing a lot.

Over the past few months we've covered, in-depth, many subjects of vital relevance to small businesses such as: How to use your MP to the best advantage. How to raise venture capital and where to start. How to find the perfect secretary, and the way to your bank manager's heart.

In the coming months our in-depth coverage continues; facts, figures, surveys, analyses no small business can afford to miss, so take out a subscription today and you could profit from our knowledge tomorrow.

You can't afford to ignore **BUSINESS MATTERS**

Available from W. H. Smith, John Menzies and all leading newsagents, or by subscription for £12 per year (£20 overseas). Write to Business Matters, ECC Publications, 30-31 Islington Green, London N1 8BJ. Tel: 01–359 7481.

167

should ideally be soundproof, particularly if they are used for interviewing, and this often occurs automatically where the premises are converted from residential accommodation with solid walls. Where small numbers of staff are grouped together in a room it will not be possible to provide them with the aural privacy that one might try to achieve in a larger open office, and there will probably be little point in putting up an expensive acoustic ceiling in this size of office.

When it comes to decoration, you will probably only be able to justify the cost of paint rather than, for instance, the use of a harder wearing and relatively expensive vinyl wallcovering. This is where lack of inhibition with regard to colour can apply. With awkwardly shaped rooms, colour can play an important role in offsetting odd visual aspects, and ugly ducts and pipework evident in older, industrial buildings could be painted effectively in contrasting colours rather than attempting to camouflage them.

It is not uncommon for office accommodation in the size range we are considering to be offered without any form of heating. In such a case careful thought should be given to the choice of a heating system. In many cases traditional central heating, whilst probably providing minimum running costs, will be eliminated on the basis of capital cost, disruption to the building, or physical constraints such as lack of gas or space for fuel storage. This leaves electricity as the most obvious answer. Sophisticated controls for storage heaters are now available which reduce the problems of inflexibility and running costs, although the units do take up valuable floor space.

In selecting appropriate floor covering many of the points made previously apply. There are a number of relatively inexpensive floor coverings on the market specifically designed for office use. Heavy duty carpet or carpet tiles are easy to clean, absorb sound and in the long term can be cheaper than, say, vinyl tiles.

It is a commonly held view that it is not economical to enlist professional help for the smaller office project. This is not necessarily true. An ingenious and inventive designer who is capable of working to a strict budget may go a long way to offsetting the cost of his fee by means of savings and short-cuts of which he will have professional experience. If the impact your office premises make on your clients is important, few people should have sufficient confidence in their creative powers to eschew outside help.

Should you decide to 'go it alone' you will have to face the problems of choosing and controlling a contractor. Be wary of using any small jobbing builder unless he is highly recommended and you can see one of his completed jobs. You should prepare a written specification against which he can quote and try to avoid changing your mind or adding in extras once the builder has started; they have a habit of costing more than the whole job put together.

Thought given and care taken during the fitting out process will repay dividends in the long run. Any business must be worth these considerations, whatever its size.

7
Benefiting from the Tax System[*]

JOE HORNER

7.1 How to halve Capital Transfer Tax liability

In sections 7.1, 7.2, and 7.3 we examine the brighter side of the tax system from the viewpoint of small businesses and point out some ways in which high tax rates might work for the benefit of the business. Here we look at the way Capital Transfer Tax might be the spur to somebody to invest in a new business.

Suppose that Mr A has a desire to form a new business but finds it hard to raise the necessary capital. Suppose, also, that Mr B is a wealthy man with a potential top Capital Transfer Tax rate of 60 per cent. It might be possible for Mr A and Mr B to join forces and form a company for which Mr B provides the bulk of the capital and acquires the majority of the voting shares.

After he has held the shares for two years Mr B would be able to transfer them as a gift to a younger generation of his family and the tax payable would be based on only half their true value.

If the amount subscribed by Mr B for the shares was, say, £30,000 the tax which it would have suffered if not invested in the company would have been £18,000. The next generation would therefore have received £12,000 net. If the value of the shares at the time they are given away is still £30,000 the tax will be £9,000 so the next generation will receive net assets to the value of £21,000.

The value of the shares may well have increased in the two years by more than the capital would have increased if held in another

---

[*]Tax rates are subject to change, but, in all cases where current tax rates differ from those quoted, the principle on which they are based remains unchanged.

form. The present law regarding the distribution of profits of close companies allows substantial amounts to be retained within the company.

Instead of his investment producing income which would be highly taxed in his hands Mr B would therefore probably prefer to let all the profit accumulate in the company, where it would suffer tax at only 43 per cent and where it would effectively increase the value of his shares.

As long as the retained profit was not used to acquire non-business assets the increased value attributable to it would bear Capital Transfer Tax at half the normal rate in the same way as the value of the original capital subscribed.

If the value of the shares fell the next generation might still receive higher net value than they could receive in the normal way. If, at the time of transfer, the value had fallen to, say, £20,000 the tax would be £6,000 leaving them with a net £14,000 which still compares favourably with the £12,000 net they would have received if the money was invested in something which did not enjoy business property relief.

The business property relief is therefore a powerful incentive for a wealthy person to invest in a new venture. It can take a lot of the risk out of what is a speculative investment and it can increase the net return.

As always of course, there can be snags. To get the full 50 per cent discount on valuation Mr B would need to have control of the company. Mr A, who would effectively be running the business, would not see that as the ideal situation and would obviously like, sooner or later, to acquire control himself.

Even if he accepted the need for Mr B to have control because this was the way Mr B and his capital could be attracted, he might be unhappy at the thought of this control later passing to other members of Mr B's family.

It would be essential for Mr A to have a contract with the company that entitled him, one way or another, to participate in the prosperity of the company.

Care would have to be taken to ensure that he did not have a binding contract for the purchase of Mr B's shares because such a contract would disqualify them from business property relief.

The exact detail of the arrangements between Mr A and Mr B would depend upon many variable circumstances, concerning the nature of the business and the family and domestic situation of each party.

It would usually be possible to give Mr A a reasonable degree of

171

security whilst allowing Mr B to take advantage of the favourable treatment which the law offers but, as with almost all financial propositions, it would be impossible to eliminate all risks.

7.2 Relief in do-it-yourself retirement schemes

Retirement annuities or 'self-employed pension schemes' as they are sometimes known are contracts under which a person who is self-employed, or in partnership, or employed in a non-pensionable employment may pay premiums towards the cost of providing benefits for himself commencing not earlier than his sixtieth and not later than his seventy-fifth birthday.

Qualifying premiums under an approved contract can be deducted from his relevant income for the purpose of calculating his tax liability and the premiums will thus enjoy tax relief at his highest tax rate.

The existence of these contracts is, of course, very widely known but what is perhaps not so widely realised is the opportunity to obtain similar tax relief on premiums paid for family income benefit or for term assurance.

A person may pay a regular annual premium to ensure either a capital sum payable on his death before a specified age (which must not exceed 75) or an annuity payable either to his spouse or other dependant for the period after his death up to the specified age.

Premiums within the approved limits will qualify for full tax relief. Thus a person who is in the 60 per cent tax bracket will receive 60 per cent relief and a premium of, say, £500 would effectively only cost him £200. For this outlay a man of 40 could ensure that in the event of his premature death his widow could receive an amount of over £7500 each year until his 75th birthday.

For this type of policy regular premiums must be maintained throughout the term and the policy can have no surrender value in the event of the premiums not being paid or the insured person ceasing to be eligible because he ceases to be self-employed or because his employment becomes pensionable.

The maximum amount of premium on which tax relief will be

allowed in any year is 5 per cent of the relevant earnings for the year.

Where a person has this type of policy and also a policy to provide a retirement annuity for himself the tax relief on the combined premiums is limited to 17.5 per cent of relevant earnings. (The percentage is higher for people born before 1916.)

A premium is deducted from the assessable income of the tax year in which it is paid. However, a person may elect for it to be treated as having been paid in the preceding year. If there were no relevant earnings in the preceding year he may elect for it to be treated as having been paid in the year before that.

7.3 Working abroad

One of the improvements to the lot of the small businessman introduced by the 1978 Budget and Finance Act is the reduction of tax for a person who is resident in the UK but who spends part of his time abroad on business.

There was already relief for a self-employed person whose business was carried on wholly abroad and for an employed person whose duties were carried on partly abroad, but until this year there had been no relief for a self-employed person who carried on business partly in the UK and partly abroad.

In the Budget and in the original Finance Bill relief was promised for people who spend 60 days of the fiscal year outside the country but the Bill was amended so that the qualifying period was reduced to 30 days, which is the same period as for an employed person.

The first thing to establish is how many days have been spent outside the UK and whether they are qualifying days.

A person will be regarded as absent for any day if he is absent at the end of it, except if he is on a sea or air trip which begins and ends in the UK.

A day of absence will be a qualifying day if it is devoted substantially to the business or to travelling wholly and exclusively for the purposes of the business. It is also recognised that a person needs rest days and a day which is spent neither on business nor on travelling can be a qualifying day if it is one of at least seven consecutive days of absence which taken as a whole are devoted substantially to the business.

For the current tax year and for later years, if a person can show that he has had 30 or more qualifying days of absence the assessable profit for the year will be divided equally among the 365 days of the year and the portion attributable to the qualifying days will attract relief. The relief will be a deduction of 25 per cent of the profit for those days. If the business is not carried on throughout the full year the apportionment will be over the period during which it is carried on rather than over 365 days.

It is the assessable profit *after* deducting any stock relief and any capital allowances which is apportioned and on which the deduction of 25 per cent is based. A decision not to claim stock relief or capital allowances, or to claim less than the maximum amount of capital allowances available, usually means that one year's profit is higher than it might otherwise have been and that the profit for another year or years is correspondingly reduced. The question of whether overseas relief is due for the year which is more highly assessed than it might be and/or for the years which are lower will now be one of the factors to be considered when deciding whether to claim stock relief and capital allowances.

If an individual is in partnership the relief is due against his share of the partnership profits. In a partnership where several partners spend two or three weeks abroad, but each fails to reach the qualifying target of 30 days it will obviously be worth considering whether one partner can take on some of the work that others would normally do and therefore bring himself within the scope of the relief.

The assessable profit for a fiscal year is usually calculated not by reference to the accounts or activities of that year, but by reference to an earlier period. The eligibility for overseas relief depends on movements during the fiscal year. There is thus no real link between the profit earned by the overseas activities and the tax relief. If a person qualifies for relief in 1980-81 it will probably reduce the tax profit which he actually earned in 1979-80 or which he earned partly in 1979-80 and partly in 1978-79 and it may be that in those years he spent no time abroad. The profit he makes this year and which may be attributed to the time spent abroad may be assessed in 1981-82 or 1982-83. Whether he then obtains overseas relief will depend upon his movements at that time.

A claim for the new overseas allowance must be made within two years after the year to which it relates.

Finally, it should be noted that the 25 per cent deduction is for tax purposes only and does not reduce the amount on which the Class 4 National Insurance contribution is calculated.

7.4 Creating settlements

This article and sections 7.5 and 7.6 look at the way in which settlements (or trusts) affect taxation liabilities.

There are different types of settlement but the main type is where one individual (the settlor) places funds or assets in the custody of another person or persons (the trustees) to hold and use on behalf of a further person or group of persons (the beneficiaries).

The settlement is usually created by a written deed which specifies what responsibilities and restrictions are placed on the trustees. In some cases they may be required to pay out the income of the settlement to or for particular individuals.

In other cases they may be required to accumulate it for a given period.

A third possibility is that they will be given discretion either to distribute or to accumulate. If there is more than one beneficiary the deed may require the trustees to treat them all equally or it may give the power to discriminate at their discretion.

In addition to saying what shall or may be done with the income the deed will also say what shall or may untimately be done with the capital. Again, the trustees may be compelled to appoint it to named persons at specified times or they may have discretionary powers of appointment.

In some cases the income of the settlement may be regarded as the income of the settlor for tax purposes. We will describe the circumstances in which this applies in section 7.6, but for the present we will restrict the explanation to cases where it does not apply.

The trustees are liable for basic rate tax on income arising to the settlement. As they do not receive the income in a personal capacity they cannot claim personal allowances and they are not liable for higher rates of tax. It is this exemption from higher rate tax which makes settlements attractive for tax purposes.

If the settlement is a discretionary one or if it provides for the income to be accumulated the 15 per cent investment income surcharge will be payable in addition to the basic rate tax.

Any income paid to beneficiaries by the trustees or used on behalf of the beneficiaries is treated as income which has suffered tax at the basic rate or, where appropriate, at the basic rate plus surcharge. The beneficiary may be entitled to reclaim some of this tax or he may be called upon to pay additional tax depending upon what other income he has and what allowances he may be entitled to.

Trustees are liable for capital gains tax on any gains made. If the settlement was made before 7 June 1978, gains of up to £500 a year will be free of tax. If the gains in a year are more than £1250 the full rate of 30 per cent will apply to the whole gain. If the gains are between £500 and £1250 in a year the tax will be 50 per cent of the amount in excess of £500. For years before 1978-79 all gains were taxed at 30 per cent and for settlements created after 6 June 1978, all gains are at 30 per cent.

In the past it was quite usual for a person who had most of the shares in a successful family company to create a settlement to hold some of them for the benefit of future generations. In this way the person could ensure that the shares benefited his children or grandchildren without letting them have control of the shares.

If the company was paying dividends because of the tax laws about close companies and if the settlor had a very high tax rate those dividends which went to the settlement rather than to him would be taxed at lower rates.

In some cases the trustees would pass the dividends on to beneficiaries straight away, but in others they would hold them for a period so that they did not become the income of any individuals perhaps until several years later.

Settlements are not quite as fashionable now, and one of the reasons is that the law which made many companies pay dividends has been relaxed considerably in the last year. The taxation position for Capital Transfer Tax has also changed in a way that makes settlements not quite as attractive as they were.

Although the tax advantages of settlements may have been diminished, there are sometimes other good reasons for creating them. A person may think that his son or grandson is too young or immature to have control of funds or assets but may nevertheless want those assets to benefit him.

Another person may want assets to benefit a number of individuals but may feel that it is too early to say which should benefit more than others.

People are particularly cautious about shares in family companies. A person with more than one child may want some shares to benefit his eldest son or daughter but may be worried that if that son married and was then killed the shares might be passed to a daughter-in-law who would then have a right to vote on affairs which the parent regards as family affairs.

By creating a settlement the parent might hope to let the financial benefit go to his son or daughter-in-law but let the voting power be held in what he regards as more mature or responsible hands.

There can be many other sound commercial reasons for creating a settlement. Even though taxation as a prime motivation may be less important now, it is still a consideration and a tax advantage may be an added bonus or a tax disadvantage may be a deterrent.

7.5 Settlement exceptions

Section 7.4 explains that income is charged to tax at the standard rate and that, if it is an accumulation or discretionary settlement, the 15 per cent investment income surcharge will also be payable.

We now look at some exceptions, where income of the settlement is regarded as income of the settlor.

Children of settlor

If any of the beneficiaries are children of the settlor, income paid out to or for the benefit of such a child at a time when the child is under the age of 18 and unmarried is treated as income of the settlor. A minor exception is if such income does not exceed £5 in a tax year. Income which is accumulated for the future benefit of the child is not included as the parents' income.

Revocable settlements

If the terms of the settlement allow the settlor, a trustee, or anybody else to revoke the settlement and if, in the event of such a revocation, some part of the property in the settlement could be returned to the settlor or his spouse the income of the settlement is treated as income of the settlor.

If only a part of the property could be returned only a corresponding part of the income can be so treated. If the power of revocation cannot be exercised within the first six years after property is settled, this treatment will not apply until such a time as the power to revoke is capable of being exercised.

A power to revoke includes a power to diminish the settlement.

Retained interest

If the terms of the settlement allow any income to be paid to, or applied for the benefit of, the settlor or his spouse, any such income which is not distributed to other beneficiaries will be treated as income of the settlor. A similar consequence will result if any of the capital in the settlement can be applied for the benefit of the settlor or his spouse.

There are some exceptions to this treatment if the power to apply the income or capital for the settlor or spouse can only arise in certain circumstances. These circumstances mainly involve the bankruptcy or death of other beneficiaries.

Discretionary power for benefit of settlor

If the terms of the settlement allow the trustees to use their discretion in a way which will benefit the settlor or his spouse the income will be treated as belonging to the settlor. If the discretionary power is limited to a certain part of the income or property, this treatment is limited to a corresponding part of the income arising.

There are, again, exceptions if the discretion can only be exercised in the event of death or bankruptcy of certain other beneficiaries.

If the discretion can not be exercised within the first six years from the time property is settled or income first arises, the income will not be regarded as belonging to the settlor until such time as the power to exercise the discretion does arise.

It will be seen that there is some overlapping between these four sets of circumstances and a settlement may be caught under more than one of them. It is obviously advisable to bear them all in mind when considering whether a settlement should be created.

Where the settlor is assessed to tax on income which he has not received he can ask a tax inspector for a certificate showing the amount of tax charged and he will be entitled to recover that amount from the trustees or from the beneficiary who actually did receive the income.

There is another circumstance (see section 7.6) in which an amount equal to the income of a settlement can be treated as income of the settlor. It is of particular significance where the settlement holds shares or debentures in a close company.

7.6 The double tax trap[*]

The situation by which a settlor can be taxed on income he does not receive contains an anomaly which can be a boobytrap for somebody who might make a perfectly reasonable commercial arrangement with no intention of obtaining a tax advantage.

The law says that if the trustees of the settlement pay any capital sum to the settlor, any undistributed income of the settlement (up to the amount of that capital sum) shall be treated as his income. If the undistributed income is less than the capital sum the income of subsequent years can be treated as his.

A capital sum is any amount which is not paid as income and is not paid for full consideration. It includes money loaned to the settlor and also the repayment of any loan he has made to the settlement.

While it is easy to see that a person should not be free to borrow money from a settlement which is receiving income and being protected from higher rate tax, it is much less easy to see why a person should be penalised for withdrawing his own money.

There is, however, an even bigger problem, and one which is likely to occur more often in practice because not many people, having created a settlement, would then wish to lend further money to it. This is where the settlement or any beneficiary of the settlement is a participator in a close company.

If the company pays any capital sum to the settlor (again including any loan or repayment of a loan) that sum can be treated as if it was paid *by the settlement* and the settlor can then be charged to tax on the undistributed income of the settlement.

It is quite common for shareholders in a close company to lend money to the company. It is also quite common for a major shareholder to want to transfer some of his shares to a settlement for the benefit of grandchildren or some other relatives.

It is the combination of these two common occurrences which has the unfortunate tax consequence. Before settling close company shares, therefore, a person would be well advised to withdraw any loan he has made to the company and to consider whether the

[*] The Finance Bill 1981 contains provisions to modify the problem described here. Some aspects of the problem will not, however, be affected, and it is wise for the settlor not to have any loan dealings with the settlement or with a company in which the trustees are participants.

situation is likely to arise in the future that he will need to make any further loan.

The need for caution with regard to this part of the Taxes Acts is not restricted to people who hold shares in a close company. If a person who is not a shareholder in the company but has lent money to it is the settlor of a settlement and one of the beneficiaries of that settlement happens to be a shareholder in the company, the law could act to treat a withdrawal of his own money as income of the settlor.

The law applies to withdrawal by, or payment to, the spouse of a settlor in the same way as to the settlor himself.

In section 7.5 we describe four cases where income of a settlement was taxable as income of the settlor. In each of those four cases the law says that the income so treated should not also be treated as the income of anybody else.

In other words, if the settlor pays the tax the person who actually receives the income receives it tax-free (although the settlor is entitled to ask him to reimburse the tax) so the income is at least taxed only once.

There is no such safeguard in the case described here. Although the amount of undistributed income in the settlement is used to ascertain how much of the capital withdrawn is treated as income, it is the capital which is taxed as income and the actual income of the settlement is still taxed in the normal way. This part of the legislation can therefore effectively impose a double charge to tax.

7.7 Producing capital gains

In this section we consider reasons (other than matching up capital gains and capital losses) for taking a close look at the time of disposals which will produce capital gains.

The first and most obvious point is that a short delay in making the contract can produce a long delay in paying the tax. If a company makes up its accounts to 31 March it will normally pay its tax on the following 1 January. If an asset is sold in the last week of March 1978 the tax on the gain will be due on 1 January 1979. If the sale can be delayed until the first week of April 1978 the tax will not be due until 1 January 1980.

A less obvious point is the effect of a capital gain on a company's status as a small company for the benefit of the lower rate of tax.

A company is a small company if its profit falls below a certain figure. For the year to 31 March 1978 the figure was £50,000. Profit for this purpose includes capital gains but, having decided that a company is small, the lower rate of Corporation Tax applies only to the income and not to the capital gains.

The government intends that capital gains shall only suffer tax at 30 per cent. To achieve this it says that only 30/52 (approximately 60 per cent) of the gain shall be taxed, but that the tax shall be at 52 per cent. Thus, if a company sells an asset at a profit of £60,667 the amount assessable will be £35,000 and the tax will be £18,200.

If the company had income of £50,000 and had no other profit, it would pay tax at 42 per cent on that income, which would come to £21,000.

If, however, the assessable gain of £35,000 fell into the same accounting period as the income of £50,000 the total profit would be £85,000 and the small company rate of tax would not apply. The tax on the income of £50,000 would be at the rate of 52 per cent which would be £26,000. The capital gain would therefore, in addition to the immediate tax of £18,200, have cost the company a further £5000 in increased tax on income.

Whether this additional tax could be saved by deferring the sale until the following accounting period would depend upon the directors' anticipation of the trading results for that period. If it was forecast that the company's income for the next year would be £100,000 and that, therefore, there would be no small company relief which could be lost the deferral of the gain would save £5000.

The amount of income in an accounting period refers to the taxable income and it must be borne in mind that the incidence of stock relief or clawback or of capital allowances can mean that the taxable income is significantly higher or lower than the true income for the period.

If a company has associated companies the figures for deciding whether it is a small company or not are reduced. If it has three associated companies the maximum profit to benefit from the 42 per cent rate is £12,500 instead of £50,000 and the level of profit at which tapering relief expires is £21,250 instead of £85,000. These figures will apply even if three of the companies have very tiny profits and the combined profits of all the companies are well below the figure of £50,000.

Some associated companies are independent but some may be within a small group of companies.

If a company has three associated companies and has income of £12,500 or just under it will want to enjoy the lower rate of tax. If it

181

has a capital gain of £9000 the benefit will be lost. However, if one of the associated companies is in the same group and if that company has very low profits or has such high profits that it cannot be considered for small company relief it is possible to transfer the asset to that company and to let that company sell it and make the gain.

It is also a pity that, in taking these steps to avoid an unfair burden of tax, the company may sometimes have to risk other pitfalls. It is essential to have good professional advice to ensure that the action being taken really is the most effective for the particular transaction under consideration.

7.8 The golden rule – a good accountant

The golden rule for any small business must be 'Get a good accountant,' and one of the very valuable early services an accountant can render is advising on the best accounting date to select for tax purposes. Very different assessments can be made on the same trading results depending on the accounting date chosen.

For the tax year in which a business starts, the tax assessment is based on the profit for the period up to 5 April following the commencement. If accounts are not made up to that date, the profit will be determined by apportioning the profit of whatever accounts are prepared.

For the first *full* tax year throughout which the business is carried on, the assessment will be on the profits of the 12 months from commencement of the business. Again, if accounts are not made for that period the profit will be calculated by apportionment of whatever accounts are made.

For subsequent years, the assessment will be based on the profit of the accounting year which ends in the tax year preceding the year of assessment. Thus, if accounts are made up to 5 April, the accounts to 5 April 1980 (ending in tax year 1979-80) will form the basis of the assessment for 1980-81. If, however, the accounts are made up to 6 April, the accounts to 6 April 1980 (ending in 1980-81) will form the basis of the assessment for 1981-82. A difference of one day in the accounting period can, therefore, mean a difference of one year in the assessment.

Sole traders and partnerships can choose any accounting date they like. Indeed, they are not compelled to keep to the same date each year but it will usually be sensible and convenient to do so. Let us now look at one example to show how the choice of accounting date can have a significant effect on the amount of profit that will be assessed. Suppose that a partnership starts a new business on 6 January 1977 and suppose that the profits made in the first five quarters are:

3 months to 5 Apr 1977	... £1200
3 months to 5 Jul 1977	... £5000
3 months to 5 Oct 1977	... £6000
3 months to 5 Jan 1978	... £7800
3 months to 5 Apr 1978	... £2200

(The first quarter of the calendar year is obviously the poor season for this particular business).

If it is decided to make up an account for the first year's business up to 5 January, 1978, the total profit will be £20,000 and the assessments will be:

1976-77 20,000 x 3/12 =	5000
1977-78	20,000
1978-79	20,000
Total profits assessed for	
first three years	45,000

If it is decided to prepare a three month account to 5 April showing profit of £1200 and then a full-year account to the following 5 April showing profit of £21,000, the assessments will be:

1976-76	1200
1977-78 1200 + (21,000 x 9/12) =	16,950
1978-79	21,000
Total profits assessed for	
first three years	39,150

A third possibility would be to make up a 15-month account showing profit of £22,000, and if that was done the assessments would be:

1976-77 22,200 x 3/15 =	4440
1977-78 22,200 x 12/15 =	17,760
1978-79	17,760
Total profits assessed for	
first three years	39,960

It will be seen that three totally different results can be produced from the same set of facts. There could, of course, be numerous

183

other variations, particularly if it was possible to analyse the flow of profits into even shorter periods than three months.

Let us suppose that the accountant was able to see that there was very heavy expenditure in April 1978 and that there was a nil profit for the month to 5 May, 1978. It might be decided that a 16-month account should be prepared which would show profit of £22,000 and the assessments would then be:

$$1976\text{-}77 \quad 22,200 \times \quad 3/16 = \quad 4,162$$
$$1977\text{-}78 \quad 22,200 \times 12/16 = 16,650$$
$$1978\text{-}79 \qquad\qquad\qquad\qquad 16,650$$

Total profit assessed for
first three years $\overline{37,462}$

In this fourth case the assessment for 1979-80 will also be in the amount of £16,650. The accountant's job is not finished when he decides which accounting date produces the lowest total of assessments for the three-year period. He must also try to judge the effect on future years of the accounting date chosen, and in addition he must consider the way the profits are allocated between the years.

For instance, the second set of figures shown above, totalling £39,150, is not necessarily better than the third set showing a total of £39,960. The difference in higher rate tax on £21,000 compared with £17,760 may more than outweigh the advantage gained in the two earlier years.

If the profits in the early years of the business do not keep increasing it is possible that it may be to the advantage of the partnership to claim a different basis of assessment for the second and third years of business.

7.9 Avoiding unnecessary tax

Section 7.8 explains how the choice of accounting date can be very important at the start of a business carried on by an individual or a partnership because of the commencement provisions which govern the basis period for assessment. There are complementary rules when a business finishes. A proper understanding of these provisions can often affect the decision as to the date a business should cease.

If a business has been operating for a few years and the commencement provisions no longer apply, the tax assessment for a year will not be on the amount of profit earned in that year, but on the amount of profit earned in the accounts year which ended in the previous fiscal year. Thus, if accounts are made up to 5 April each year the assessment for 1980-81 will be on the profit earned in the year to 5 April 1980 but, if accounts are made up to 6 April, it will be on the profit earned in the year to 6 April 1979.

For the fiscal year in which a business ceases the assessment is made on the profit earned in that year. If accounts are not made for the period from 6 April to the date of cessation the profit is calculated by apportionment of whatever accounts are prepared.

For the two fiscal years preceding the year of cessation the tax inspector will also calculate the profit for the actual years (by apportionment if necessary) and if the total of such profit for the two years exceeds the total of the two years' assessments on the 'previous year basis' he may amend those two assessments.

In the case of a partnership which makes up its accounts to, say, 30 April the assessment for 1979-80 will have been made on the profit of the year to 30 April 1978. If the partnership finishes on 30 April 1980 the 1980-81 assessment will be on the profit for the period from 6 April 1980 to 30 April 1980 (a little under one-twelfth of the final year). If the inspector decides not to revise the years 1978-1979 and 1979-80 the profit of the period between 1 May 1978 and 5 April 1980 will not be assessed at all.

If the inspector does revise the assessments for 1978-79 and 1979-80 he must take the profit for the years beginning 5 April 1978 and 1979. The assessment for 1977-78 will have been on the profits to 30 April 1976, so the profit of the period between 1 May 1976 and 5 April 1978 will escape assessment.

It will be seen that, whatever action the inspector takes, a period of nearly two years will be free from assessment. The inspector merely decides which of the two periods it will be.

The 'tax-free' period is merely a *quid pro quo* for the several assessments which will have been made on the profit of one period in the early years. Whether the partnership gains or loses overall will depend substantially on whether the profit which has been assessed more than once is greater or less than those which have not been assessed at all. The comparison may also be affected by such considerations as the profit sharing agreement between partners; what personal allowances or other deductions were available in different years; what other income was assessable; and difference in tax rates from year to year.

185

It is not always possible to control the date of cessation of a business. A death, a fire and termination of a lease are some of the possible causes but there are many other cessations which are controllable. It is advisable to give the accountant for the business the fullest possible information about future intentions. His advice on the actual date of termination may be invaluable.

For instance, there may be an intention to finish near the end of March 1981. As this is in tax year 1980-81 it will give the Inland Revenue the chance to revise assessments for 1978-79 and 1979-80. If 1978-79 happens to have a particularly low assessment because of poor results in its basis period it may pay to prolong the business a few days so that the cessation is in tax year 1981-82 and 1978-79 therefore becomes safe from revision.

On the other hand, there may be occasions when, the decision to terminate having been taken, the tax consequences make it desirable to finish earlier than may be required for other purposes.

7.10 Tax on business profits

Generally, a tax assessment will only be on the actual amount of profit earned for the year in which the business commences and the year in which it finishes.

For the first *complete* tax year in which a business is carried on (which will therefore be the second tax year except for the few businesses which commence on April 5) the assessment is on the amount of profit earned in the first 12 months' trading. For all other other tax years the assessment is on an amount equal to the profit of the accounting period ending in the tax year preceding the year of assessment.

For the second and third tax years in which the business is carried on the proprietor can elect for the assessments to be based on the actual profits instead of on this normal basis but after that there is no choice. He will obviously only wish to make such an election if the profits of later periods are lower than the profits of his first trading year.

For the two tax years preceding the tax year in which the business finishes the tax inspector can choose to alter the assessments he has made and to assess the actual profits earned instead of the amounts calculated on the normal basis.

The choice for the taxpayer at the beginning and for the tax inspector at the end must be exercised for both years or for neither.

In a few businesses which are carried on for only a short period the amount of profit assessed will be equal to the amount of profit earned in the whole period of trading, but for the majority of businesses some profits will be assessed more than once and other profits will not be assessed at all. Whether a person is assessed on more profit than he has earned or on less will depend on the particular sequence in which profits arise.

In the following examples we look at three businesses, each of which commences on 1 May 1974 and carries on for six years until 30 April 1980. During the six-year period each makes total profits of £26,000, but the sequence in which these profits are earned varies for each business.

Although the businesses are active for only six years they spill into seven tax years and we have shown what amounts will be assessed for tax each year. There are two columns shown for business B. The column headed B(2) would probably be the figures used, but column B(1) could apply if the taxpayer or his agent failed to elect for the lower basis in the second and third tax years.

It will be seen that the assessments on business A come so far less than the total profits earned. This is because the very low profit in the first accounts year forms the basis of two years of assessment and of the 11 months in the first tax year while, in the years before cessation, a full year and a further 11 months' profit at the rate of £6000 per annum escape assessment.

Business B is assessed on more or less the right amount unless the foolish mistake of failing to elect is made.

Business C starts with high profits and finishes on a low note and the effect is the opposite of business A. The profits assessed exceed the profits earned.

Very few businesses will be carried on for only six years. Over a much longer time span there will still be a difference between the amounts earned and the amounts assessed, but the difference will usually not be such a large percentage of the earnings as it is in examples A and C. However, it is the business which looks promising and fails after a few years which is likely to have the shorter life and therefore the situation in C may be more likely to arise than the situation in A.

A similar basis of assessment used to apply for trading companies as, prior to 1965, they were assessed to income tax. With the introduction of Corporation Tax these artificial basis periods disappeared for companies.

Three traders each commence on 1 May 1974, and carry on for six years to 30 April 1980.

Profits

Year ended 30 April,		A	B	C
	1975	500	6000	6000
	1976	1500	3000	7000
	1977	6000	3000	6000
	1978	6000	4000	3000
	1979	6000	4000	3000
	1980	6000	6000	1000
Total profits in 6 years		26,000	26,000	26,000

Assessments

	A	B(1)	B(2)	C
1974-75	458	5500	5500	5500
1975-76	500	6000	3250	6000
1976-77	500	6000	3000	6000
1977-78	1500	3000	3000	7000
1978-79	6000	4000	4000	6000
1979-80	6000	5833	5833	3000
1980-81	500	500	500	83
Total assessments for 7 tax years	15,458	30,833	25,083	33,583

7.11 Transferring assets for capital gains

Capital gains are taxable at 30 per cent (sometimes, as in the case of individuals, at a lower rate). However, where a gain is realised on an asset held by a company the tax is effectively higher than 30 per cent if one looks at it from the standpoint of shareholders in the company.

It is probably particularly relevant to do that in the case of a close company. The company will pay 30 per cent of its gain in tax, which will therefore leave it richer by only 70 per cent of the gain. If the shareholders wished to spend the money arising from the gain they would have either to sell their shares or liquidate the company. The value they would get would reflect the 70 per cent of the gain which was left to the company after tax.

This additional value would, however, be taxed as a capital gain again in the hands of the shareholders. Thirty per cent of this net value would be equal to 21 per cent of the original gain, and, therefore, the total tax suffered before the value of the asset was available to the shareholders would be 51 per cent of the original gain.

In some cases a gain may be realised by a company which is itself the subsidiary of another company. In such a case there could even be a third point of taxation before the gain was available to the shareholders. The subsidiary company would pay 30 per cent on its gain and when the parent tried to turn the subsidiary into cash (by selling or liquidating it) another 30 per cent of the net figure would be payable. This would leave only 49 per cent of the gain in the parent company.

When the shareholders came to realise their investment in the parent company they would have to pay a further 30 per cent of the net amount, which would be almost 15 per cent of the original gain. The total tax taken in the three operations would therefore be about 66 per cent. If the group of companies contained more than three tiers it is possible that there could be four, five, or more charges to tax before the cash from the gain was available to the shareholders.

It must be accepted that in most cases the double charge to tax will apply, but of course there may be some relief of the second charge because the individual shareholders may be liable to lower rates, or may be entitled to some relief. It is often possible, however, to avoid further charges by transferring the asset within the group of companies before making a disposal. Where one company is at least 75 per cent subsidiary of another company, the Taxes Act provides that no tax shall be charged when a chargeable asset is disposed of by one company to the other.

A similar law applies regarding any transfers within a group, provided that both the company making the transfer and the company receiving the asset are controlled as to at least 75 per cent by some parent.

It is possible, therefore, for the company which is about to make the sale of the asset to transfer it first of all to its parent or some other company higher up the group, at such a price that the gain falls in that higher company. In this way it can be ensured that the gain is only taxed once within the group of companies, but there will be the likelihood of a further tax charge on the shareholders as individuals.

The transfer of ownership of assets within a group of companies before sales outside the group may be made for other reasons. For instance, another company in the group might have allowable capital losses brought forward, or may be about to make a disposal within the same accounting period which will produce a capital loss. In such an instance it might be prudent to transfer the asset into the company with the loss, so that when the gain is made the loss can be set off against it.

Another reason for transferring assets within a group might be to preserve the benefit of small company relief. Certain small companies can be taxed on their income at only 42 per cent instead of 52 per cent, or can be taxed at a rate which is effectively somewhere between 42 per cent and 52 per cent.

Although this reduced rate applies only to income, the question of whether there is an entitlement to it is determined by reference to the company's total profit which includes chargeable gains. Thus the presence of a gain in one company may deprive it of its title to the relief. If there is another company in the group which is not entitled to small company relief it might be prudent to transfer the asset to that company and let it bear the tax on the capital gain. The Inland Revenue accepts that transfers of assets within the group in this way are normal prudent tax planning, and does not try to upset the arrangement.

If assets are transferred in such a way that they take value out of a company, with the result that when that company is liquidated or sold there will be a capital loss, there is provision for the tax inspector to regard the transfer as a 'depreciatory transaction' and to refuse to treat the loss as an allowable loss for tax purposes.

There may be a further problem if the asset in question is land or buildings. There is a section of the Taxes Act which enables the Inland Revenue to treat as income any capital gain made in certain circumstances from land or from an asset deriving its value from land. One of the circumstances is where the land is acquired with a view to realising a profit on its disposal.

It seems possible, therefore, that if a building or some land was transferred by one company to another to avoid a multiple charge to tax, the receiving company might be receiving it with the sole purpose of realising a profit on disposal, and might be putting itself in the position where tax could be levied as a tax on income rather than on a chargeable gain. Although this interpretation may be possible in theory, the Inland Revenue says it will not seek to use that argument except where it believes the transaction was part of a more extensive scheme of tax avoidance which it considered to be undesirable.

7.12 Capital gains tax needs foresight

Some companies may pay tax on capital gains, which, with a little foresight, might have been avoided.

Whenever a company disposes of an asset which is within the definition of chargeable assets a computation should be prepared which will show whether the transaction resulted in a gain or a loss. If there is a loss it may be used to cancel a similar amount of gain in the same accounting period or, if there is no gain or too small a gain, it may be carried forward and deducted from gains in later periods. The loss cannot be set against income and it cannot be carried back to be set against gains of earlier periods.

A company which makes a capital loss of £2000 in year 1 and a capital gain of £2000 in year 2 will pay no tax. If it makes both the gain and the loss in year 1 or in year 2 it will, similarly, pay no tax. If it makes the gain in year 1 and the loss in year 2 it will have to pay £600 tax.

Whenever it is proposed to dispose of some asset on which a gain will arise it is advisable to consider whether there might be a disposal of some other asset in the following year. If there is to be a later disposal which will result in a loss, it might be worth trying to defer the profitable one or advance the date of the unprofitable one so that they fall within the same accounting period.

It will not always be easy to achieve this. Delaying a sale might mean that the purchaser is lost. Alternatively, it may not always be possible to advance a sale because the asset might be needed for use in the business for a slightly longer period. Sometimes, however, these difficulties can be surmounted by making full use of the wording of the legislation.

A sale is deemed to take place when an unconditional contract is made. If the contract is conditional, the sale does not take place for tax purposes until the conditions are fulfilled. Physical possession or use of the asset may be transferred before or after the contract is made or has become unconditional. Thus, if the vendor needs the use of an asset but wants to advance the sale date for tax purposes he may make a contract in year 1 for completion or delivery in year 2.

If the vendor wants to delay the effective tax date of a sale he may include a condition in the contract which will not be fulfilled until some time within the next accounting period. It must be a condition which stands some chance of remaining unfulfilled. If there was no such chance it would probably not be possible to interpret it as a condition at all. There is nothing, however, to prevent it from being a condition which has only a very remote chance of being unfulfilled.

It must be appreciated that, if there is a conditional contract or a delay between contract and completion or delivery, one of the parties may be at risk in the event of a breach of faith by the other or in the event of an unexpected change in the position or fortunes of the other. It is essential, therefore, that competent legal advice is obtained regarding the contract.

A company which makes a gain may not, of course, have another sale pending which will show a loss. It may, however, own some asset which has lost some of its value but which it wished to retain. If these circumstances do apply it is sometimes possible to arrange a sale which will crystallise the loss and then to buy the asset back again. If this happens there will of course be a smaller loss or maybe even a gain if the asset is subsequently sold. This type of arrangement is the equivalent to the 'bed and breakfast' sales which are a feature of stock exchange activity just before the fiscal year end.

A few words of caution are again necessary. It would be no good selling an asset at an artificially low price in order to establish a loss because the tax inspector would be entitled to ignore the contract price and treat the transaction as taking place at open market value. The scheme would therefore only work with an asset which had genuinely fallen in value from its cost (or, in certain cases, from its deemed cost) price.

Second, the sale and repurchase must be genuinely independent transactions. If they are, it will follow that one party to the first transaction might change his mind or be prevented from entering into the second transaction and the other party may therefore be at risk.

Third, the sale which produces the loss should not be a sale to a connected person.

Where an asset is transferred from one company in a group to another company in the group a capital gain or loss is not calculated. The asset is treated as having been sold at the figure which gives no gain or loss to the company making the disposal. If the acquiring company later disposes of the asset the whole of the gain or loss accruing during the ownership of both companies will be attributed to it.

7.13 Property income: the right approach

Here and in sections 7.14 and 7.15 we examine the tax aspects of income and other profits or gains from land and buildings.

The main type of tax liability on income or profits derived from property (ie land and buildings) is assessed under Schedule A. The law provides that the amount assessed for any year shall be the rent which becomes due for the year less the expenses which are actually paid during the year.

This basis of assessment can create a very unfair situation. Suppose that the owner of property lets it for £5000 per year but that in one particular year the occupier is having financial difficulties and does not pay his rent during the year. Suppose also that in that year the owner spends £5000 on repairs for which he receives the bills, but which he does not pay during the year.

On a normal concept of income the expenses incurred should be deducted from the rents becoming due and therefore the income for the year is nil. The actual amount received during the year is also nil. Under the Schedule A provisions, however, the income assessable is £5000.

The rent is assessable even though it has not been received, but the expenses are to be ignored until they are eventually paid. It may be that in the following year there is further expense on repair and maintenance and the tax relief for the expenses may, therefore, be deferred for quite a while.

The expenses can be carried forward to later years to the extent that they exceed rents. There is not, however, any provision for setting off losses on this type of income against any other type of income. If losses or excess expenses are carried forward and if the future rents are not large enough to absorb them, the tax relief on those expenses may be lost entirely.

The Inland Revenue recognises that there is an injustice in having the receipts side of a profit and loss account based on an 'earnings' basis whilst having the expenses side based on a 'cash' basis.

In practice, therefore, they will allow the profit and loss account to be made up on an earnings basis for both sides, but they will only do this if the method is adhered to for every year and if the property owner supplies full accounts including a balance sheet each year.

Many people do not supply a balance sheet for this type of income and do not realise that there can be a problem until the circumstance arises where both receipts and payments are delayed and the injustice becomes obvious. Such people are in danger of being required to pay tax on income for a year earlier than the year in which it arises, or in fact on income which they never receive or become entitled to.

The calculation of rents receivable less expenses should be made for the year to 5 April, but the Inland Revenue is also prepared to depart from the strict legal position in some cases. Where full accounts including a balance sheet are made up every year to some date other than 5 April, inspectors will often be prepared to accept those accounts as though they were accounts for the tax year in which the accounting year ends. Accounts for the year ending 31 December 1977 could, for example, be accepted as though they were accounts for the year ended 5 April, 1978.

Tax under Schedule A is due on 1 January during the relevant tax year. As the income for the year cannot be known until the year ends, the law empowers the tax inspector to make a provisional assessment. This is made on an amount of income equal to the income of the preceding year.

When the tax year has ended and the correct amount of assessable income is known, the assessment will be either reduced or increased and tax will be repaid or further tax demanded.

The owner of the property cannot claim that he should not pay the tax on the provisional assessment, because he knows that the assessment will eventually prove to be too high because of heavy expenses. However, if he can show that the receipts side of his profit and loss account will be lower in the year of assessment than in the previous year, a proportion of the tax charged on the provisional assessment will be held over at his request.

7.14 The best way to slice the property cake

Section 7.13 looks at the taxation of rental income from property. Here we examine other receipts.

It is not only rents that are taxable under schedule A. Some premiums and other items are also taxable. The premiums to which this applies are premiums paid for a lease of less than 50 years. Whether the whole of the premium or only a part will be treated as income depends on the length of the lease. If the lease is for less than two years the whole will be regarded as income. If it is for between two and three years only 98 per cent of it will be so regarded. If it is for between three and four years the figure is 96 per cent and so on. There is a reduction of 2 per cent for every complete 12 months after the first 12 months.

If the owner of the property is an individual (ie not a company or a trustee of a settlement), the effect of having a premium, which is in effect akin to advance rental for several years, taxed in one year may be to take him into higher bands of taxation than he would normally be in. He can, therefore, claim that the tax should be reduced on what is known as a 'top slicing' calculation.

In this calculation the amount of the premium is divided by the number of years in the lease to give a yearly equivalent. Tax is then calculated on this yearly equivalent as though it is the most highly taxed slice of the individual's income for the year. The amount of tax on the yearly equivalent is then multiplied by the number of years in the lease and the tax charged in the assessment is reduced to the resultant figure.

The law provides that some types of payment which are not premiums shall be treated as premiums for the purpose of schedule A taxation. One example is a payment for the variation of the terms of a lease. Another is the payment for the assignment of a lease which was originally granted at an undervalue.

Another item which may be taxed in the same way as a premium is a requirement that a tenant should carry out improvements to the premises. In this sort of case the amount to be regarded as a premium is the value added to the landlord's interest in the property by virtue of the requirement to carry out the improvements. This is not necessarily the same as the amount which the tenant spends on the work. It may be either more or less.

Where premiums or similar payments are assessed as income on the lessor, the lessee will be entitled to treat some of the premium as rent paid. If he is carrying on a business he will therefore be able to deduct this notional rent paid as an expense of his business. The amount which he can deduct each year is the amount on which the lessor is assessed divided by the number of years in the lease.

The length of a lease for tax purposes is not necessarily the term shown in the lease agreement. There are provisions which enable the tax inspector to take account of rights to extend a lease or of various other circumstances which make it unlikely that the occupation will actually be for the term stated.

7.15 Land disposal and the tax man

This section looks at the taxation of profits from disposing of land. It does not deal with Development Land Tax, which I hope to refer to at a later date, but confines itself to Corporation tax and Capital Gains tax and tax on income.

If somebody carries on a business of building or property developing there is no great problem. Purchases and sales of land will be taken into account in calculating the trading income. The problems arise when profits are made in transactions which fall short of being a trade.

Before 1965, if a profit was made and the tax inspector could not show that there was a trade or 'an adventure in the nature of trade' the profit would escape tax. Since 1965 we have had Capital Gains Tax and the profits on isolated, non-trading transactions will normally fall within this tax.

Usually it is better to be assessed on a capital gain than on income, but just occasionally it can be worse. This is because some expenses which might be deductible in computing income from a trading adventure would not be deductible for Capital Gains Tax. Another possibility is that the person in question might have some loss in another trade or an allowance for interest payment which could be deducted from income but not from a capital gain. Apart from these rare situations, however, the lower rate of tax makes Capital Gains Tax preferable.

With the near certainty that property values would rise consistently, it was still a good investment for a potential high-rate taxpayer to buy land rather than to place his money elsewhere. In 1969 the situation changed when legislation was introduced which enabled the Inland Revenue to treat some capital profits on land as if they were income. The relevant section of the Taxes Acts is headed 'artificial transactions in land' but it covers some transactions which the taxpayer may consider are not properly described by those words.

A capital gain can be treated as income if any land or any property deriving its value from land (eg shares in some companies) is acquired with the main aim of making a profit in disposal. Thus, it is the intention when the land is acquired which can influence the method of taxation when it is sold. If the person acquires the land for the purpose of using it in his business or to let for the production of rental income a subsequent sale at a profit should be taxable as a capital gain. Even if the purpose is to hold the land in order to prevent somebody else acquiring it a gain should escape being treated as income.

It is not always obvious what a person's primary purpose may be when he acquires land. There may be a mixture of motives or he may even have no clearly formulated motive. Even if his motive is a subsequent profitable sale he may say it is something else. Other actions both before and after the event may have to be discussed in order to try to discern the main aim at the time of acquisition and, of course, it is open to the person to point to changes in circumstances to demonstrate that he had one motive but later had to abandon it.

If a property which is bought with the intention of resale at a profit is used as a private residence, tax will be assessed as a capital gain. This contrasts with the more usual sale of a private residence which is free of all tax.

Another circumstance in which a capital gain can be assessed as income is where land which has been acquired without the main aim of profitable disposal is later developed with the object of selling. Again, the motive is critical at the time the development is done. If it is done for some other purpose and the decision to sell comes later the gain will probably be a capital gain. Again also, surrounding facts and actions may indicate a different motive from the one which the person claims is the primary one.

An assessment can be made if a person does not make the profit himself but, directly or indirectly, transmits the opportunity to make it to somebody else.

The law does not lay down precise methods of calculating the assessment where this legislation on 'artificial transactions' applies. It simply says that such methods shall be adopted as is just and reasonable. The taxpayer and the tax inspector may very easily differ on the interpretation of this phrase.

In many ways it is regretable that the law should be so imprecise and that two people who do exactly the same thing with the same result should be taxed in different ways and charged different amounts. This particular legislation was produced in response to activities which the Inland Revenue obviously thought gave some people an unfair advantage, but to what extent those activities were themselves responsive to injustices and anomalies in the Taxes Acts it is impossible to say.

7.16 Self-administered benefit schemes

One of the happiest aspects of our tax system, from the point of view of small companies, is the encouragement it gives to the provision of retirement and associated benefits for employees including shareholder/directors.

It is possible to set up and obtain approval for a fund (or several different funds) for one small group of employees or even for a single employee. If approval is obtained the company can treat its contributions to the fund as deductible expenses for tax purposes to the extent that they are 'ordinary annual contributions'.

If additional contributions are made these also may be deductible, but there will sometimes be a requirement to spread them over several years. If the employee makes contributions, these will similarly be deducted from his earned income for tax purposes.

The fund itself will be exempt from tax on the investment income generated by the investment of the contributions. It will also be exempt from Capital Gains Tax.

Benefits paid out by the fund will either be tax-free or treated as earned income.

The principal requirements for a fund to be approved are:

1. That it is in connection with a trade or undertaking carried on at least partly in the UK.
2. That the employer contributes to it. (It is not essential that the employees should contribute, although they may do so.)
3. That all members entitled to join are informed and given relevant particulars, (as stated above, the membership may be limited to a certain class of employees of whom there may, in fact, be only one).
4. That there is a trustee or body of trustees resident in the UK, who is responsible for the proper administration of the fund.
5. That the fund exists for the genuine purpose of providing approved benefits within certain limits.

It is not a statutory requirement that the trustee should be a person in the pension or life assurance business, but it will normally be sensible to have at least one such trustee and it may well be easier to convince the approving authority (the Superannuations Funds Office) of the *bona fide* purposes of the scheme if there is such a trustee. The SFO does have quite wide discretionary powers of approval.

The allowable contributions are limited to the amounts needed to fund benefits up to an approved maximum. The older the members are at the commencement of the fund the higher the contributions will be needed to ensure that the fund will be able to provide the benefit. In some cases where a company has had no pension provisions and the directors or employees are on high incomes and not too far away from retirement age, very large amounts can be contributed. The problem is not how much can be approved, but how much can be afforded.

The following are the benefits which can be funded. It is not obligatory to provide them all or to provide up to the maximum.

1. A lump sum, not exceeding four times pensionable salary, on death in service. It can be arranged that this sum is not subject to Capital Transfer Tax.
2. A widow's pension on death in service. This can be up to four-ninths of salary and is available also for widowers and certain other dependants.
3. A retirement pension of up to two-thirds of final salary on retirement after at least 10 years service. Smaller fractions apply for shorter service. There are various ways of calculating final salary. This is discussed more fully in section 7.17.
4. A tax-free lump sum on retirement. This can be up to one and a half times final salary. If this is taken it reduces the amount which can be paid as a retirement pension.
5. A widow's or dependant's pension on death after retirement. This can be up to two-thirds of the individual's own pension.

7.17 The pension benefits for those with a stake in the business

Section 7.16 looks at the type of benefits which a company can provide under an occupational pension scheme. Now we examine the private company where the employees for whom the scheme is operated may well be directors and shareholders.

The benefits which can be paid by an approved fund are limited to amounts calculated by reference to final salary so it is important to know what final salary means.

One definition is the highest remuneration for any of the five years preceding retirement or, for death in service benefits, preceding the death. This definition is not available for use in the cases of directors who can control over 20 per cent of the voting power in the company.

When deciding what votes a person can control he is deemed to have control of shares held by his wife, his minor children and the trustees of any settlement.

The other definition is the average of a period of at least three years ending within 10 years before retirement or death.

In making the calculations it is permissible to take into account not merely the actual amount of the remuneration for the various years but the amount for each year (except the latest) revalued in accordance with the retail price index.

For example, assume that the index went up by 12 per cent in each of the last two years; by 14 per cent in the two years preceding them; by 12 per cent in the next four years back; and by 8 per cent in the next two years back.

Consider a person who had remuneration of £3000 in 1968/69 and who has had increases in the region of 10 per cent each year. His salary progression, revalued on the index, is discussed below.

If this person was about to retire, his pension could be based on a salary of £9181, although he had never actually had more than £7700. He could, therefore, have a pension of up to £6120. Alternatively he could have a tax-free lump sum of up to £13,770 and a reduced pension.

Let us now think about a more successful person for whom all the figures in the chart are trebled. Based on a final salary of £27,543 (although he may never have taken more than £23,100), the major attraction to him of a pension scheme may not be the opportunity to have a pension of over £18,000 but the right to have death in service cover of over £110,000 free of Capital Transfer Tax.

With many family companies, directors have not been accustomed to pay themselves at salary levels commensurate with people having similar ability and responsibility but working for an 'armslength' employer.

This has largely been due to the higher rates of tax on personal income. A person could see that money left in the company would be taxed at a lower rate and would still indirectly belong to him or his family. Over the last few years, since controlling directors have been able to be members of company pension schemes, there has been a gradual realisation that by underpaying himself a person was reducing the pension and death benefits which the company could provide for him.

There has, therefore, been a conflict between the wish to take high remuneration and qualify for high benefits on the one hand and the wish to restrict remuneration and reduce current taxation on the other hand. The reduction of the higher tax rates in the 1979 Budget reduced the area of conflict very significantly.

Pension and death benefit schemes should not be thought of primarily as tax-saving devices. They are sound prudent arrangements which various governments have decided should be encouraged by tax incentives.

While it is very nice to realise that the law allows a company to provide this security for its employees and directors, the pension fund will not be able to pay out these generous benefits unless it has received the contributions to build up its funds.

While the company might like to take advantage of all the opportunities, the real problem is frequently that it does not have the money available to make the necessary contributions. This is not a real difficulty and can on occasions be exaggerated (see section 7.19).

7.18   Pensions for controlling directors

Until a few years ago it was not possible for controlling directors to be members of occupational pension schemes. They were free to make their own retirement arrangements by way of retirement annuity contributions, but in many businesses the overriding need in early years is to find enough cash to meet immediate bills so that drawings are kept to a minimum and such matters as providing for a distant future are given low priority.

Many people, therefore, find themselves half or three-quarters of the way through their working lives with no provision for old age or disaster, although they are in their own prosperous and solidly based company. Some realise this only as they are practically at retirement age.

For such people the company is permitted to pay large sums into a retirement fund in order that sufficient resources may be available to meet the types of benefits described in sections 7.16 and 7.17.

The problem for many family companies is that, although they are successful and may have valuable assets, many do not have much available cash. The directors appreciate the wisdom of looking after their retirement years, but regret that the cash flow position of the company does not permit them to take advantage of the opportunities available. However, in some such cases they may not realise that contributions to a retirement fund can sometimes be built up with very little immediate call on the company's cash resources. A fund may even improve the company's cash flow.

The trustees of a fund have a duty to invest the resources at their disposal as securely and profitably as they are able. In many cases, an investment in the employing company may be as secure and profitable as any other. If so, such an investment may benefit both the company and the fund.

For example, let us assume that a company is about to buy some shop premises for its business at a cost of £50,000. Let us also assume that it would be permitted to pay £50,000 into a retirement fund for the directors but feels that the cash for this contribution is simply not available.

If the £50,000 is paid into the fund rather than being used to buy the shop it may be possible for the fund to invest the money by buying the shop and letting it to the company.

The company will only have parted with the same amount of money. The contribution to the fund will save tax of perhaps £26,000 a little over a year later so that the company will actually be in a better cash position. It will, of course, have to pay rent over later years and it is essential that this rent should be at a proper market rate.

Instead of buying a building, the fund may lend cash to the company at a commercial rate of interest and again the effect on the company's cash flow will not be too hard.

The Superannuation Funds Office has wide discretionary powers to approve funds and to impose conditions. They have said that they do not object to the principle of a fund investing in the employer company but they are naturally anxious that the method of doing this is not abused.

They must be satisfied that the object of the fund is to provide benefits and not merely to give tax advantage to the company. They must also be satisfied that the investment is so arranged that the fund will have access to cash when it becomes responsible for paying out benefits.

As a broad guide it seems that if no more than half of the fund's resources are lent to the company the SFO will not object, but it must

Independent advice

on self-invested pension schemes
for controlling directors – and
pensioneer trustee facilities –
available from consulting actuaries

DUNCAN C. FRASER & CO.

24-28 Cheapside, London EC2V 6AB Tel: 01-248 6981

BIRMINGHAM	021-455 7485	LEEDS	0532 443753
DUBLIN	0001 720764	LIVERPOOL	051-236 9771
EDINBURGH	031-226 4115	MANCHESTER	061-832 5688

be pointed out that they make individual judgements in individual cases.

If a new fund is set up the SFO will not normally mind if all the contributions for the first three years are invested in property provided that the ages of the fund members are not such that the fund is going to be short of ready cash when needed.

I have been asked if a retirement fund is allowed to invest in works of art or assets such as yachts which do not produce an income. The attitude of the department seems to be that these might be suitable investment for a small (say 5 per cent) part of a fund, but that they would be unlikely to approve a fund which wishes to invest more substantially in this area unless the trustees could show that their ability and expertise were such that this really was the safest and most profitable area of investment.

If the trustees could show this they might still be courting problems because it might be deemed that their activities amounted to trading. In such a case the profits would be taxable because it is only investment income of an approved fund which is exempt from tax, not trading income.

It is to be hoped that not many companies are tempted to invest in these unorthodox areas. The department will inevitably be suspicious of arrangements which suggest that the aim is to give present benefit rather than future security. Not only will such schemes probably be refused approval, but they may affect the presently very reasonable attitude of the department and that would be to the detriment of the whole small business sector.

7.19 Raising capital

A young man who wishes to start a business making hand-made jewellery has written to ask whether he is being unrealistic in hoping that he can find some way of financing himself and his business for a period until he can make sufficient to live on and develop the business. He lives in a town small enough to interest CoSIRA (The Council for Small Industries in Rural Areas) and hopes that he may get some assistance from that source, but for various reasons he thinks that any help will be delayed for quite a while.

His is a very common problem; probably the commonest of all faced by aspiring businessmen. They believe that they can fulfil a public demand, but need some capital before they prove it. In this particular case the nature of the commodity adds to the difficulty of finding finance through traditional channels. Anybody thinking of lending him money would have to make a judgement of his talent and of the merit of his jewellery, and very few people would regard themselves as qualified to do that. Moreover, they would probably feel that, in times of austerity and incomes freezes, luxury products would be less attractive than more fundamental supplies.

Anybody trying to develop a new business of an artistic nature from scratch should obtain a job to provide basic income and develop the other interest in his spare time. However, we assume that this correspondent is either unable or unwilling to do that. We also assume that he has no capital of his own, such as a house which he could sell and buy another with a mortgage, and that he has tried and failed to get loan or overdraft facilities from his bank.

If he has any relations or friends who, although not wealthy, may be able to raise capital he should ask himself why he does not try to borrow from them and he will probably come to the conclusion that the investment would be too risky and he is not willing to put them in a position where their savings or borrowed capital may be lost. The obvious question following this admission is why anybody else

RUNNING A SMALL BUSINESS?

CoSIRA can point the way to

• HIGHER EFFICIENCY
• GREATER PROFITABILITY

in the manufacturing and service industries

NOTE! You **must** – be operating in an English rural area
– be employing under 20 skilled people
You must **not** – be a member of the professions
– be in agriculture, horticulture
or any retail business

For further information write or phone our County Offices
(in Yellow Pages) or Head Office:

**(Dept. G) 141 Castle Street, Salisbury, Wilts, SP1 3TP
Tel. (0722) 6255**

would be prepared to put money into such a doubtful venture. Why should his patron or financier put his money into this business rather than invest it in a bank or building society where it would be safe and would earn a guaranteed amount of income?

The answer must lie in the risk/reward ratio. An investor will put his funds into a project which might lose his capital only if he can see a possibility, should the business be successful, of a better return than he could get on a safe investment. If the capital is put in as a simple loan this usually means that a high rate of interest is required.

There are, however, some situations where an investor will take a different view of risks and rewards and these are largely created or influenced by our quaint taxation system.

Many wealthy people are very conscious of Capital Transfer Tax. If such a person knows that on his death the top part of his estate will be taxed at 60 per cent he is often prepared to discount the risk in an interesting or 'fun' investment by that much. When putting up £1000 which he does not need during his lifetime he thinks that, if it should be lost the Exchequer will lose £600 and his heirs will lose £400.

Another possibility is that a wealthy person will not want regular annual interest on an investment because his income tax rate is so high that it leaves very little in his hands. He would prefer either to let

205

interest accrue and take it in such a way that it became taxable in years when his tax rate may be low or invest in a way that would enable him to take his return on the investment in the form of a capital profit which would be taxed at only 30 per cent. If the investment could be arranged to achieve this he may be satisfied with a gross rate of return no higher or even a little lower than interest rate on a secure investment.

It is not possible in a short article to explain how the financial arrangements would need to be concluded to achieve these taxation aims because the methods would vary according to a large number of factors but accountants and solicitors are familiar with the concepts and solutions. I regret that it is very seldom as simple as a mere loan agreement.

Most solicitors, accountants and bank managers know a few people whose finances put them in the position where they are interested in finding tax advantageous, rather than traditional, forms of investment and this young man should try such contacts. He might also perhaps be able to use the tax system as a selling point to potential customers as well as a potential patron or partner.

It is not always true that the demand for luxury goods falls in times of financial difficulty. Good quality, non-perishable goods have an attraction as an investment as well as for the enjoyment their owners will derive. If there is a reasonable prospect of them appreciating in value, the appreciation is more attractive to a high-rate taxpayer than income would be.

Ultimately, success in any commercial venture must depend on convincing the public that what one is selling is worth having and, in a competitive sphere, is better than what the opposition is offering. If our reader can persuade people of that, our fiscal laws which cause so much grief to many others may prove to be useful allies to him.

7.20 The way to take the tax sting out of perks

One difficult area of income tax law is the question of the taxation of benefits or perquisites arising to a person (or to his family) by reason of his employment office. Some items are assessable regardless of the seniority or status of the employee. Others are assessable only if

MAKING A SMALL BUSINESS BIGGER

Six ways we can help you expand

1 Enterprise Loans A scheme designed to help you raise money for new plant, equipment, premises … anything that involves expansion or diversification. Loans in the range of £25,000 to £250,000 (or more), with interest linked to base rate. Repayments up to 10 years. Money when you need it, to pay back as your expansion programme begins to pay back.

2 The Lloyds Bank Finance Series A series of free handbooks about starting, developing and running a business. 'Making a small business bigger' is full of advice, subjects ranging from marketing to tax and legal problems. And it will also help you present a clear and convincing financial proposition when you come to ask us for money.

3 Leasing Borrowing money to buy equipment outright is not always the answer. You may be better off leasing. We'll help you understand why.

4 Factoring As your business expands, you'll find money going out faster than it's coming in, often because customers aren't paying on time. By factoring debts, through our associated companies you could turn them into immediate cash (with 100% bad debt cover).

5 Selling Overseas You can't be everywhere at once but we can – through our world-wide group network. We can provide information on overseas territories and help find reliable agents and buyers. Some helpful information can be obtained from our new booklet – 'Exporting for the smaller business,' one of our Lloyds Bank Finance Series. Copies are available in all our branches.

6 Business Advice Our Business Advisory Service can show you how to turn information in your audited accounts into a control system. This will help remove the uncertainty of day-to-day financial control and assist you to get on with building up your business.

If you're planning to expand your business, your nearest Lloyds Bank manager may well be able to help. Call in and see him.

More help for business At the sign of the Black Horse

LLOYDS BANK

Lloyds Bank Limited, 71 Lombard Street, London EC3P 3BS

207

the person is a director of the employing company or is highly paid. It is the first group of items which we consider now and the others will be dealt with later.

The first thing to emphasise is that money and benefits are assessable whether they are paid by the employer or by some other person. The criterion is whether they are a reward for services, not the immediate source of payment. It is for this reason that in certain jobs tips are assessable.

Apart from the payment of money, there are five types of emolument which will be assessable on any employee, and these are categorised below.

Vouchers
This includes stamps or other documents and the amount assessable is the cost of providing the voucher plus the value of money, goods or services for which it can be exchanged.

Medical insurance
The amount assessable is the cost of providing the insurance. Where there is a group scheme the premiums must be allocated 'as is just and reasonable' between the persons covered. The assessment does not extend to premiums covering the cost of any treatment received outside the UK in connection with illness or injuries while outside the UK on business.

Living accommodation
There are five circumstances which are exempt from assessment:

1. Where it is necessary for the proper performance of the duties that the employee resides in the accommodation provided.
2. Where the accommodation is provided for the better performance of the duties and where it is customary for employers to provide accommodation for employee of that type.
3. Where there is a special threat to the security of the individual and he resides in the accommodation provided as part of the security arrangements.
4. Where the employer is an individual and he provides the accommodation in the normal course of his domestic, family or personal arrangements (ie for a domestic employee or relation).
5. Where the employee is a local authority employee and he occupies the accommodation on terms comparable with people of similar circumstances who are not employees.

Unless one of these five circumstances applies, the employee is assessable on the annual value of the property he occupies. He need not, however, feel too aggrieved by this as the annual is, in effect, the rateable value which will normally be less than the rent he would need to pay for equivalent accommodation.

If the employee pays some rent for the accommodation the assessable benefit is reduced by the amount of the rent.

Debts or liabilities
The amount assessable, where an employee's liability is settled for him, is the amount of that liability.

Money's worth
Where something is provided which is capable of being converted into money the amount assessable is the amount of money into which it can be converted (except if the employee comes within the definition of director or higher paid employee, in which case it is the cost of making the supply).

These principles can lead to some curious anomalies.

For instance, if an employer wishes to provide a suit or some other clothing for an employee the tax liability of the employee will depend upon the way the employer chooses to carry out his intention. If he gives the employee the money to buy it the money will be taxable in full. If he tells the employee to order it and then accepts the tailor's bill, it will similarly be taxable in full because he has settled a liability incurred by the employee.

However, if the employer places the order himself and then accepts the bill the employee can only be taxed on the amount which he could receive from a sale of the suit.

If an employer provides meals for his staff, in a canteen or otherwise, the employees will only be assessable on the realisable value of the food. Normally the employees will be free to eat or to leave the food but will not be able to take it and sell it and, therefore, the realisable value and the tax assessment will be nil.

On the other hand, if the employer gives the employee a meal allowance the allowance will be taxable in full. There is just one exception to this rule. That is in the case of luncheon vouchers. These are not taxed, up to a limit of 15p per person per day, provided that they are available to all employees or, if there is any restriction on the people who receive them, they are available to the lower paid employees.

7.21 Spreading the tax net for directors

Section 7.20 describes the benefits which will be assessable on any employee if bestowed on him by reason of his employment. Sections 7.21 and 7.22 look at the additional legislation which relates to senior employees.

It is first necessary to be clear which senior employees are within the additional legislation. The law refers to directors and to persons in an employment with emoluments at a rate of £8500 or more a year.

The word 'director' is extended to some people who might not enjoy that title but who exercise the equivalent rights and privileges of a director. This is to prevent a person who has a directorial say in the running of the company from escaping from the provisions which tax certain benefits (and also from other provisions of the Taxes Acts).

On the other hand, a director will be outside the provisions if he has an interest in no more than 5 per cent of the ordinary capital and if he is required to devote substantially the whole of his time to the company (but he may be brought back within the provisions by virtue of the level of his emoluments).

The word 'emoluments' is important because it signifies that, in deciding whether a person is within these provisions, it must first be assumed that he is and the benefits must be quantified accordingly. If the total of these benefits plus his remuneration fails to reach the figure of £8500, the benefits will be left out of account but if that figure is reached he is in the net.

Where there are several associated companies, the emoluments of all of them are added together to apply the £8500 test. If a person holds the office or employment for only a part of the year the figure of £8500 is reduced proportionately.

Once it has been decided that a person comes within the senior employee legislation he will be assessed not only on benefits but on expenses paid to or for him. These expenses will include, for instance, travelling and subsistence payments. He will not necessarily pay tax on them because he will be entitled to an expense allowance if he can convince his tax inspector that the money was paid out by him wholly, exclusively and necessarily in the performance of his duties. Some or all of the money added in to his assessment by the senior employee legislation may therefore be taken out again as an expense allowance.

An employer is welcome to discuss with the tax inspector the basis on which he meets expenses payments and if the inspector is satisfied that the basis is reasonable and that certain items, if assessed, would then be deductible again he may issue a 'dispensation' for those items. A dispensation will then remove those items entirely from the application of the senior employee legislation.

A dispensation can be very useful because it may save several individuals from having the nuisance of conducting separate negotiations with the tax officials. It will not, however, be given if the effect of giving it would be to prevent a person who would normally be treated as a higher paid employee from being so treated.

For people just below the threshold of the senior employee legislation there can sometimes be a situation akin to the 'poverty surtax' of people in the area where social security limits and tax thresholds start to overlap. A pay increase may reduce his take-home money rather than increase it.

A person may, for instance, have a salary of £7000 and there may be benefits of £1200 which would be assessable on him if he was within the senior employee legislation, but which are not assessable because they raise his emoluments to only £8200.

If this person receives a salary increase of £350 the total emoluments will be £8550 and he must pay tax on the benefits. The tax on £1200 benefits and on the £350 salary increase, will, at 30 per cent be £525. In addition, he would pay a further National Insurance contribution, so that the increase of £35 would leave him with *less* cash to spend.

If this person had other income (say from investments) which took him into the higher tax brackets it could be even more undesirable to give him the pay rise which took him over the threshold.

7.22 The tax man and the house perk *

If a person is provided with living accommodation by reason of his employment he will be assessed for tax on the value of the accommodation to him. The value would be taken as the gross rating value, and this is true where the employer or the other person providing the accommodation owns it, but I should have added that a different figure can apply if that person pays rent for it.

In such a case the value will be taken as the higher of the gross rating value or the rent paid by the person providing the accommodation. If the employee is required to pay rent, the amount assessable is reduced by the amount of rent he pays.

In the case of senior employees, including directors, there will be a further assessment if additional facilities are provided. The provision of furniture or other equipment will be assessed at 10 per cent of its market value at the time it was provided. This assumes that the asset remains the property of the person providing it. If the asset is actually given to the employee the assessment will be on the full amount of the market value at the time the ownership changes.

A combination of the law taxing the use of assets and the law taxing the gift of assets produces an interesting situation.

Suppose that an employer acquires an asset of a type which depreciates by 40 per cent in its first year and that he lets the employee have the use of it for a year and then gives it to him. In the first year the employee will be assessable on 10 per cent of the cost because he only has the use of the asset. In the second year he will be assessable on 60 per cent of the cost because that will be the market value at the time ownership passes. He will therefore have acquired full rights in the asset but will have been taxed on only 70 per cent of the cost.

The 10 per cent valuation of the use of assets applies to all items except land and buildings (where the annual value applies) and to cars.

If the employer pays the rates on the employee's accommodation, the full amount will be assessed on the employee because rates

---

* Since this article was written the law has changed if the employee enjoys the use of an asset. The assessment is now on 20 per cent (not 10 per cent as previously) of the original value of the asset. Moreover, if the asset is later given to the employee the assessment will now be on the original value less any amounts taxed as benefits in earlier years.

are the responsibility of the occupier. The provision of heating, lighting, cleaning or other facilities is also assessable on senior employees, and the value assessed is normally the cost to the employer or to the other person who provides the facilities.

There is however an exception. There are certain circumstances in which the provision of the accommodation itself would not be taxed:

1. Where it is necessary for the proper performance of the duties that the employee resides in the accommodation provided.
2. Where the accommodation is provided for the better performance of the duties and where it is customary for employers to provide accommodation for employees of that type.
3. Where there is a special threat to the security of the individual and he resides in the accommodation as part of the security arrangements.

If a person can convince his tax inspector that he comes in one of these categories he will not only escape taxation on the value of the accommodation but a limit will be placed on the value of the ancillary facilities which are provided for him. The limit is 10 per cent of the amount of his emoluments from the employment in question and from any other employment with a company associated with his employing company.

This limit applies to the total benefits which would otherwise be assessable in respect of heating, lighting, cleaning, repairs, maintenance, decoration and the provision of furniture and other effects which are normal for domestic use.

It should be noted that the 10 per cent valuation basis referred to earlier covers all types of assets but the limitation of assessment on people in categories (1), (2), and (3) above covers a more limited range of assets. Television sets, refrigerators and washing machines are presumably regarded as normal domestic effects, but stereo and hi-fi equipment or other items of a hobby nature are not. On the other hand, all furniture is included and it does not seem to matter how expensive it might be.

8
Franchising

8.1 Introduction

Clive Woodcock

One of the fastest growing areas of the small business sector in Britain today is the system known as franchising. The aim of this chapter is to examine that growth and try to define what franchising is and what it offers to the prospective small businessman and to describe some of the individual operations. As with any form of business venture readers are urged to take professional advice before entering into any financial commitments.

Reliable statistics on the industry are difficult to come by and virtually the only ones available come from the British Franchise Association itself. Current BFA membership accounts for more than £280 million in retail sales and backed by the growth in new franchising opportunities the association expects sales to exceed £1000 million by 1985.

Since the BFA was formed in 1977 its membership has grown from the eight founder members to close on 40 companies, all of which conform to standards of business practice laid down by the Association and are generating proven business format franchises.

The number of retail outlets operated by members doubled from 1906 in 1978 to 3969 in 1980. Sales have risen from £154 million to £285 million — an increase of 84 per cent — and sales for 1981 are estimated to grow by a further 15 per cent. Such high percentages tend to reflect the BFA's own growth in membership terms but, discounting this growth in size by the Association, the increase in outlets over the past two years averages 9 per cent and the increase in retail sales 10 per cent.

The total number of staff directly employed in franchising by members of the Association is more than 20,000, an increase of 24 per cent since 1978. Fifty-six per cent of prospective franchisees come from the ranks of people who are already employed. Unemployed or redundant executives account for 8 per cent of the intake, and 36 per cent previously worked in a self-employed position. There are clear signs that the intake from unemployed executives is on the increase and could well double in 1981.

Married couples account for 29 per cent of franchisees and individual female franchisees are only 5 per cent of the total, although significant growth in the number of women franchisees is anticipated in the near future.

The average initial cost of a franchise is £16,000, excluding fast food for which the average cash requirement is £55,250. However, franchised opportunities vary from an investment as low as £2500 for a domestic cleaning business up to £250,000 for a major fast food operation. Prospective franchisees who obtain their initial cash requirements through savings or redundancy payments account for 31 per cent of the total. Almost 25 per cent of the remainder used bank loans and only 7 per cent went to a finance company.

The average service fee paid to the franchisor by the franchisee was 11.14 per cent of the gross turnover. The main services provided to the franchisees for this service fee included initial training, on-the-job training, training manual, aid in launching an outlet, advice on selling prices, quality control, day-to-day business advice, national advertising and research and development of new products or services.

Franchise contracts are most frequently of five years' duration, which usually includes an option to renew while more than half of the BFA members operate internationally.

The average Association franchisee is 39, has had some business experience previously either as an employee or self-employed. More than one-third of their wives work in the business and the main reason for entering a franchise was to own and operate a business and have independence.

Problems experienced in operating a franchise relate principally to staffing, cash control and the initial adjustment to working for themselves. Less than 1 per cent of franchisees ended their agreements in 1980, the major reasons given being domestic problems and retirement.

Franchisors ended twice as many contracts but still less than 1.5 per cent, the reasons in the main being unwillingness of franchisees to conform to the system and breaking of contractual agreements. Franchisors monitor franchisees very carefully because one poor operator can adversely affect the public reputation of all the others, and franchisors are very sensitive about reputations.

The one thing that franchising is not is a licence to print money, even though the understandable tendency of franchisors in their literature is to emphasise the potential profitability of their method of business.

Much of that can, of course, be put down to the traditional hyperbole of the salesman but the franchising industry has to be particularly careful in view of the unpleasant publicity it gathered in the 1960s and early 1970s when it was bracketed with the pyramid selling operations. Those were no more than exercises in parting the gullible from their money: an investor bought a distributorship for a product or service but could only earn profits by recruiting yet more distributors. Many of those taken in by this lost not only their savings but their homes as well because they financed themselves with second mortgages.

Legislation has outlawed the most blatant examples of this type of operation but there are still fringe schemes which almost qualify for the description 'franchise' but are in fact unethical, if not illegal.

Any one of these could quickly destroy the hard won respectability of the many reputable business format franchise operations in this country who have benefited from the improved image nurtured by the British Franchise Association. During its two years of existence the BFA has attempted to repair the earlier damage by bringing some kind of order to the scene. It has had a fair degree of success, though changing a bad image is always an uphill job.

But once it is accepted that reputable franchise operators simply offer a less lonely way of getting into business, by a method which irons out a few of the bugs but in no way reduces the hard grinding slog necessary to achieve success in any form of small business, franchise or non-franchise, then the credibility gap narrows.

It also has to be remembered that like any other business, even *bona fide* franchising operators can get it wrong. They can be wrong in their choice of franchisee and find that they have a square peg in a round hole, or their own market research can be at fault.

An ice cream parlour franchise, for example, which was launched in Britain in the long, hot summer of 1976, found that the British public was not as interested as the American in buying

50 or more different flavours of ice cream, summer and winter. A proven franchise in the United States did not work when translated to Britain and a number of investors have found that although a franchise usually offers an improved chance of success it does not guarantee it.

The possibility of a franchise failing to work is obviously not something on which promoters lay emphasis but it is fairly certain — in the absence of precise reliable figures — that the failure rate is nowhere near that of non-franchised, independent small businesses.

And with more and more people leaving jobs with redundancy payments, often of substantial sums, there is likely to be a considerable boost to the already rapidly growing franchising business in this country as they look for alternative methods of earning a living.

Franchising takes a variety of forms, a factor which makes it difficult to define with precision. Primarily, it is a means of marketing a product or service and achieving a greater and faster rate of expansion than would otherwise be possible.

The owner of the product or service — an organisation or an individual entrepreneur, known as the franchisor — develops a type of business but lets others — the franchisees — run it in return for royalty payments or the right to supply them exclusively with the raw materials.

The franchisee finances his own business from his own resources and buys or rents premises with help from the franchisor, who also receives a fixed, once and for all, sum for the trade name and training. The franchisee is essentially paying for what he can reasonably expect to be a proved business format, backed by professional advice and national promotion.

There is, in fact, a mixture of working for oneself and working for a large organisation because the franchisor will want maintain the national name and reputation of his business by a fairly strict standardisation, which after a while might become irksome to the franchisee. There is a need, therefore, to be able to cope with both independence and maintaining a working relationship with the promoter.

Franchising is, in fact, not as new a system of doing business as might be thought. Probably the first examples of it were British breweries a century or more ago with tenanted but tied public houses; but the major developments came in the United States, where there are now said to be about 500,000 franchised outlets with sales of more than $300 billion a year, accounting for about

217

30 per cent of all retail sales.

The names of franchising operations in the United Kingdom are familiar to most people — though many probably do not realise that they are in fact franchises — but the industry is at a relatively early stage of development compared with the US. Growth is accelerating however.

The most familiar names are probably the fast food operations such as Wimpy and Kentucky Fried Chicken (both of which are American imports) and car hire franchises like Budget Rent-a-Car. The Dyno-Rod drain cleaning service is well known, while home-grown operations such as the instant printing chain, Prontaprint, are becoming increasingly familiar.

Most things can be franchised — the list already runs from weight-watching to selling trucks — and good franchises can provide benefits for both the franchisor and franchisee as well as the economy as a whole. Provided the self-discipline urged by the BFA can be maintained it seems likely that franchising will provide an increasingly important part of the development of the small business sector in Britain.

8.2 The franchisee

John Stanworth Director of the Small Business Unit, Polytechnic of Central London, and
James Curran Senior Lecturer in Industrial Sociology, Kingston Polytechnic

A brief look at any of Britain's established franchised operations shows that franchisees vary considerably in their levels of success. For some, franchising means a good income and steady capital appreciation, while for others in seemingly similar territories it can mean a hard struggle or even failure. Obviously, a lot depends on the personal qualities of the franchisee and, equally, the franchisor's success is crucially dependent on picking franchisees who will succeed.

Not surprisingly, a good deal of folklore has developed in the franchise industry about what sort of person is ideally suited to make a successful franchisee. American franchisors, for example, requently claim that ex-servicemen make particularly good franchisees. Yet, the most reliable United States research —

sponsored by the US government's Small Business Administration — has reported that only 3 per cent of franchisees are ex-servicemen and that they are among the least successful.

Similar claims have been made concerning women and members of minority ethnic groups in the United States, but, again, independent research shows little support for these claims. In Britain, however, research does indicate that franchising, particularly in fast food, may offer an important outlet for the entrepreneurial ambitions of members of minority ethnic groups. It provides a sheltered independence well suited to those with ambition and capacity for hard work but limited previous business experience.

Franchisors often claim that franchisees with no previous experience in the operational area of the franchise are the most suitable. 'Individuals new to the business have no preconceived ideas' argued a former head of Wimpy International. They are usually considered to be more receptive to company training and, no doubt, more grateful for the opportunity for self-advancement offered by franchising. But our research in Britain and the US shows that, in fact, they are no more successful than franchisees with previous relevant experience.

One British authority on franchising claimed some years ago that franchising would never take off in Britain, unlike America, since people with sufficient capital would rather receive an investment income than risk their money in a business where they would have to work hard. The rapid expansion of franchising in Britain during the last 10 years suggests that this comparison is groundless.

Our own research shows that franchisees come from a wide variety of former occupations — accountants, policemen, firemen, chemists, plumbers, shop-floor workers — and most have no previous experience of self-employment. As with small business-men generally, their main incentive is not usually the hope of hard financial gain but escaping from the frustrations of working for someone else. And, in spite of the supervisory role exercised by the franchisor, the great majority stress that franchising does give them the feeling of independence they seek. However, a franchisor's profits are related to his franchisee's turnover and, as such, there is pressure to grow.

There does appear to be a positive correlation between previous earnings and success as a franchisee.

The average franchisee is in his late thirties or early forties and is married with children. His wife often takes an active role in running the business. Indeed, in some franchises the wife's importance to the business is crucial, which means that husband and wife must be able to work effectively as a business team.

Our research shows that in spite of the important differences between franchising and the conventional small business, there are also similarities. The loneliness, stress and risk of a small business have to be coped with since the franchisor only provides an overall supervision and general framework; franchises can ail in the same way as any independent small business even if they do so rather less frequently.

One quality required of a franchisee is the ability to manage his own franchise outlet and, at the same time, maintain an amicable working relationship with the franchisor as part of a larger organisation. One leading British franchisor has claimed: 'The only restriction we impose on a franchisee is a withdrawal of the right to mismanage his business'. But, for some would-be entrepreneurs this, in itself, could remove a good deal of the zest from self-employment.

8.3 Fast food

Rod Chapman

Should the spreading recessionary cloud have any silver lining, it may lie in the continuing boom in the fast food business — one of the few discernible growth businesses in this country, as any observer of the litter scene will attest.

The well-established giants like Kentucky Fried Chicken and Wimpy are currently ploughing money into promotional efforts aimed at maintaining their hold on the market (and, in the case of the latter, at shaking off some of the 'junk food' connotations).

The success of the fast food chains stems partly from the product and partly from the franchising concept. In the first place the cheap Chinese and Indian takeaways of yesteryear have become the £5 touches of the inflationary 1980s — while the trattorias and other courting haunts appear to have added several noughts to their bills.

Secondly, fast food folklore teems with anecdotes of those who bought their franchises and became millionaires almost overnight. Some, according to sources within the business, even made it by investing their redundancy money — an idea which would appear to have practically infinite possibilities in present-day Britain.

However, the fast food idea is derived from the US, where massive sales volume has enabled the growth of chains like Kentucky Fried, with over 6000 outlets there, and some 8000 worldwide, and McDonald's. It is the volume which has provided the base for the expansion of these companies and for the enrichment of their franchisees.

In Britain,the market is still regarded as virtually untapped, by North American standards, although it is now estimated to be worth over £500 million a year. 'The market is enormous, and we're only scratching the surface' says Wimpy's marketing director, Mr Peter Smale. He feels that most of the potential lies in areas where the hundreds of thousands of small cafes throughout the UK are 'satisfying the consumer to a certain extent', but where his and other chains could both score off the old 'Greasy Spoon' operations and generate extra business.

Wimpy pioneered fast food franchising in this country in the 1950s when J Lyons, of Corner House fame, brought it from it from its US parent. United Biscuits took it over in a £7 million deal three years ago, and it now has an annual turnover of almost £70 million with some 600 outlets in Britain.

Following a fairly sluggish period of market growth in the early 1970s, other groups took the fast food route in the UK. Colonel Sanders' benevolent visage began to grace high streets and waste paper bins, along with the big M of McDonald's. More American folksiness arrived when Grand Metropolitan concluded a deal with the US company Burger Queen in July last year which led to the launch in Britain of the Huckleberry's chain of franchised stores, complete with Twain-inspired logo.

A fast growing sector of the market of late has been pizza restaurants, with Pepsi-Cola's Pizza Huts opening up over here along with Pizza Express and Pizza Land — the last named part of United Biscuits' DS Crawford division.

Most of these mastodons are promoting heavily this year, with Kentucky Fried talking of opening new 3000 to 4000 square feet high street outlets similar to that in Kensington High Street, London, an 84-seater which has cost more than any other KFC outlet to set up.

Wimpy is spending £750,000 on national advertising in an attempt to 'pull ourselves up by our bootlaces' according to Mr

221

Smale. 'One of the problems' he says 'was that standards were allowed to fall over the years as we had no competition; it took people to come in with American standards to jolt us'.

Some of the problems arose, as Mr Smale admits, from having 'the wrong sort of franchisee in the system'. Some 40 Wimpys were closed down last year for a variety of reasons — many of which nonetheless came back to standards. Wimpy franchisees pay a £5000 'up front' fee for an outlet offering table service, and double that for one with counter service. The average cost of a Kentucky franchise is about £30,000.

For this sum, new entrants get the strength of a big company around them. Wimpy, for example, finds the site, draws up the plans, advises on staff recruitment and sends managers on a Wimpy training course. It then supplies the outlet with meat at a marked up price — representing an average 8½ per cent royalty on turnover.

Wimpy is now moving into company-owned stores, flagships which it will use for training and development. It expects up to 20 per cent of its stores to fall into this category eventually. But the main question against the majors is when, or if, McDonald's will move in the other direction and bring in franchise operations: all of its British stores are company-owned at present, and many competitors feel they always will be — to guarantee standards.

However, the theory that the only future for fast food franchising is for new entrants to join one of the big chains and use an identifiable name is discounted by some. 'When you're smaller, you've got more control, and other chains act as support', says Mr Alan Lorenz, joint proprietor of My Old Dutch.

Mr Lorenz, a solicitor, and his partner, Mr Martin Roach, have opened three outlets so far offering large Dutch pancakes at table service. 'One-item restaurants don't work — so we'll include other foods', he says. 'We'll also put together a franchise package. Even during a recession people have to have their luxuries, and we provide an inexpensive meal at a proper place where you could take your insurance man for example'.

If the legal profession and pancakes seem an unlikely alliance, the British School of Motoring is joining an Edinburgh-based operation called Spud-U-Like to expand a fast food chain offering baked potatoes with a variety of fillings. The deal augurs well, being masterminded by Mr David Acheson, who helped to build up Wimpy and then Kentucky Fried, where he effected a financial turnaround.

BSM will provided the corporate infrastructure, and Mr Acheson is looking for relatively small outlets, where initial capital investment should be around £25,000 and margins on 40p to 50p potatoes should give a capital payback in two years. The chain will use franchises but also have its own company stores.

8.4 Motoring

James Erlichman

The pitch is brash, unabashed, and straight-to-the-point. 'We'll fix your exhaust without exhausting your wallet.' Such corny puns are the hallmark of the American hard sell. They seek to evoke confidence by assuring Mr Joe Public that here is a product and a salesman that can be trusted. The origins of this sales technique can be traced straight back to the covered wagon from which frontier hucksters sold elixirs and snake oil, and occasionally got tarred and feathered for their trouble by irate customers not entirely pleased with the product.

Now, this kind of American sales pitch is being heard on Britain's airwaves advertising Midas Mufflers (exhaust systems). Not that Midas is in the snake oil category, far from it. Midas is the largest retailer of exhausts in the world and is one of America's oldest and most respected franchise businesses. The advertising slogan is the brainchild of Mr Dick Crook, a 53-year-old Mormon and godfather (in the Christian sense) of the motor industry franchising business in Britain.

The roots of motor industry franchising, like those of the fast foods business, are thoroughly American, and US corporations still control much of the action in the UK. The American's fondness for his stomach and automobile are as legendary as his zeal for making money. It is, therefore, not surprising that so much of his franchising energy was focused on food and cars and has now spilled over into this country.

The variety of motor industry franchises in Britain is impressive. The list includes: Rustproofing (Ziebart, Tuff-Kote Dinol, Body-shield, End Rust, and Total Protection); exhaust fitting (Midas); car hire (Budget-Rent-a-Car); engine tuning (Autrac and Home-Tune); paint re-spraying (Envirogarde and Textron). Several firms, including Envirogarde (which operates Ziebart), also fit sunroofs, and one firm, Protexcar, is setting up franchises which offer a novel anti-theft system.

Dick Crook left a US naval career when he was 37 to join Budget-Rent-a-Car in 1964. Within 18 months Budget sent him to Britain to establish its presence on this side of the Atlantic. Not all the credit belongs to Mr Crook, but Budget today claims to have overtaken Avis as the second largest car-hire firm in Britain (behind Godfrey Davis).

After several years with Budget Mr Crook became a freelance consultant — teaching the gospel of franchising to anyone who would listen. One firm that listened was Midas, which was so impressed with his message that Mr Crook became managing director in April of TI-Midas (UK), the recently established joint venture with Tube Investments.

Until Mr Crook was hired Midas had not allowed any of its United Kingdom outlets to be franchised. For such a huge organisation, built on the franchising ideal, this was most exceptional. But Midas, apparently, was not prepared to entrust its good name to British franchisees. Now with Mr Crook at the helm it has franchises in the UK and hopes to have 25 by the end of next year.

'Finding enough people with £50,000 who want to open a franchise is no real problem,' said Mr Crook. 'Finding people here prepared to work their tails off isn't hard either. But finding both in the same British person ... now that isn't easy.'

Not everyone would agree. Ziebart, another US-owned organisation, has successfully franchised in Britain for a number of years and now has 120 outlets. Its arch-rival, British-owned Bodyshield, has established 54 franchise outlets in seven years and is now beginning to expand abroad.

But the motor repair trade in Britain is notorious, and deservedly so, for the number of its dishonest practitioners. Is franchising then the best way to improve its image? Perhaps. Motor industry franchising, after all, adheres strictly to the same business bible which has put McDonald Hamburgers and Kentucky Fried Chicken franchises on high streets everywhere from Kansas City to Wolverhampton. And according to the gospel everyone, the franchisor, franchisee, and the customer, benefits.

The franchisor benefits because he can expand rapidly without borrowing heavily, since his franchisee has stumped up much of the cash to establish his own outlet. The franchisee benefits because he has the benefits of a big operation backing him yet most of his profits are his own. And the customer benefits because the system cuts out costly middle management and he can depend on the franchisee 'to work his tail off' providing a cheap and reliable service.

Unfortunately, franchising itself has been tarred in the past by shady operators who have used its perfectly legitimate practice of 'selling territories' as a guise to run pyramid selling rackets. The British Franchising Association concedes that motor industry franchising is particularly susceptible to this kind of infiltration, although no pyramid seller has ever succeeded in getting its seal of approval. And, presumably the beleaguered motorist, with grim experience of the anonymous back street mechanic, would prefer to trust his precious vehicle to a nationwide franchisor who guarantees the quality of the repairs done under his banner.

If you want to become a franchisee in the motor industry you will need typically around £15,000 in starting capital. About half goes to the franchisor for the licence, training, and advertising. The rest covers a few months of rent, equipment, and working capital. Midas is the exception, charging £50,000 since it requires franchisees to buy the sub-lease on its premises, although the company does help with about 75 per cent of the financing.

Motor industry franchisors then either take an annual percentage of the turnover (commonly 10 per cent) or charge their franchisees an admittedly inflated price for their products which the franchisee is under contract to buy exclusively.

Franchisees, as a breed, tend to grumble whichever way the tithe is extracted. Said one: 'It's a love-hate relationship. You love your franchisor in the beginning because he has set you up in business, Then, as you find your feet, you become convinced you are being robbed blind, working until you drop while he sits back and creams the profit off the top.'

No doubt the franchisor, ever vigilant lest his franchisee lets him and the customer down, sees things rather differently.

8.5 Services

Margaret Dibben

Services, as opposed to goods, which are offered by franchisees come very much in the mountain to Mohammed category. They are the jobs which have to be carried out *in situ* and provide ideal candidates for a franchise operation.

The range of services is growing but perhaps the most widely known is drain cleaning. Then there are other services for the home such as cavity wall insulation, cleaning carpets, and repairing vinyl coverings.

Since the operator is mobile and takes his services to the client, it is a very suitable business to run from home, particularly in the early days while the franchise is being built up. Moreover, everyone else living in the house can help by taking telephone messages or helping with the clerical work. It is possible to build a franchise up to sales as high as £50,000 a year before the operation outgrows the front room.

Dyno-Rod has been a pioneer in clearing pipes and drains since it started in 1963. The franchisees are trained to use the latest technology to provide a service 24 hours every day of the year.

The outfit has grown steadily and now provides a range of franchising consultancy services through its subsidiary, Franchise Developments International. Dyno-Rod has also moved into the motor industry by offering a cosmetic car refinishing process called Texon Autopainting.

The original business uses the latest electro-mechanical equipment combined with high pressure water jetting units, electronic drain tracing, and TV surveying. A blocked domestic toilet is now only a very small part of the work and most of the turnover comes from commercial, industrial and public authority contracts. The jobs could include work on a North Sea oil rig or in a luxury hotel.

The franchises vary enormously in size. A small country area can be handled by a team of three people; the largest, in a city, would have sales of £500,000 a year with a fleet of radio controlled vans and using the most modern pipework cleaning techniques.

The minimum investment in a small franchise is £10,000 and, for the largest, might be £30,000. The royalty is 23 per cent. In the past three years, Dyno-Rod reckons to have grown by 35 per cent a year.

Power Rod is a smaller and younger drain cleaning outfit. The investment required varied between £7500 and £20,000 and the royalty is about 23 per cent.

The office cleaning business run by Global Franchise Services operates differently and gives the franchisee the opportunity to use managerial talents. He is not involved in the cleaning work itself but organises others and negotiates contracts.

The franchisee's job is to act as a cleaning and maintenance consultant and to obtain contracts which he sells to the cleaners. He provides management and administrative services for both the cleaner and the customer. Cleaners who work for the franchisees at present include bank clerks, nurses, accountants and teachers who need to supplement their wages.

Both sides of the arrangement pay the franchisee. His money comes from selling the contracts to the cleaners and also from fees for his management services. His investment with Global is £12,000 made up of £6000 for the franchise fee and £6000 working capital for the first year.

The franchisee has a two-week training course to learn how to win contracts and how to place them. He also learns how to calculate the cleaning time of a building to the minute.

Cleaning carpets and curtains *in situ* is done by several franchise operators. Service Master began in the United States in 1952, came to Britain in 1959 and is now operating in 23 countries with a worldwide turnover of some £155 million. The investment needed is £500 with fees at 10 per cent of gross sales.

Thuro-Steam provides at-home cleaning to wealthy home owners. An industrial cleaner, Safeclean International, is expanding overseas and asks for a minimum investment of £2500.

Another growing area for franchise opportunities is in the repair and cleaning of chairs made with vinyl, such as those found in hospitals, libraries and schools. One is Vinylmaster where the minimum investment is at least £7000 and the royalty around 10 per cent. Another is Uticolor which repairs, recolours and restores vinyl coverings.

In these energy saving days, dry cavity wall insulation is gaining popularity. Isodan, originally a Danish system, has 40 outlets in the UK. The franchise costs £4500 made up of £3500 franchise fee, £650 for the Isopump and a £350 Agrément Board fee. The franchise also needs to provide a small van, ladders and tools. If the installer wants to leave Isodan after a minimum period of 18 months, the company will repay 80 per cent of the fee when they resell the territory he has been operating.

8.6 Outlets

Margaret Dibben

To run a shop under a franchise agreement gives an independent retailer additional protection against the vagaries of high street spending. Someone can expand a hobby or interest without taking the risks of a novice.

There is the opportunity to start from scratch with the benefit of someone else's wider experience and larger cash resources. The goods for sale through franchised outlets take customers from the friendship bureaux to the bridal wear shops, past the hairdresser and the invitation printer to the kitchen equipment supplier.

The introduction bureaux idea is relatively new and operated by Prestige Partners. It does not want to be thought to be a marriage bureau, and caters for professional and executive people who are too busy to build an organised social life for themselves.

Wedding dresses are sold by Pronuptia which originated in France. Four years ago Pronuptia teamed up with Young's Dress Hire and now has 270 branches around the world.

The initial franchise fee is calculated at £5 per 1000 population in the catchment area, giving exclusive rights to that area. The payment includes initial training and help in finding premises and fitting out the shop. Pronuptia reckons its franchisees do not have to pay prime site rates because brides will seek out the Pronuptia shop.

With the boost from national advertising, magazine features and outdoor posters, the shops get wider publicity than an individual outlet could afford. The head office pays half the initial advertising costs for the opening of each shop. The fee charges to the franchisee is 10 per cent of the value of orders and is paid monthly.

One of the most successful shops is in the north-east. The Newcastle outlet rang up sales of £120,000 in its first year. For the fee, the franchisee gets advertising artwork, public relations help, bi-monthly meetings in London, and training (many Pronuptia franchisees have little or no previous fashion experience).

The menswear side is now being developed with the expansion of the formal menswear hire business.

Toppy's Salons look after both ladies' and men's hair and work with the Steiner hair products company.

High-speed printing is an increasingly popular franchise. The largest chain in the UK is Prontaprint which started in Newcastle in 1971. The group has over 100 outlets and is still looking for more.

Prontaprint is British but is modelled on similar American operations. In the United States franchise operations account for nearly one-third of all retail turnover (around £100 billion) employing 4 million people.

Although it started in the north-east and is still strongest there, the chain now stretches from Aberdeen to Plymouth. The service offers basic photocopying, including colour, quality printing, duplicating, and collating. The jobs include printing programmes, menus, tickets, price lists and brochures. The chairman, Mr Edwin Thirwell is, like all franchise operators, optimistic. He is currently chairman of the British Franchise Association.

He says: 'Franchising will be a tremendous growth area in the 1980s in spite of the forecast of economic gloom. Franchised chains in the retail and service sectors in particular can usually operate much more efficiently and profitably than either company-owned and managed networks or independently owned single units.'

He feels that the range of franchises available can offer redundant executives and workers the opportunity to strike out on their own with a better than average chance of success. Statistics in the United States show that individuals starting up business have a 90 per cent failure rate within five years, whereas, of new franchises, only 12 per cent fail in the first five years.

The largest instant print franchise in the world is Kall-Kwik. There are 500 outlets altogether and 15 centres in the UK. The UK operation was set up last year with help from the Industrial and Commercial Finance Corporation.

The Flying Printer circulates its franchisees with a regular newsletter and league tables comparing the shops' performances. The company reckons that the total investment will be £17,500 and suggests that an average size unit of 700 sq ft with a turnover of £75,000 a year can produce a profit of £15,000 after overheads and royalties. The licence fee is £14,000.

The Cookmate Reject Kitchen Shop, established five years ago, has 25 outlets of which 11 are franchised. The minimum investment is £20,000 and the shops sell cookware, fun giftware, and bankrupt stock of glass and china.

The French-based Phildar shops sell knitting wool and handicraft products. There are 30 company owned outlets and 10 franchised units in the UK. There are no franchise fees or royalties but the franchisee has to buy Phildar products.

A commitment to health foods is demanded from franchisees by Nature's Way. Ten of the company's 14 shops are franchised and the minimum investment is £12,000.

Apollo Window Blinds charges no franchise fee or royalty. The investment is £3000 plus £2000 for an advertising launch and the shops sell Apollo's own make of venetian and roller blinds.

Photomarkets is described as halfway between a full franchise and a voluntary trading association. The 100 Photomarket photographic retailers pay £250 towards kitting out the shop and a flat fee of £100 a month.

9
Further Information

SMALL FIRMS CENTRES:
Small Firms Division
Department of Industry
Abell House, John Islip Street
London SW1

Scotland:
57 Bothwell Street
Glasgow G2 6TU

Wales:
16 St David's House
Wood Street
Cardiff CF1 1ER

Northern Region:
22 Newgate Shopping Centre
Newcastle NE1 5RH

North-west Region:
320-5 Royal Exchange
Manchester M2 7AH

Liverpool Sub-office
1 Old Hall Street
Liverpool L3 9HJ

Yorkshire and Humberside Region:
1 Park Row
City Square
Leeds LS1 5NR

East Midlands Region:
48-50 Maid Marian Way
Nottingham NG1 6GF

West Midlands Region:
Ladywood House
Stephenson Street
Birmingham B2 4DT

Eastern Region:
24 Brooklands Avenue
Cambridge CB2 2BU

London and South-eastern Region:
Bulstrode Street
London W1

South-western Region:
Colston Centre
Colston Avenue
Bristol BS1 4UB

COUNCIL FOR SMALL INDUSTRIES
IN RURAL AREAS (CoSIRA):
141 Castle Street
Salisbury
Wiltshire SP1 3TP

ASSOCIATION OF BRITISH
CHAMBERS OF COMMERCE:
6-14 Dean Farrar Street
London SW1H 0DX

SCOTTISH DEVELOPMENT
AGENCY:
Small Business Division
102 Telford Road
Edinburgh EH4 2NP

WELSH DEVELOPMENT AGENCY:
Small Business Unit
Treforest Industrial Estate
Pontypridd
Mid Glamorgan CF37 5UT

DEVELOPMENT BOARD FOR
RURAL WALES:
Ladywell House
Newtown
Powys SY16 1JB

SOUTH WEST DEVELOPMENT
BOARD:
County Hall
Truro
Cornwall

HIGHLANDS AND ISLANDS
DEVELOPMENT BOARD:
Bridge House
Bank Street
Inverness

9. Further Information

NORTHERN IRELAND:
LOCAL ENTERPRISE
DEVELOPMENT UNIT
Northern Area
17 The Diamond
Londonderry BP48 68R

Western Area
14 Mountjoy Road
Omagh

Southern Area:
5 Downshire Place
Newry

Eastern Area:
Lamont House
Purdy's Lane
Belfast BT8 4TB

LONDON ENTERPRISE AGENCY:
69 Cannon Street
London EC4N 5AB

ENTERPRISE NORTH:
Mill Hill Lane
Durham DH1 3LB

COMMUNITY OF ST HELENS
TRUST:
PO Box 36
St Helens
Merseyside

EXECUTIVE STAND-BY LTD:
310 Chester Road
Hartford
Northwich CW8 2AB
Cheshire

FOUNDATION FOR
ALTERNATIVES:
10 Grenfell Road
Beaconsfield
Bucks

UNION OF INDEPENDENT
COMPANIES
71 Fleet Street
London EC4

ASSOCIATION OF INDEPENDENT
BUSINESSES
Trowbray House
108 Weston Street
London SE1 3QB

ALLIANCE OF SMALL FIRMS:
279 Church Road
London SE19 2QQ

FORUM OF PRIVATE BUSINESS:
Ruskin Rooms
Drury Lane
Knutsford
Cheshire WA16 0ED

NATIONAL FEDERATION OF
SELF-EMPLOYED:
32 St Annes Road West
Lytham St Annes
Lancashire WA16 0ED

NATIONAL UNION OF SMALL
SHOPKEEPERS:
Western Buildings
Theatre Square
Nottingham NG1 6LH

TEESIDE SMALL BUSINESS CLUB:
16-20 Marton Road
Middlesbrough
Cleveland TS1 1HS

CO-OPERATIVE UNION:
Holyoake House
Hanover Street
Manchester M60 0AS

INDUSTRIAL COMMON
OWNERSHIP MOVEMENT:
31 Hare Street
Woolwich
London SE18 6JN

SCOTTISH CO-OPERATIVES
DEVELOPMENT COMMITTEE:
100 Morrison Street
Glasgow G5 8LP

CRAFTS COUNCIL:
12 Waterloo Place
London SW1Y 4AU

NATIONAL RESEARCH
DEVELOPMENT CORPORATION:
Kingsgate House
66-74 Victoria Street
London SW1 6SL

10
Select Bibliography

Added Value: The Key to Prosperity E G Wood, Business Books
Basic Business Management M A Peters, Jordans
Bigger Profits for the Smaller Firm E G Wood, Business Books
Complete Guide to Managing Your Business Eaglemoss Publications, 87 Elystan Street, London SW3 6RL
Cooperatives and Community David H Wright, Bedford Square Press
Croner's Reference Book for the Self-Employed and Smaller Business Croner Publications, 46-50 Coombe Road, New Malden, Surrey KT5 4QL
Essential Business Law series (paperback), Sweet and Maxwell
Guide to Small Business Systems Computer Guides, 30-1 Islington Green, London N1 8BJ
Rapid Company Growth A C Hazel and A S Reid, Business Books
The Small Business Casebook Dr Sue Birley, Macmillan Press
Starting and Running A Small Business Alan Sproxton, United Writers Publications, Zennor, St Ives, Cornwall
Tax Facts Joe Horner, Oyez Publishing Ltd
Understand Your Accounts A St J Price, Kogan Page
VAT Made Easy A St J Price, Kogan Page
Working for Yourself Godfrey Golzen, Kogan Page
The Working Office Geoffrey Salmon, The Design Council

Index

235

Index of Advertisers